OXFORD MODERN LANGUAGES
AND LITERATURE MONOGRAPHS

Editorial Committee

SCHILLER
AND THE HISTORICAL
CHARACTER
Presentation and Interpretation in
the Historiographical Works and in
the Historical Dramas

by

LESLEY SHARPE

OXFORD UNIVERSITY PRESS
1982

Oxford University Press, Walton Street, Oxford OX2 6DP

London Glasgow New York Toronto
Delhi Bombay Calcutta Madras Karachi
Kuala Lumpur Singapore Hong Kong Tokyo
Nairobi Dar es Salaam Cape Town
Melbourne Auckland
and associates in
Beirut Berlin Ibadan Mexico City Nicosia

Published in the United States
by Oxford University Press, New York

British Library Cataloguing in Publication Data

Sharpe, Lesley
Schiller and the historical character.
—(Oxford modern languages and
literature monographs)
1. Schiller, Friedrich—Criticism and
interpretation 2. Historical drama, German
I. Title
832'.6 PT2496.H5

ISBN 0-19-815537-9

Typeset by DMB, Oxford.
Printed in Great Britain at the
University Press, Oxford
by Eric Buckley, Printer to
the University.

PREFACE

This book is an attempt to analyse the impact of historical study on Schiller's dramatic practice, and to demonstrate his continued interest as a dramatist in the relation of the individual to the movement of history. It is substantially based on a doctoral thesis for Oxford University, and was written under the supervision of Mr F. J. Lamport, whose guidance, support, and sustained interest over five years of work were invaluable. I should also like to thank colleagues and friends at the University of Exeter for many useful suggestions and for practical help with work on the manuscript and proofs.

Quotations from Schiller's works follow the text of *Schillers Werke*, Nationalausgabe (= NA). This edition is supplemented by *Schillers Sämtliche Werke*, Säkular-Ausgabe (= SA), where the work in question has not yet appeared in the Nationalausgabe. *Schillers Briefe* (edited by F. Jonas) will be referred to as J, followed by the volume and letter numbers. Orthography follows the edition being used. (It should be noted that the Nationalausgabe modernizes spelling in some works and retains the original spelling in others, while the Säkular-Ausgabe modernizes spelling throughout.)

November 1981   L.S.

CONTENTS

Introduction   1

CHAPTER 1   *Fiesco* and *Don Carlos*   9

CHAPTER 2   Schiller's historiography
             I 1785-1788   35
             II 1789-1792   54

CHAPTER 3   *Wallenstein*   72

CHAPTER 4   *Maria Stuart*   106

CHAPTER 5   *Die Jungfrau von Orleans*   127

CHAPTER 6   *Wilhelm Tell*   142

CHAPTER 7   *Demetrius*   174

Conclusion   184

Notes   189

Bibliography   201

Index   209

INTRODUCTION

For some twenty years or more, helped no doubt by the celebrations of 1955 and 1959, Schiller's reputation has been undergoing radical revision. It was appropriate that the many articles, speeches, and monographs, which appeared to mark those years, should have presented a new picture of Schiller, because it was the first centenary celebrations of 1859 which did so much to distort the image of Schiller and to cause him to be rejected during much of this century. Schiller's works were flagrantly misused in the nineteenth century by those who wished to proclaim liberal political ideals or to call for national unity, and *Don Carlos* and *Wilhelm Tell* were particularly useful for this purpose. This particular form of misuse was, however, only part of a general tendency, which established itself even during Schiller's own lifetime, to regard his plays as containing unequivocal statements of his own ideals. A refinement of this tendency was the practice in criticism of seeing the plays as embodying certain philosophical ideas, which were to be found in Schiller's own theoretical works. This tendency is obvious in the major monographs of the decades around the turn of this century, in Berger, Minor, and Bellermann.[1] It survives in recent criticism also. Fritz Martini has discussed *Wilhelm Tell* in terms of the *Ästhetische Briefe* in his article, '*Wilhelm Tell*: der ästhetische Staat und der ästhetische Mensch'.[2] He admits that the play does not re-enact dramatically the substance of the *Ästhetische Briefe*: 'Jedoch ist richtig, daß die dichterischen Strukturen das poetische Analogon zu den philosophischen Ideen darstellen, der Philosoph und der Dichter eine gemeinsame Person sind.'[3] Even more recently a similar approach has been taken to *Maria Stuart*: 'Maria hebt die Differenz zwischen äußerer Vollkommenheit und menschlicher Unvollkommenheit in ihrer Todesstunde auf. Sie wird zur schönen Seele.'[4] In other words, Schiller's plays have been taken to relate so closely to his own theoretical writings that categories defined in those works, such as the 'schöne Seele', are taken to be exemplified in actual dramatic characters, whose behaviour can then be interpreted in terms of those theoretical works.

The long life which this critical approach has enjoyed would seem to be due to several factors. First, Schiller's work became extremely unfashionable from about the 1920s onwards. When interest in Schiller began to revive, some thirty years later, it was reasonable to expect that older critical approaches would also be be revived, while new ones also developed. Secondly, Schiller's theoretical writings demand attention, and it is more than tempting to apply them to the dramas, in particular because several of them are directly concerned with the nature of tragedy. However, a number of the most frequently quoted—*Über Anmut und Würde, Über die tragische Kunst, Über das Pathetische*—were written several years before Schiller returned to the drama as a playwright. Therefore, although they shed light on his choice of subject matter and on the effects he was trying to create, they do not exhaust the possibilities of tragedy. In fact, it is altogether conceivable that his actual engagement with particular subject matter produced results which did not accord with, were even radically different from, the results which his theory would suggest. Thirdly, Schiller's works are enormously varied. Amongst the plays it is hard to imagine two more different in outer form than *Die Räuber* and *Maria Stuart*. It is also difficult at first sight to understand how a man who could express confidence in the future of mankind through the power of aesthetic education, could, a few years later in *Wallenstein*, present such a tragic vision of the world of action. The application of Schiller's theory to his dramatic practice can be seen as an attempt to penetrate to some underlying unity in his artistic and philosophical works. The quotation above from Martini illustrates this desire to unite Schiller's activity as a creative genius and as a theoretician and philosopher.

Some of the most fruitful lines of criticism of Schiller's dramas since the 1950s have been those which recognize the essentially non-confessional nature of his later drama and the fact that he is neither voicing his ideals through the characters of the drama, nor simply dramatizing philosophical ideas. As Gerhard Storz says:

Der Blick von den philosophischen Schriften auf die Gedichte und die Dramen hat das dichterische Werk Schillers schon allzuoft zur versifizierten Darstellung eines Gedankensystems zusammenschrumpfen lassen. Diese Verzeichnung ist die scharfsinnigste, aber auch schädlichste unter den mancherlei Verunstaltungen gewesen, die Schillers Dichtung ... erlitten hat.[5]

Storz is one of a number of critics who have, since the mid-1950s, stressed the fact that Schiller the dramatist was concerned above all not with ideas but with aesthetic effects and that his dramas are all informed by his strong sense of the theatre. This is obviously true of the early dramas, written specifically for immediate performance. (Even in the case of *Don Carlos*, the original subject matter was suggested by Dalberg, the 'Intendant' of the Mannheim theatre, though the play's protracted development and final length hampered stage performance.) It is no less true of the later dramas. Schiller's ten-year dramatic silence after *Don Carlos* was a period of varied activity for him. He became a professional historian, formulated his ideas on aesthetic education, and strove for greater theoretical clarity about the nature of tragedy. He also matured as a man at a time of great political upheaval in Europe. All these things must be considered in approaching the later plays.

In addition to the present emphasis on reading the dramas as products of an artistic rather than a philosophical imagination, there has also been an attempt to correct the impression that Schiller himself was committed in later life to a highly abstract form of philosophical idealism. It has long been recognized that his idealism was counterbalanced by a contrary impulse. In his study of this dualism Kurt May calls the two poles 'Idee' and 'Wirklichkeit'.[6] It is to this tension that May attributes Schiller's failure to finish his *Geschichte des Abfalls der Niederlande*. While Schiller began the work with a highly speculative notion of demonstrating the inevitable progress of mankind towards freedom, the contrary impulse to see people and events in a more realistic light asserted itself.[7] More recently, however, Käte Hamburger has suggested that this dualism is an inadequate explanation. In her article, 'Schiller und Sartre. Ein Versuch zum Idealismus-Problem Schillers',[8] she argues that Schiller was not concerned so much with purely abstract moral philosophy but with the world of experience. Freedom, rather than obedience to the moral law, as in Kant, was his main concern. Hamburger points out how in *Über naive und sentimentalische Dichtung*, where Schiller discusses the idealist and the realist, the realist is not criticized to the advantage of the idealist. Schiller maintains the balance between them when he says: 'Es ist also offenbar, daß der Realist würdiger handelt als er seiner Theorie nach zugiebt, so wie der Idealist erhabener denkt als er handelt' (NA 20, 500). In other words, Schiller is concerned more with the world of action than with the world of pure speculation: 'Der Dramatiker Schiller hat es mit dem Bereich der Existenz zu tun ... mit dem des Handelns, der Tat.'[9] Different orientations to the world of action come into conflict in the dramas.

Two critics who have contributed valuable and original studies on the world of action in Schiller's dramas, and who have opened up the approach to Schiller taken in this thesis, are Max Kommerell and, more recently, Paul Böckmann. If Käte Hamburger has pointed out how Schiller wished, as it were, to reinstate the world of action or of phenomena as valid, Kommerell and Böckmann have considered his presentation of dramatic character within that world. Kommerell's two studies, *Schiller als Gestalter des handelnden Menschen*[10] and 'Schiller als Psychologe'[11] are no longer than essays but are strikingly original in their approach and rich in interpretative suggestions. Rather than seeing Schiller's characters as philosophical types, as was then the prevalent view, Kommerell pointed to the characters as active in the world, and brought to light the way in which that world forces roles upon them. Rather than expressing his personality in action, a man finds that his decisions create a personality which he must assume, and so Kommerell formulated the conclusion: 'daß die Tat den Charakter schafft und nicht der Charakter die Tat.'[12] Predisposition is not, therefore, the determining factor in a character's behaviour, despite the long-standing notion that Schiller created dramatic characters according to the types of the idealist and realist, schematically presented in *Über naive und sentimentalische Dichtung*. For example, E. L. Stahl's study, *Friedrich Schiller's Drama: Theory and Practice*,[13] focuses on the central dramatic characters, all of whom he calls either realists or idealists. Indeed, in his introduction Stahl discusses what he considers to be Schiller's preoccupation with the idealist and his problematic nature. As we shall see in discussion of *Don Carlos* (Chapter 1) the psychology of Schiller's early dramas differs radically from that of the later. Paul Böckmann has also contributed to this investigation of Schiller's presentation of character and action in two essays, 'Gedanke, Wort und Tat in Schillers Dramen'[14] and 'Politik und Dichtung im Werk Friedrich Schillers'.[15] (In addition, his study of *Don Carlos* in its early forms has shed valuable fresh light on that particular drama.)[16] Like Kommerell, Böckmann stresses Schiller's interest in role-playing in the political world and the ambiguity of that world, where there is a constant discrepancy between appearance and reality, deed and intention. Most recently Kenneth Dewhurst and Nigel Reeves have studied Schiller's early training in medicine and psychology and applied their findings to the early dramas.[17] They have drawn attention to his interest in those early dramas in the portrayal of certain extreme dispositions and have made a number of very acute observations on the springs of action in his early heroes. However, they were not able to extend their discussion to cover the later dramas, and indeed their consideration of *Don Carlos* fits that drama too firmly into the psychological pattern of the earlier plays, whereas this present study attempts to show how *Don Carlos* marks a move away from that psychological pattern.

Both Böckmann and Kommerell have tended to stress the specifically political aspects of the world of action in Schiller's dramas. They have opened the way for more extensive studies of the development of Schiller's conception of character and its relation to action. Kommerell in particular focused on the later dramas, and so on Schiller's mature psychology. This present study aims to examine its development in two of the early dramas, *Fiesco* and *Don Carlos*, the second being the vital transitional work, where Schiller first presents characters in an ambiguous political world. *Don Carlos* is also the first drama where he attempts to interpret the past, where he ceases to treat his source material as anecdotal and instead presents both the private and the public aspects of his characters' lives. This present study focuses on the historical dramas in particular, because it was in his turning to serious source study that Schiller changed his conception of *Don Carlos*. It was through his attempt to interpret the action of the play in a broader political and historical context that he first started to create the ambiguous world which became characteristic of the later historical dramas, and in which his distinctive psychology becomes apparent. The writing of *Don Carlos* was closely connected with the production soon after of the *Geschichte des Abfalls der Niederlande*. The various merits and demerits of Schiller's two major historiographical works have been fully discussed elsewhere.[18] What has not been considered is their place as a stage in the development of Schiller's view of character and action. While his observations on the historical Wallenstein in the *Geschichte des Dreißigjährigen Kriegs* have frequently been drawn into discussions of the later *Wallenstein* trilogy the historiographical works as a whole reflect a gradual change in Schiller's understanding of how historical figures stand in relation to the events of history, how far they create history and how far it creates them. As works of historiography both the *Abfall der Niederlande* and the *Geschichte des Dreißigjährigen Kriegs* were, of course, superseded very quickly. In Schiller's own development, however, they were important in sharpening his sense of the dependence of historical figures on their circumstances.

Schiller was interested in history not just as source material for his dramas but in its own right. His words to Caroline von Beulwitz, 'Die Geschichte ist überhaupt nur ein Magazin für meine Phantasie' (J2, 350), appear to support the view that Schiller was not seriously interested in history, nor, with the possible exception of *Wallenstein*, in presenting the historical world in his dramas.[19] These words are, however, more properly understood as a reassurance to a friend that he had not forsaken his vocation as a poet, and are wrongly applied to the later dramas, on which Schiller embarked some ten years after writing those words. The later chapters of this study attempt to show how Schiller uses the medium of drama to bring the historical world to life.

The title of this book inevitably raises the question of what the term historical drama means. The genre is so varied that the task of precise definition seems impossible. In the introduction to her study of *Fiesco* and *Don Carlos* Ursula Wertheim lists a range of the meanings of the word 'historisch' as applied to the drama, meanings ranging from 'vergangen schlechthin', 'antiquarisch', portraying historically genuine characters in invented situations, to historical in the sense of interpreting the past in a way which invests it with significance for an audience in the dramatist's present.[20] Dramatized anecdotes from the past, such as *Fiesco*, cannot in her view properly speaking be called 'historisch'.[21] Certainly *Fiesco* stands alone amongst Schiller's dramas which take historical (i.e. as opposed to contemporary or wholly invented) material, in that it predates Schiller's study of history as such. It reflects a comparative lack of interest in the source material in itself, and Schiller's preoccupation with the hero as a personality. The other historical dramas are historical in varying senses, but they are all historical in a way which *Fiesco* is not; they all (including *Don Carlos* in the final two acts) display an emphasis, not on portraiture of the central character or characters, but on situation. This is true even of *Die Jungfrau von Orleans*, where Johanna is seen in and against the movement of events in which she becomes involved. They all, in addition, present an image of the complexity and ambiguity of the historical world.

In his study of historical drama, Herbert Lindenberger[22] does not attempt to define the genre, but rather to bring to light its characteristic forms and insights, and to give an account of how both the dramatist perceives the historical matter and the audience perceives the play. In doing so Lindenberger has illuminated some of the aspects of historical drama which apply particularly to Schiller. One such aspect is the mystery surrounding the relationship of historical characters to the events around them. Schiller's distinctive psychology gives a certain elusiveness to a number of his characters (e.g. Posa, Wallenstein, Elisabeth), which springs from our sense that their actions and words do not issue from a clearly defined personality in any obvious way. 'The particular "wisdom" of historical drama comes from the insight that the springs of human action are unfathomable, that there is no necessary correlation, for instance, between intention and event, between the ability of the human will to govern action and the power of actual circumstances.'[23] Another aspect to be stressed in this study is the sense the audience has of the complexity of the world which Schiller presents. This complexity springs from the dramatist's ability to allow validity to the various and often conflicting viewpoints and judgements of the characters in the play. No single character has complete insight into the events around him; the claims of conscience cannot be seen unequivocally to overrule the demands of the moment, nor the demands of legitimate authority to destroy admiration for the usurper. Of the clash of legitimate authority with the usurper, a central theme in Schiller's historical drama, Lindenberger says, 'through our ambivalence of response we often feel we are experiencing not merely our own complexity of attitude but also the complexities of history itself.'[24] The various ways in which Schiller produces that sense of ambivalence through dramatic presentation emerge in the course of the later chapters of this study.

The two quotations from Lindenberger sum up in general terms much of Schiller's interest in and use of historical drama. He is not interested in creating historical drama to celebrate the past, as Goethe was in his *Götz von Berlichingen*. There, Lindenberger suggests, the very Shakespearian chronicle form of the play implies dissatisfaction with, and rejection of, the values of the eighteenth century.[25] Schiller's wide choice of subject matter indicates that he did not wish to dramatize his own nation's past. Nor did he wish to put forward any philosophical view of the ultimate meaning or goal of history, even though the plays necessarily suggest an interpretation of the movement of events, which springs from the dramatic organization of the subject matter. In his historical dramas Schiller shows his fascination with the phenomenon of historical greatness. From *Wallenstein* onwards he was fascinated also by the mystery surrounding action in the world, a mystery which finds its fullest expression in historical figures. In other words, how can we separate what a man is from what a man does? Do his actions in any sense belong to him, and how far can one speak of guilt or innocence if he acts not freely but under pressure of circumstances? When Max Piccolomini is on the point of leaving him, Wallenstein challenges him with the question:

> Bist du dein eigener Gebieter
> Stehst frei da in der Welt, wie ich, daß du
> Der Täter deiner Taten könntest sein?
> (*Wallensteins Tod* 2180-2)

In the context of the whole play this question is ironical. Wallenstein tries to force Max to obey him when it is he himself who has already lost all control over his own destiny. At the same time it is a question which hangs over the whole play. Can people in the world of action, forced to act on the stage of history, ever perform actions which spring from their inner selves? Are they not manipulated by events and by other people into roles which they must play? Having dealt with the vital transition in the presentation of character and action in *Don Carlos* and in the historiography, this study looks at the various forms which Schiller gives to this central issue in the historical dramas from *Wallenstein* onwards, and the various dramatic techniques—particularly those of juxtaposition and manipulation of the audience's sense of superior insight into events—by which he makes the historical world transparent. Since Schiller's dramatic work is characterized by its very experimental nature, this study does not aim to impose on it any artificial unity but rather to show how certain insights into the historical world continually re-emerge while the dramatist carries on experimenting with form.

CHAPTER 1

FIESCO AND DON CARLOS

FIESCO

A discussion of *Fiesco* is a useful introduction to Schiller's development in the presentation of historical characters in the drama, mainly by virtue of the contrasts between it and *Don Carlos*. *Fiesco* is the first play in which Schiller makes use of historical material, characters and setting. *Die Räuber* before it and *Kabale und Liebe* after it both reflect Schiller's concern at this stage not with the past but with the present. Yet at the same time *Fiesco* has many features in common with these two dramas, particularly in its exploration of the potentially destructive aspects of the idealist hero, and so provides illuminating points of comparison between *Don Carlos* and Schiller's earlier dramatic method.

Critical opinion is at the same time unanimous and conflicting on the subject of *Fiesco*. No one will claim that it is a good play, though here and there critics such as Professor Fowler[1] have tried to rescue its merits from the overwhelming weight of condemnation. The play's faults are patent—an unsatisfactory ending, unevenness of tone, an excess of rhetoric, oversimplified characterization. On all these points critics are agreed; the play is a failure. How the play stands in relation to the other dramas, particularly those of the early period, and whether it is a temporary digression from Schiller's main preoccupations are questions which receive various answers. Kurt May, for example, sees Fiesco as a successor to Franz Moor, though less abstract in conception than Franz.[2] Ilse Graham sees in him an early treatment of the theme of aesthetic contemplation and so implies strong affinities between *Fiesco* and *Don Carlos* and *Wallenstein*.[3] Gerhard Storz sees the play primarily as the product of pressure from Dalberg; it is purely theatrical and does not reflect a stage in Schiller's artistic development: 'Fast nur um dieser Begegnung willen, die Schiller mit dem Theater und der Zeitwelt zu bestehen hatte, ist ein Werk heute noch merkwürdig: der *Fiesko*. Er liegt seitwärts und ferne vom inneren Gesetz und Wachstum des dichterischen Schaffens.'[4]

Ursula Wertheim notes the fact that the play marks the beginning of Schiller's interest in historical subject matter.[5] She will not, however, apply to it the adjective 'historisch' because Schiller has not chosen subject matter which represents a significant historical moment. The Fiesco incident is merely an anecdote from the past, a coup which failed. This argument is not entirely satisfying. A dramatist can take historical subject matter of an anecdotal nature and invest it with significance. The Fiesco material could, for example, be adapted to demonstrate the clash of the old order with the new, despotism with republicanism. Schiller did not choose, or at least did not feel free, to exploit this possibility fully. Whether he has in fact explored any historical problems is the question to be tackled here.

Storz terms *Fiesco* 'ein Jugendwerk'. What he means is that the play was a pot-boiler, an attempt by Schiller to maintain his connection with the Mannheim theatre. So he aimed to impress Dalberg with the choice of subject matter: 'ein ganzes groses Gemählde des würkenden und gestürzten Ehrgeizes' (J1, 40). Certainly the play was written with the Mannheim theatre in mind, but in saying that it is not necessary to deny it any significance as a stage in Schiller's development. *Fiesco* is undoubtedly a very theatrical work in the sense that it abounds in movement, intrigue and disguise, as well as in rhetoric. The historical setting can be seen as part of the theatrical paraphernalia. The minor characters tend to be stereotypes—Verrina the stern republican, Bourgognino the hot-headed youth, Gianettino the boorish despot. The list of 'Personen des Stücks' indicates that Schiller chose for his play certain pre-established types. Bourgognino, for example, is described as 'Jüngling von zwanzig Jahren. Edel und angenehm. Stolz, rasch und natürlich' (SA 3, 159). This way of presenting character accounts for the fact that all characters are subordinate to Fiesco himself, who can manipulate them successfully. Both *Fiesco* and *Don Carlos* are plays involving complicated intrigue. In *Don Carlos*, however, the characters interact with each other and with events to a far greater extent than in *Fiesco*, with the result that the intrigue is beyond the control of any one man. In *Fiesco* the intrigue is more controlled and mechanical, with Fiesco always at the helm. Although he is at one point betrayed by the Moor, this episode is more a *coup de théâtre* than part of a complex chain of action and reaction; it has no serious repercussions and Fiesco can proceed with his plans.

It is in fact because Fiesco is such a successful intriguer that he has to be brought down eventually by assassination. There is nothing in the order of things, as presented in the play, which exposes a weakness in Fiesco's method of action. The death of Leonore appears as an unhappy accident, an instance of the mechanism going wrong, but even that does not affect the course of the action. The 'Mannheimer Bühnenfassung' omits the death of Leonore altogether and some stage productions, based on the 'Buchfassung', also omit the incident without making any appreciable difference to the play.

The motif of masks, which is important in *Fiesco*, is one which reappears in Schiller's later drama, notably in *Wallenstein*. The use of the motif of masks corresponds to the differing presentation of action in *Fiesco* and *Wallenstein*. Both men try on various disguises so that we are left to wonder which, if any, reflects the real man. Fiesco, however, wears masks to gain freedom to act by extending his influence into as many spheres as possible. At the perfect moment he will show his true colours and take charge when all is ready for him. Wallenstein wears masks in order to remain inactive. To show his true face would limit his freedom to contemplate further the possibilities of action. He mistakenly believes that the false impressions he gives do not affect his position or his potential freedom.

Of *Fiesco* Paul Böckmann says:

Wie sehr in den Jugenddramen gerade auch der politisch Handelnde sich in den Schein verstrickt und die Unbedingtheit der Freiheitsidee sich gegen ihn selbst kehrt, zeigt sich vor allem im *Fiesco*. Der Entschluß zur Befreiung Genuas vom Tyrannen führt nicht nur zu einem Spiel der Listen und Intrigen, sondern droht, eine neue Gewaltherrschaft zu begründen ... Je mehr er sich verlarvt, je klüger er rechnet, je mehr er sich hinter den Worten versteckt, um so zweideutiger und undurchschaubarer wird sein Handeln, bis er sich selber die Frage stellt, ob es ihm mehr um die Befreiung vom Tyrannen oder um die Begründung der eigenen Macht geht.[6]

Böckmann is perhaps too sweeping. He fails to point out the vastly more subtle and complex nature of the problem as posed in *Don Carlos*. While indicating the important motif of 'Schein', and its connection with masks, Böckmann does not point out that 'Schein' operates on a different level in this play, and in a way which is different from the later drama. Fiesco does not fall victim to 'Schein'; he is not prey to the 'Doppelsinn des Lebens', because the world of *Fiesco* is not portrayed as the essentially hostile and ambiguous world which emerges in the later drama, and also in *Don Carlos*.

There is, none the less, an ambiguity in *Fiesco*, the ambiguity of the hero himself. This he shares with Ferdinand and Karl Moor. These are all characters who are capable of bringing destruction to themselves and others as a result of their own extremism. Inherent in their idealism is a ruthless element which can be turned against individuals (as Ferdinand turns against Luise) or against the world in general, as in the case of Karl Moor. Fiesco is a man of less violent and extreme reactions than Karl or Ferdinand. He is, however, aware that his own best impulses, his republican ideals and love of freedom, can easily turn into despotism, freedom at the expense of others. As the conspiracy progresses, Fiesco contemplates in a soliloquy (II, 19) the conflicting impulses within him: 'Republikaner Fiesco? Herzog Fiesco?—Gemach—Hier ist der gähe Hinuntersturz, wo die Mark der Tugend sich schließt, sich scheiden Himmel und Hölle' (SA 3, 224). It is in the examination and portrayal of this figure that Schiller seems primarily to be interested. Fiesco carries within himself the seeds of his own salvation *or* destruction. The fact that Schiller was more interested in the character of his hero than in his interaction with other characters and with events is indicated by the existence of three versions of the ending. The 'Buchfassung', normally taken as the primary version, ends with the murder of Fiesco by Verrina. Here Schiller takes the historical fact of Fiesco's mysterious death by drowning, moves it to a point after the political coup and gives it a plausible explanation. The 'Mannheimer Bühnenfassung' ends with Verrina's successful attempt to persuade Fiesco to renounce his dukedom and become Genoa's 'glücklichster Bürger'. The third ending, that of the 'Leipziger Bühnenfassung', is the 'Julius Caesar' ending, where Fiesco is stabbed by Verrina in the senate. This ending is closer to the 'Buchfassung', where the hero's tendency towards despotism brings about his downfall. However, the existence of various endings suggests that Schiller was trying them out for theatrical effect, but that he had not created the kind of play where one particular ending would seem necessary or inevitable. Schiller obviously favoured the assassination ending but also considered himself free to choose whichever suited his purpose.

The existence of various endings to *Fiesco* highlights the essen-

tially unhistorical nature of the play. Schiller's emphasis on portraiture of the hero has given rise to a drama where the hero has so
little interaction with the world around him that no outcome to the
sequence of events seems necessary or inevitable. In two versions
he succumbs to the temptation of despotism, while in the third he
experiences a change of heart. Circumstances impinge on Fiesco's
freedom of action so little that up to a very late stage in the drama
he can still choose which of the two impulses he is going to follow.
Fiesco does not, therefore, offer an interpretation of man's place in
an authentic historical (or political) world and for this reason it is
doubtful whether it can legitimately be called a historical drama.

DON CARLOS

Don Carlos may be regarded as a transitional work for a number
of reasons. First, it is Schiller's first attempt to write a play in verse.
By choosing Shakespearian blank verse he demonstrated its merits
and advantages for the German dramatist. Although he recast the
play in prose for stage performance, verse was the original medium.
Secondly, as in all of the dramas of the first period there is a complex intrigue. In *Don Carlos*, however, Schiller moves away from
creating a conventional stage villain and from making a sharp
division between good and evil characters. Certainly at the beginning
of *Don Carlos* it looks as though Philipp may be a conventional
villain, but by the middle of the play he is shown to be isolated and
perplexed, and finally suffers his own tragedy. Thirdly, Schiller
may indeed have written to Dalberg, 'Carlos würde nichts weniger
seyn, als ein politisches Stük' (J1, 106), but after the long process
of writing, this emerges as a play which deals not only with love and
intrigue, but also with the clash of ideologies. Schiller comes to
interpret the historical moment at which the action takes place as
being significant for the future of Europe—in particular its political
future. Although a wholly invented character, Posa comes to
represent the forces of change which threaten Philipp's mode of
government. Philipp's role develops from that of the jealous
husband and tyrannical father into an exploration of the isolated
and insecure absolute monarch, who knows that the world is
changing and that his sun is setting. For these reasons *Don Carlos*,
rather than *Fiesco*, deserves the title of Schiller's first genuine
historical drama. Fourthly, and closely connected with these historical aspects of the play, *Don Carlos* is the first play in which

action no longer develops out of pre-established character, but rather reveals itself and develops through action, to a greater extent than perhaps even Schiller himself realized. Thus the play portrays not only the tensions between the characters and between the political philosophies of Posa and Philipp, but also expresses, in this interaction of character and event, the nature of political involvement.

Because of the complicated genesis of the play, it is helpful here to state briefly how *Don Carlos* arrived at the form which is now the standard text. The idea of using the Abbé de St. Réal's *Dom Carlos, nouvelle historique* as material for a drama came from Dalberg. He suggested it to Schiller when the latter made a brief visit to the Mannheim theatre before his flight from Württemberg. Schiller began work on the play in Bauerbach in 1783, and it is from this period that the 'Bauerbacher Plan' and Schiller's enthusiasm for Carlos as hero date. Work was interrupted on Schiller's return to Mannheim, but after preparing *Fiesco* and *Kabale und Liebe* for stage performance, he eventually finished Act I, which he published in his own *Rheinische Thalia* in March 1785. The second and third acts (now Act II, 1-13, and Act II, 14, 15–Act III, 7, line 2886) were published during 1786 in the *Thalia*, numbers 2 to 4, a journal which succeeded the *Rheinische Thalia*. The play was finally completed and published in book form in 1787. New editions were produced in 1801, 1802, and 1805, for each of which Schiller made cuts, so that the final approved version of 1805 is some thousand lines shorter than the 1787 version.[7] The 1805 text is, however, essentially the same play as the 1787 text. The major changes take place between the *Thalia* stage and the 1787 version.[8]

Don Carlos is a play which has always posed severe critical problems. As a result of its lengthy development and of Schiller's change of plan, with the shift of interest from Carlos to Posa, the play seems to lack the unity and consistency which a well-executed play should have. It appears to raise expectations of seeing the development of a love intrigue between Carlos and the Queen, only to move on to a portrayal of the idealist Posa and his involvement with Carlos and the King. Schiller himself was aware of this lack of unity and tried to defend himself in the *Briefe über Don Carlos* by suggesting that a thematic unity, in the ideal of humanity, underlies the play:

Und was wäre also die sogenannte Einheit des Stückes, wenn es *Liebe* nicht
sein soll und *Freundschaft* nie sein konnte? Von jener handeln die drei
ersten Akte, von dieser die zwei übrigen, aber keine von beiden beschäftigt
das Ganze ... Rufen Sie sich, lieber Freund, eine gewisse Unterredung
zurücke, die über einen Lieblingsgegenstand unsers Jahrzehents—über
Verbreitung reinerer, sanfterer Humanität ... unter uns lebhaft wurde ...

(NA 22, 161 f.)

This is not entirely satisfactory as a solution to the play's form.
The theme of humanity is present at the beginning of the play but
not in the same measure as in the final three acts. Schiller admits
to a decline in his interest in Carlos—'Karlos selbst war in meiner
Gunst gefallen, vielleicht aus keinem andern Grunde, als weil ich
ihm in Jahren zu weit vorausgesprungen war' (NA 22, 138)—and to
a significant change in himself, of which his reduced interest in
Carlos was the result.

Although Schiller argues for the unity of *Don Carlos* in the *Briefe
über Don Carlos*, he nevertheless admits elsewhere to radical
changes in his own perception of his material during composition.
One month after the publication of *Don Carlos* he describes in
a letter to Körner a conversation with Herder:

Er [Herder] fragte mich, wie ich arbeite und da ich ihm sagte, ich hätte das
Unglück während einer weitläufigen poetischen Arbeit mich selbst zu
verändern, weil ich noch im Fortschreiten wäre und also am Ende eines
solchen Produkts anders als bei deßen Anfang zu denken und zu empfinden,
so rieth er mir schnelle Brouillons hinzuwerfen und dan erst langsam darinn
nachzuarbeiten.

(J1, 207)

A change of plan and a change within Schiller himself are evident
in *Don Carlos*. Exactly what the change of plan was and its relation
to Schiller's original conception is another of the thorny problems
of criticism. Until quite recently the accepted view of the thematic
development of *Don Carlos* was that Schiller originally intended to
base the play on a love intrigue but that in the lengthy process of
composition he decided to introduce a political/ideological dimension in the form of conflicts at a moment of crisis for the future
of the Netherlands. The old regime was to be pitted against the
younger generation. Such a view is expressed by Herbert Lindenberger:

it [the complicated love intrigue] is a result of Schiller's shifting conception
of the play, during his many years of work on it, from the relatively simple

love—and—political conspiracy in his source ... to the high-minded expo-
sition of political idealism which was central to his final intention.[9]

Similar opinions, such as those of H. B. Garland, who divides the
characters into political and non-political,[10] stem from Schiller's
undoubted sympathy for Carlos in the Bauerbach stage of composition and in the first two acts of the *Thalia* version. The 'Bauerbacher Entwurf', along with the letter to Dalberg, is usually taken
to indicate that at that stage (1783) Schiller had not yet contemplated
a political dimension to the play, certainly not one beyond the level
of conspiracy and intrigue. Böckmann, however, has argued
recently that a political element was in fact part of Schiller's original
conception of the material, but that his idea of the means by which
his conception could be realized changed considerably. Even in the
Bauerbacher Entwurf Böckmann sees evidence for the intertwining
of the personal and political which is characteristic of the final
drama.[11] So Böckmann sees consistency in the themes of the play
but inconsistency in the dramatic form, which changes as Schiller
tries to find the appropriate way of executing his idea: 'Statt
verschiedene Konzeptionen gegeneinander auszuspielen, sollte vor
allem die Thematik beachtet werden, der eine eigene Struktur
entspricht, die durch die bestimmenden Motive abgewandelt wird
und der Darstellung eine innere Konsequenz gibt.'[12] This brings
Böckmann close to Schiller's own defence in the *Briefe über Don
Carlos*, although Böckmann is not so much defending the form
as suggesting an alternative reason for its inconsistency.

Whatever Schiller's early plan for his material, he was obviously
a different person in 1786/7 from the one who made the 'Bauerbacher
Entwurf' of 1783. He had developed an interest in historical study,
in part the result of his realization that he must give serious attention
to background reading if his characters were to have any authenticity as personalities, and if he were to understand how they should
behave in certain situations. In October 1785 Schiller writes to
Huber, 'Ich lese jezt stark im *Watson* und meinem *Philipp* and
Alba drohen wichtige Reformen' (J1, 144). By the time *Don Carlos*
was published, he was already at work on the *Geschichte des Abfalls
der Niederlande*. Historiography was popular reading at the time
and Schiller no doubt knew he would make some much needed
money from his historical researches for *Don Carlos*. His turning
to historiography indicates also the need he felt after *Don Carlos*

to reach a proper understanding of the complex period he had tried to depict in the play.

Schiller's gradual loss of interest in Carlos and his increasing concern for historical breadth bring Posa to the fore.[13] Here again, critical opinion has undergone considerable revision in the last three decades. The expansion of Posa's role raises the question of Schiller's dramatic purpose in bringing him to prominence and in putting into his mouth the sentiments he expresses to Philipp in the famous audience scene (III, 10). The most obvious answer is that Posa is an idealist who gives all for his ideal, a man filled with love for humanity, for his friend and for his vision of the future of mankind. Thus Posa has frequently been taken to be Schiller's mouthpiece and his death an example of self-sacrifice for an ideal which may be realised through it. There is no doubt some truth in this. Schiller's own idealistic belief in the progress of mankind, which shows itself again in the *Abfall der Niederlande*, does indeed seem to shape Posa's utterances to the King. However, the matter becomes more problematic when we examine not only Posa's words but also his role in the drama. The problem lies in the fact that Posa finally betrays not only Carlos but also the King, in whom he extinguishes all humanity. By seeming to set his ideal above all other considerations he uses others as his tools and finally brings disaster to the whole royal family.

In an article 'Friedrich Schiller's Marquis Posa', André von Gronicka gives a survey of the development of opinion on this character.[14] Some fairly early commentaries on Schiller by Julian Schmidt and Emil Palleske take note of Schiller's own criticisms of Posa in the *Briefe über Don Carlos*. Palleske, for example, feels that Posa's flaw is pinpointed in Letter 11, where Schiller says, 'nichts führt zum *Guten*, was nicht *natürlich* ist',[15] while Schmidt sees the play as prophetic of where the pursuit of ideology was soon to lead, i.e. the French Revolution.[16] The Schiller centenary of 1859, however, did much to promote the idea that Posa was Schiller's own mouthpiece, so reducing him to something of an abstraction. A typical centenary lecture puts forward this view: 'Und dieser Marquis Posa selbst—wohl hat man ihn getadelt; denn er ist nur ein verkörperter Gedanke, der Gedanke des Lichts und Rechts und edler Menschlichkeit, der Gedanke dieses zukunftsfreudigen achtzehnten Jahrhunderts!!'[17] By the turn of the century established critics such as Berger and Bellermann were basing their estimation of Posa purely on his words rather than on his actions and role in the drama. Berger calls Posa's actions 'peinlich und unnatürlich'.[18] He recognizes the problem but rejects the possibility that Posa is not meant by Schiller to be an ideal figure. This approach naturally makes the play look as if it is first and foremost a political manifesto. The tendency to take the ideology as dominant and the characters as secondary to it still survives in criticism and leads to the view that *Don Carlos* is, if not a political manifesto, at least a play of ideas. George Steiner puts forward this view:

The defect of 'Don Carlos' is not an excess of melodrama but rather the sacrifice of poetic form to the claims of ideology. In defiance of historical fact, Schiller made of Don Carlos a victim in the political struggle between absolutism and liberty. And in the Marquis von Posa (the true hero of the play), he dramatised his vision of the ideal man: noble, liberal, immensely alive, yet prepared to sacrifice his life to the romantic ideals of freedom and masculine friendship ... But the rhetoric of 'Don Carlos' comes to overshadow the drama. In the light of such ultimate philosophic conflicts, the characters tend to abstraction. Over their lives hangs too vivid a cast of thought.[19]

Steiner's view illustrates how an over-emphasis on ideology prevents the reader or audience from appreciating the clash not of ideas but of personalities. It is this very approach to the plays which Oskar Seidlin so firmly rejected 100 years after the 1859 centenary, an event which did so much to distort the image of Schiller. Seidlin says:

The nineteenth century ... was mistaken in forcing Schiller into a posture which was that of a tribune of the people rather than that of a poet. Yet underneath the spurious overlay there exists a genuine and fundamental level upon which Schiller and politics meet ... his plays ask decisive and basic questions: What and where is man's place in this vital and fateful game called politics? How does he master it and how does it master him?[20]

Seidlin's article is one of a number of pieces of research, most of them written comparatively recently, which take account of the apparent discrepancy between Posa's professed ideals and his actual behaviour. They try to explain how and why a man who claims to love mankind rides roughshod over the lives of his friends, Elisabeth and Carlos, and reduces finally to nothing Philipp's regard for humanity. As Max Kommerell says, 'so erscheint der hohe Liebende am Ende als der Lieblose'.[21] Some critics (e.g. von Gronicka,[22] Graham Orton[23]) are more ruthless towards Posa than others (e.g. Frances Ebstein[24]) and it is interesting to note that much that has been said against him has already been said by Schiller himself in the *Briefe über Don Carlos*. Schiller, under pressure to explain Posa's behaviour, admits that Posa is guilty of 'Schwärmerei', that he is concerned not only with humanity but also with his own heroic reputation, and that by thinking he can do everything himself he is untrue to his friend and destroys him. Schiller attributes this to the fact that political idealism of Posa's sort is not naturally present in the human heart, and that not being a natural product it is dangerous in a personality already prone to pride and self-assertiveness:

Schon allein dieses, daß jedes solche moralische Ideal oder Kunstgebäude doch nie mehr ist als eine Idee, die ... an dem eingeschränkten Gesichtspunkt des Individuums teilnimmt ... schon dieses allein, sage ich, müßte sie zu einem äußerst gefährlichen Instrument in seinen Händen machen: aber noch weit gefährlicher wird sie durch die Verbindung, in die sie nur allzuschnell mit gewissen Leidenschaften tritt, die sich mehr oder weniger in allen Menschenherzen finden; Herrschsucht meine ich, Eigendünkel und Stolz, die sie augenblicklich ergreifen und sich unzertrennbar mit ihr vermengen.

(NA 22, 171)

Posa certainly does make an ambiguous impression. He is spokesman for laudable ideals. Ursula Wertheim is one critic who points out how Posa is in many ways a man of the Enlightenment, a man who looks forward to a better world with the optimistic assurance that he is moving in the direction in which history itself is going.[25] Posa's love for humanity is impressed upon us from his first appearance on stage, when he says to Carlos (I, 2)

Ein Abgeordneter der ganzen Menschheit
Umarm' ich Sie

(157-8)

He gives an impression to the world of great independence. He is a man gifted with many talents, yet one whom no one at court envies, much to Philipp's surprise. He has a breadth of vision and a lack of personal ambition which enable him to envisage an ideal future for mankind. As Schiller points out in the *Briefe über Don Carlos*, he finally dies for his ideal, doing the most he can do to ensure its, rather than his own, survival: 'er stirbt, um für sein ... Ideal alles zu tun und zu geben, was ein Mensch für etwas tun und geben kann, das ihm das Teuerste ist' (NA 22, 174). Amid the prevalent criticism of Posa in recent studies it can be easy to lose sight of his undoubted nobility, even though it is not flawless.

The negative aspects of Posa's behaviour must, all the same, be recognised. Though inspired by a lofty ideal, he nevertheless becomes a manipulator, in spite of the fact that, with his independent spirit, he cannot bear to be manipulated by others. This is what he tells Philipp, who cannot understand why Posa will not seek advancement at court:

> Sie wollen
> Nur meinen Arm und meinen Muth im Felde,
> Nur meinen Kopf im Rath.
>
> (3025-7)

Posa wants to feel that he is in control of his own life and actions, not someone who plays a small part in someone else's grand design. He is not, however, slow to manipulate others, especially Carlos. He has created a certain role into which Carlos must be fitted. A certain amount of critical argument surrounds the extent to which Posa manipulates Carlos from the very beginning. The argument hinges on the value given to the letters, discovered after Posa's death, which make known that a Turkish fleet is already on its way to Spain. If the letters are to influence our whole reading of the play then we must say that they show that Posa was under great pressure of time to persuade Carlos to support his plan. Orton says: 'When we accept the authenticity of the letters we must as a corollary reject a popular and attractive reading of the play ... The letters prove Posa to be a consistent intriguer both before and after his audience with the King.'[26] Orton gives a fairly damning account of Posa's part in the action on the strength of the letters. Böckmann, more convincingly, argues that their value is not to be overstated, in fact that it is a misunderstanding of the nature of the dramatic movement to assume that we have to begin our reading of the play with the discovery of Posa's plot. Böckmann's view is that the letters are an example of the *coup de théâtre*, a theatrical device to unravel intrigue quickly and to give Schiller scope for trying out dramatic effects.[27] The latter explanation is more satisfactory than Orton's view, though Böckmann is interpreting with Schiller's supposed compositional methods strongly in mind, while Orton works on the principle of interpreting the text as it stands as a finished product.

Certainly Orton's interpretation indicates just how negative a view of Posa the text itself can seem to justify. The very least one can say is that Posa wishes at all costs to advance his vision for the freedom of the Netherlands and is dismayed to see Carlos absorbed by his hopeless love for Elisabeth. Posa and Carlos may be friends but, as Schiller points out, this is not an equal relationship but rather one of mentor and pupil: 'Dieser schöpferische und feurige Geist mußte bald einen Stoff haben, auf den er wirkte; konnte sich ihm ein schönerer anbieten als ein zart und lebendig fühlender, seiner Ergießungen empfänglicher, ihm freiwillig entgegeneilender Fürstensohn?' (NA 22, 143). Carlos is to be educated by Posa, with the result that Posa can be criticized for seeming not to respect Carlos's freedom. This lack of respect for Carlos's freedom comes in a readily recognizable guise, that of the master wishing to protect his pupil by shielding him from unhappy discoveries. Posa will not take Carlos into his confidence and remains inscrutable to him almost up to the last moment. Realizing after their encounter in Act IV, Scene 7, that Carlos is actually capable of doubting him, Posa decides still to keep secret what is going on:

> Warum
> Dem Schlafenden die Wetterwolke zeigen,
> Die über seinem Scheitel hängt?—Genug,
> Daß ich sie still an dir vorüber führe,
> Und, wenn du aufwachst, heller Himmel ist.
> (3648-52)

Posa genuinely seems to believe he is acting in Carlos's best interests. His pride—the belief that he knows best and must do it all himself—is mixed with benevolence, however much he overestimates his capacities.

While Posa appears to behave badly towards Carlos, he is even guiltier with regard to Philipp. Frances Ebstein rightly says that Posa's 'real betrayal of the King lies in the fact that he wins his confidence in the first place'.[28] Certainly it is a tempting opportunity for a man like Posa, filled with enthusiasm for his ideal, to try to win over the King. But immediately he becomes involved in deception and betrayal and appears to use the King as callously as he accuses Philipp of using others. His manipulation of others inevitably casts doubt on that ideal of humanity which he professes. Obviously his effect on the King is to shatter any confidence in humanity at all and to drive him back finally to the Großinquisitor and his doctrine that

> Menschen sind
> Für Sie nur Zahlen, weiter nichts.
>
> (5225-6)

To judge with hindsight, one might claim that Posa should have realised that to disillusion the King would be to bring greater disaster than simply to remain aloof from him. When Philipp's grief gives way to feelings of revenge there is the threat that a great deal of suffering can be inflicted before Posa's dream of the future becomes reality:

> .Er brachte
> Der Menschheit, seinem Götzen, mich zum Opfer;
> Die Menschheit büße mir für ihn!
>
> (5086-8)

Posa, then, is a highly ambiguous figure. While capable of the highest moral idealism, the greatest self-sacrifice, and while possessing both charm and brilliance with independence of spirit, he brings devastation to the lives of Carlos, Elisabeth, and Philipp. In her article, 'In Defense of Marquis Posa', Frances Ebstein identifies the fact that modern criticism, recognizing the problematic side to Posa's actions and the fact that it has long been ignored, has caused the pendulum to swing in the opposite direction. Whereas once Posa met with whole-hearted approval, now adverse criticism is tending to obscure his undoubted stature and nobility. Miss Ebstein, therefore, attempts a new and more sympathetic psychological interpretation of Posa's behaviour. By this method, however, the same impasse is reached as we find in the *Briefe über Don Carlos*, an impasse not to be cleared by fitting Posa into any psychological type. The reason is that Posa's ambiguity is not so much a function of his own character as of the whole situation as it develops in the second half of the play. Here the vital difference between Posa and the idealist figures of Schiller's early dramas emerges. The behaviour of Karl Moor, Ferdinand, and Fiesco is explicable in terms of the inner contradictions of the idealist type. Cruelty and despotism constitute the 'shadow' side of such personalities. Posa's behaviour can no longer be explained in these terms. We must look beyond character to dramatic situation.

The weakness of the psychological argument, with its emphasis on Posa's character flaw or flaws, is demonstrated by Schiller's own *Briefe über Don Carlos*. These letters are, of course, a retrospective examination of the play. Schiller obviously recognizes the fatal results of Posa's involvement in the action and accounts for the catastrophe by pointing to Posa's pride in his ability to achieve his great goal alone—'Geräuschlos, ohne Gehülfen, in stiller Größe zu wirken, ist des Marquis Schwärmerei' (NA 22, 170). In Letter 11 he accuses Posa roundly of 'Despotismus'. However, such criticism of Posa's flawed character obscures his nobility. It seems, in fact, likely that Schiller himself had not fully grasped how his own dramatic technique, indeed his own perception of the dramatic action, had changed in the course of *Don Carlos*. Certainly he gave up dramatic work after *Don Carlos* in order to devote time to the study of, amongst other things, how certain dramatic effects were to be achieved. He had to give time to the most fundamental questions regarding the nature and effect of tragedy, having found *Don Carlos* so difficult to execute. His turning away from dramatic creation suggests that he was dissatisfied with the somewhat haphazard, inspirational mode of writing which had produced his early work and believed it necessary to achieve greater theoretical clarity. While Schiller attributes Posa's disastrous involvement in politics to his tendency towards despotism, he finds in Letter 12 of the *Briefe über Don Carlos* extenuating circumstances. Justifying Posa's precipitate self-sacrifice he asks: 'Unter welchen Umständen schreitet er zu diesem Entschluß?—In der drangvollsten Lage, worin je ein Mensch sich befunden ...' (NA 22, 175). Here Schiller comes closer to identifying the source of Posa's ambiguity than in his psychological portrait, though he gives little weight to this argument from circumstances. He does, however, at least identify the part played by *situation*, as opposed to character. It is in the change of dramatic technique, rather than in psychological interpretation that the key to Posa's ambiguity is found.

It is necessary first of all to look again at how *Don Carlos* was originally conceived dramatically. In 1783 Schiller tells Dalberg that it will be 'ein Familiengemälde in einem fürstlichen Haußbe' (J1, 106). These words have usually provoked interest as an indication of whether Schiller envisaged any political dimension in his early plan of the play. They do, however, positively imply other things about Schiller's early plan, such as his mode of presentation.

This is to be 'ein Gemälde', a portrait; in other words, this is to be a play which depicts the relationships between members of a royal family. Böckmann regards Schiller's use of the term 'Familiengemälde' not only as an attempt to convince Dalberg that his *Don Carlos* will be a popular product for the theatre, but also as an indication of his interest in the dramatic theories of Diderot. Diderot's *Le Fils naturel, Le Père de famille, Entretiens sur le Fils naturel*, and *De la Poésie dramatique* had been translated by Lessing and published in 1760 under the title *Das Theater des Herrn Diderot.* The correspondence of Lessing's translation of Diderot's terminology and the terms in which Schiller writes about *Don Carlos* in letters of 1783 leads Böckmann to see a strong link between them.[29] This is particularly true of Schiller's term 'Familiengemälde', for it was the 'tragédie domestique' which Diderot had been defending in his theoretical writings. Diderot advocated that the family drama should be composed of a series of tableaux, showing people in typical circumstances. These tableaux should be held together by a complex intrigue and interest should be maintained and movement achieved by the clashes of interest and personality in this depiction of the middle-class 'condition'. Böckmann says of Schiller:

Er hat sich auf sehr selbständige Weise mit den Erörterungen über die 'tragédie domestique' auseinandergesetzt und sich nicht im Sinne der moralisierenden Familienstücke seiner Zeit mit einem Gesellschaftsausschnitt begnügt, sondern die grundsätzlichere Frage Diderots nach der 'condition de l'homme' aufgegriffen und am exemplarischen Fall der Königsfamilie entfaltet.[30]

Now this method of presenting a situation requires that the dramatist form in advance a complete picture of the characters he will portray. When they are put into the drama their deeds issue from these predetermined personalities. This is certainly what Diderot's theory suggests. Intrigue and conflict of interest are important because they create the situations which expose people's true nature: 'Die Bestimmung der Charaktere aber hängt von den Situationen ab ... Alsdenn sind die Charaktere gut getroffen, wenn die Situationen dadurch verwirrter und schwieriger werden.'[31] This was Schiller's method in *Fiesco* also, where the list of 'dramatis personae' contains detailed descriptions of each character, to lead the audience to expect a certain type of behaviour from them. In fact it is this way of regarding the relation of character to action that emerges from the *Briefe über Don Carlos*. Schiller describes, for example, how he came to create Carlos: 'Die Rede war also davon, einen Fürsten aufzustellen ... diesen Fürsten nur zu *zeigen*, den Gemütszustand in ihm herrschend zu machen, der einer solchen Wirkung zum Grunde liegen muß' (NA 22, 164). In other words, Schiller decides what sort of character Carlos is to be and then attempts to portray that in the play itself. Carlos needs a negative counterpart and so Philipp is created:

Da aber mein eigentlicher Vorwurf war, den künftigen *Schöpfer des Menschenglücks* aus dem Stücke gleichsam *hervorgehen* zu lassen, so war es sehr an seinem Orte, den *Schöpfer des Elends* neben ihm aufzuführen und durch ein vollständiges schauderhaftes Gemälde des Despotismus sein reizendes Gegenteil desto mehr zu erheben.

(NA 22, 166)

These words are hard to reconcile with Schiller's comments on Philipp in the *Thalia* Preface of 1785 where he recognizes the need to avoid creating stereotypes. The passage above from the later *Briefe über Don Carlos* seems accurately to explain the static quality of the first half of the drama. This static quality stems from the conception that the characters have fixed personalities from which reactions are provoked by the dramatist's choice of appropriate situations. Intrigue creates a form of movement but essentially there is little development in this conception of drama because there is no interaction of characters with one another and with the events around them except on a mechanical level.

While, however, this is true of the opening two acts of *Don Carlos*, it is not true of the final three. Whereas the first two acts are principally concerned with exploring the tensions between a group of characters, the final three acts present a much more complex interaction of characters with each other and with the events around them, from which their personalities emerge more convincingly and, sometimes, in a different light from that of the portraiture of the early part of the play. In this new development the crucial scene is the audience scene (III, 10) between Philipp and Posa. Posa speaks his mind to the King, and the King, not used to such directness, asks:

> Bin ich der erste,
> Der euch von dieser Seite kennt?

The Marquis replies

> Von dieser—
>
> Ja!
>
> (3082-4)

This reply is patently untrue. Carlos and the Queen, we may assume, are well aware of Posa's ideals and they can easily be inferred from Posa's first meeting (I, 2) with Carlos. But what is Posa to say? He cannot betray his friends. Those very qualities of independence of spirit and lack of self-interest which complement his political ideals are exactly the qualities which Philipp, exasperated by the manipulations of Alba and Domingo, is seeking. So Philipp summons Posa out of the blue and Posa now finds himself caught between the King and Carlos. Whatever the conflicting assessments of the importance, ideologically speaking, of the audience scene, from a dramatic point of view it sparks off a course of events in which intrigue still plays a large part, but where there is a much more vital presentation of human involvements. Indeed, it is vital for the very reason that new facets of each personality emerge as the drama unfolds.

The most notable example of this is in the portrayal of Philipp. Schiller was at an early stage of composition aware of the need to avoid simple caricature in his portrayal of Philipp and points this out in his preface to the original first act, published in 1785 in the *Rheinische Thalia*:

> Wenn dieses Trauerspiel schmelzen soll, so muß es—wie mich deucht—durch die Situation und den Charakter König Philipps geschehen ... Man erwartet—ich weiß nicht welches? Ungeheuer, sobald von Philipp dem Zweiten die Rede ist—mein Stück fällt zusammen, sobald man ein solches darin findet ...
>
> (NA4, 217)

The Philipp of the original Act I is, however, a tyrant. He insists on his wife's presence at the *auto da fé* and loudly forces her to attend while she pleads vainly with him. Schiller, probably seeing that the incident was crudely melodramatic, reduces it for the 1787 version, but still retains the Queen's attempt at refusal. The scene ends with Philipp's words to Elisabeth, who protests she is 'ein Mensch':

> Auch eine Christinn hoff' ich—Kommen Sie
> es zu beweisen
>
> (NA 6, 55, lines 1034-5)

In the 1805 version the King announces the *auto da fé* (lines 744-9) but no altercation with the Queen follows. The Philipp of Acts I and II stands, therefore, in somewhat sharper contrast to the Philipp of the second half of the play in the 1787 version than in the final 1805 text. From Act III onwards, however, it is a much more finely drawn portrayal of Philipp that emerges from his encounters not only with Posa, but later with the Großinquisitor and with Lerma, after the King's sleepless night (III, 2). Through the more complex and more authentic interaction of personalities and events in the final three acts there emerges more than the simple 'Schöpfer des Elends', to whom Schiller alludes in the *Briefe über Don Carlos*.

It is in the context of this much more complex world in the final three acts of the drama that we encounter the problem of Posa's ambiguity most fully. In creating a world which is a much more authentic reflection of how people act and reveal themselves in life than is the tableau world of the first two acts of the play, Schiller also lays his characters open to the sort of ambiguity which surrounds the world of history and politics. This is a different ambiguity from that which we can see in earlier idealist heroes. In a world of stereotyped figures, such as the early part of *Don Carlos*, it was easier to fit Posa into the mould of the early idealist heroes of Schiller's dramas. Like Ferdinand of *Kabale und Liebe*, Posa professes high ideals but at the same time puts his friends at risk to further his own plan. So Posa arranges for Carlos to see Elisabeth, though it endangers Carlos's life to do so. He shares with Ferdinand that vulnerability to the charge of inconsistency; he voices high ideals but fails to live up to them and his actions are at variance with the intention behind them. However, Ferdinand is an idealist who carries in him the seeds of his own destruction. Inherent in his personality are the contradictions which account for his behaviour, as in the case of Fiesco also. The fault in Posa lies not so much in him as a personality as in the world itself. Posa is not essentially the idealist tragic hero with as much capacity for evil as for good, he is rather a man forced about by the complex pressures of the world of politics, a man whose actions can no longer be taken as authentic products of his personality. His personality indeed becomes increasingly elusive as character portrayal gives way, from Act III onwards, to the type of dramatic movement where characters reveal themselves in, and are in turn moulded by, the network of circumstances and relationships which surrounds them.

The audience's perception of this ambiguous world of politics, which casts the shadow of ambiguity over the characters, is partly disturbed by the fact that Schiller is hampered in the second half of the play by the complex intrigue which he has set in motion in the first half. He is committed to the resolution of the intrigues he has begun and seems unable to bring the action forward without the aid of various *coups de théâtre* and without implicating the characters of the drama in some unbecoming activities. Garland notes, for example, how the very finely drawn Elisabeth 'deteriorates into a politician'[32] in the final stages of the play. Here she seems to be moulded by the exigencies of a complicated plot which must be brought to some sort of conclusion. The same can be said of the sudden discovery of Posa's letters in Act V, 7. Plot and counter-plot tend, therefore, to exaggerate, but also to obscure the ambiguity of this political world, which emerges from the shift to this new mode of drama from Act III onwards. In adopting the *coup de théâtre* as a means of extricating himself from the intrigues of the play, Schiller was abandoning Diderot's principles. Diderot deprecated the introduction of *coups de théâtre* because they were less true to life than the tableau presentation he advocated. Peter Szondi[33] suggests that the *coup de théâtre* was foreign to Diderot's theatre because the unexpected turn of events did not belong to the bourgeois world, for which the *drame* was intended. The sudden unexpected turn of events belonged rather to the aristocratic world: (Die *coups de théâtre* sind am Hof zuhaus, sie spiegeln die Wandelbarkeit fürstlicher Launen, die Unbeständigkeit der Koalitionen dort, wo jeder auf der Jagd ist, nach Macht, nach Gunst, nach Glück.'[34] Yet in spite of the obvious artificiality of the *coup de théâtre* as a dramatic device, the second half of *Don Carlos* is undoubtedly more authentic in its depiction of the world of action than the first, primarily because Diderot's emphasis on 'conditions' required the presentation of characters as types. Also, Schiller may be said to be employing the *coup de théâtre* in what Szondi suggests is its correct milieu, even though it tends to obscure the relationships between the characters.

In *Don Carlos* we can see Schiller advancing towards a type of drama which resembles the later plays. *Don Carlos* demonstrates Schiller's need to tackle the problem of dramatic form. Despite its manifest flaws *Don Carlos* is a highly significant work, however, because of this very change of technique which it exhibits. In the later plays Schiller again creates a complex world where even the most apparently noble and pure characters, even Max and Johanna, are implicated in the 'Doppelsinn des Lebens'.[35] The world of political action is recreated, after Schiller's ten-year dramatic silence, in *Wallenstein*, where he takes up again the problem of the relation of character and action. In *Don Carlos* Schiller begins to move towards that conception of character and action which emerges strongly in *Wallenstein*, namely that character is not fixed in advance, with appropriate actions issuing from preconceived dramatic personalities, but rather that character and action are so inseparable that it is virtually impossible to say which produces which. The question asked in *Wallenstein* is whether a man's 'character' can in any way be distinguished as some kind of abstract collection of traits and predispositions, since it is so bound up with action and decision issuing not from free choice but from pressure of circumstances.

The world of action in *Don Carlos*, Acts III to V, where response to situation in characters appears to be much more spontaneous, is a much more complex world than that of the beginning of the play, where the characters began as stereotypes. The world of *Don Carlos* can therefore be contrasted with the world of *Fiesco*. In *Fiesco* Schiller was primarily concerned with portraiture of the hero. Dalberg was to be offered 'ein ganzes groses Gemählde des würkenden und gestürzten Ehrgeizes' (J1, 40), and it is interesting to note the use of the word 'Gemählde', with its implications for the mode of drama we expect. In *Don Carlos* the main intriguer has lost the power to control the consequences of his actions and the power to predict what others will do. It is true that Fiesco is finally caught out by Verrina and betrayed by the Moor, but essentially he knows his men and how they can be manipulated. The characters in *Fiesco* are stereotypes, who neither evolve nor reveal new facets of themselves during the action. For this reason the play has a very rhetorical quality, already noted. Only Fiesco himself is in any way problematic because of the closeness of the liberator to the despot. Fiesco presents deceptive appearances but these lie on the surface only. There is a real Fiesco underneath, who emerges when the time is right. It is not until *Don Carlos* that Schiller presents the phenomenon of the character who, even when not intentionally deceiving, behaves in a way which is somehow worse than he ought to, if actions and personality are to be consonant. This discrepancy does not emerge from inner contradictions of personality but from the pressure of circumstances. Posa himself is a perfect example of the phenomenon of which Hofmannsthal spoke when he discussed the nature of Schiller's heroes. He credits them with greatness, but this greatness does not lie in their actions: 'Nicht die Gestalten also, aber etwas, das in ihnen ist: mehr ihre Allüren als ihre Handlungen, *die nicht immer ganz aus ihnen fließen.*'[36] This statement is true not of the early idealists, whose behaviour could be explained in terms of the inner contradictions of the idealist type, but of the later characters, such as Posa. The ambiguous, indeed hostile, nature of the world creates a gulf between a character and his actions, so much so that his own personality becomes virtually undiscoverable. Far from being a stereotype, he is elusive, presenting ever-changing facets of himself through action.

The fact of this ambiguity in Schiller's presentation of Posa indicates a growing objectivity on the dramatist's part towards his subject matter. This was certainly not true of the early conception of the play in the Bauerbach period, when Schiller writes to Reinwald of his involvement with Carlos: 'Ich trage ihn auf meinem Busen— ich schwärme mit ihm durch die Gegend um—um Bauerbach herum' (J1, 65). Even in the original first two acts of the play Carlos domi- nates the action with his hopeless love for Elisabeth. The increased complexity of the play from Act III onwards seems bound up with a greater degree of objectivity. By objectivity is meant the ability of the dramatist to avoid making his own sympathies for the characters apparent and/or using characters to propound his own viewpoint. It is generally acknowledged that Schiller achieved a far greater degree of objectivity in *Wallenstein* than in any of the plays of the early period up to *Don Carlos*. Signs of its growth are nevertheless present in *Don Carlos*. While admitting in the *Briefe über Don Carlos*, 'dieser Charakter ging mir nahe' (NA 22, 170), Schiller's sympathy for Posa does not prevent him from portraying Philipp with sympathy and insight, nor from allow- ing the problematic aspects of Posa's political involvement to become apparent. *Don Carlos* is not an objective play in one sense, for we cannot help hearing Schiller's voice in the noble words of Posa, and he is somewhat idealized at the beginning of the play. However, the ambiguity in Schiller's presentation of Posa, and the complexity of the political world in which Posa acts, indicate how Schiller is beginning to withdraw from the world of his play and to

hold himself more aloof from it. This greater ability to hold himself
aloof is the prerequisite for the increased objectivity of *Wallenstein*
and is the basis of that ironical distance which can be discerned in
the later dramas.

One indication of this growth of objectivity is in the question
that hangs over the ending of the play. Is this a play which looks
forward to the triumph of the ideal of humanity, in spite of the
destruction of its representatives, or is it a play which casts doubt
on the value of pursuing ideals and trying to realise them in human
society, in particular in politics? Posa is confident that he is march-
ing in the direction in which history is going and indeed he seems
at the end of the play to be vindicated. A criticism levelled against
Don Carlos as soon as it appeared was that Posa was not a credible
product of the sixteenth century. Schiller denies this in the second
of the *Briefe über Don Carlos*, though it is undeniable that Posa
gives voice to sentiments which were current in the eighteenth
century and his confidence in progress towards freedom is shared
by Schiller himself as he embarks on the *Geschichte des Abfalls der
Niederlande*. The audience, of course, knows anyway that Philipp
and his tyrannical government are on the wane[37] and that Posa's
vision of freedom for the Netherlands is eventually fulfilled. There
is an optimism in this view of history, and the play seems to suggest
that history does vindicate the good cause, that in fact it is almost
a natural law that nations assert their sense of their own independence and that history is moving towards humane and tolerant
government.

Yet despite the fact that Posa's ideal will be vindicated in a future
of which the audience is aware, the play ends in catastrophe. One is
forced to ask whether that catastrophe is simply the temporary
triumph of the forces of tyranny, or whether the catastrophe does
not suggest something deeper about the involvement of the individual in the movement of history. While Posa's vision of the future,
though not realized, retains its dignity at the end of the play, his own
attempts to put it into force have had disastrous results. It seems
that if any vision becomes reality, it will be by a long and painful
process, not by the intervention of people even as noble as Posa.
There is, in fact, a double perspective on history in *Don Carlos*,
a confidence in progress but a lack of confidence in those who think
they can bring it about. It is doubtful whether Schiller himself fully
recognized this double perspective, because his statements in the

Briefe über Don Carlos seem to be conflicting. In Letter 9 Schiller explicitly states that the fulfilment of the author's intention is to be found at the end of the play, and quotes the final interview between Carlos and Elisabeth:

> —Ich habe
> in einem langen schweren Traum gelegen.
> Ich *liebte*—jetzt bin ich erwacht. Vergessen
> sei das Vergangne. Endlich seh ich ein, es gibt
> ein höher wünschenswerter Gut, als dich
> besitzen—Hier sind Ihre Briefe
> zurück. Vernichten Sie die meinen. Fürchten
> Sie keine Wallung mehr von mir. Es ist
> vorbei. Ein reiner Feuer hat mein Wesen
> geläutert—Einen Leichenstein will ich
> ihm setzen, wie noch keinem Könige zuteil
> geworden—Über seiner Asche blühe
> ein Paradies!
> KÖNIGIN. — — So hab ich Sie gewollt!
> Das war die große Meinung seines Todes.
>
> (NA 22, 167)[38]

The implication is, as Benno von Wiese says: 'Von dem toten Posa geht eine erweckende Kraft aus, die den Königssohn zu der gleichen selbstlosen Aufopferung fähig macht.'[39] More recently, F. M. Fowler has also interpreted the ending of the play as including 'the promise that Posa's hope of a better future must eventually be fulfilled.'[40] He reaches his view through a study of gesture in the play (here Philipp's action of turning his back on his son in the final scene) and the imagery of growth and nature, which runs through it. In his interview with the Großinquisitor, Philipp receives the Church's sanction on the destruction of his son, but is aware of his sin against nature:

> Ich frevle
> An der Natur
>
> (5272-3)

In destroying Carlos, Philipp destroys himself and so there is hope for the future. While this is true, from the action of the play it is by no means clear that Posa's vision will be realized by such as Posa. Again, we can turn to the imagery of the play to illustrate this.

In the last scene of the play Carlos, in his leave-taking, is the last person to use the word 'Natur', which has been a key term in the play. It is generally used to denote an ideal state of human society, in which affections are neither spoilt by political machinations nor crushed by etiquette. Carlos complains of the distortion of nature of which his father is guilty by marrying Elisabeth:

> Sie waren mein
> . . . .
> Mir zuerkannt von Himmel und Natur
>
> (671, 673)

Philipp's violation of his natural role as father in destroying Carlos is merely the culmination of a rule which has constantly violated nature and caused Philipp's own isolation, as Posa boldly tells him,

> Unselige
> Verdrehung der Natur!—Da Sie den Menschen
> Zu Ihrem Saitenspiel herunter stürzten,
> Wer theilt mit Ihnen Harmonie?
>
> (3118-21)

The concept of 'Natur' carries over into the *Briefe über Don Carlos*. Schiller attributes Posa's despotism to the fact that the ideals which men set out to realise do not spring up naturally in the human heart, but are constructs of the mind. Inevitably, then, there is a discrepancy between the ideal itself and the pursuit of it by individuals. According to Schiller, Posa's attempt to impose his way on others was bound to end in disaster, 'denn nichts führt zum Guten, was nicht natürlich ist' (NA 22, 172). This seems to be at variance with what he states in the passage quoted above about his intention, for if Posa is estranged from nature, then he cannot serve as a model for Carlos and token of a happier future. This discrepancy seems again to spring from Schiller's uncertainty about Posa, his sympathy with Posa's ideals and nobility, but his recognition at the same time of the problematic side to his actions.

In the final scene Carlos makes a very significant statement:

> Jetzt geh' ich
> Aus Spanien, und sehe meinen Vater
> Nicht wieder—Nie in diesem Leben wieder.
> Ich schätz' ihn nicht mehr. *Ausgestorben ist*
> *In meinem Busen die Natur* ...[41]
>
> (5338-42)

In view of the connotations of the word 'Natur' in the drama and in the *Briefe über Don Carlos*, this statement casts great doubt on

Carlos's fitness to carry out the commission which Posa has left him. Indeed his coldness towards Elisabeth in the final scene (e.g. lines 5352-8) suggests already that he is estranged from nature. There is, therefore, a more complex perspective on history than is at first apparent, for alongside the dignity of Posa's ideals is the doubt cast on the possibility of effective human action to bring in a new and better world. Posa's involvement in politics has led him into the entanglements and final disaster which cast on him an ambiguous light. Would this not also happen in Carlos's case? Certainly the play provides no easy solution to the problem of how even the noblest individual can engage himself for a more enlightened future without, at least in the short term, in fact achieving the very opposite of what he intended.

The question of the progress of mankind to political freedom and enlightened government, and the role of the individual in bringing it about, continued to interest Schiller. If individual action is ineffective, as the example of Posa suggests, perhaps communal effort will be effective. This certainly is the idea with which Schiller begins his discussion of the *Geschichte des Abfalls der Niederlande*.

CHAPTER 2

SCHILLER'S HISTORIOGRAPHY

I. 1785-1788

Schiller's main period of work as a historian is confined to about seven years, from 1785 to 1792. During most of this time he found himself in considerable financial hardship, having finally left Mannheim for Dresden. Forced at first to rely on the kindness of his new friends Körner and Huber, he then had to attempt to make his own living by writing, but he found himself constantly burdened with debts and hampered by ill health. During this period Schiller aimed to make his money primarily from journals, from his own *Thalia* (begun in 1785 as the *Rheinische Thalia*), and from his contributions to Wieland's *Teutscher Merkur*, in which, for example, the *Briefe über Don Carlos* were published in 1788. The first of his two major works of historiography, the *Geschichte des Abfalls der vereinigten Niederlande von der spanischen Regierung*, was published by Crusius in Leipzig in 1788. The second major work, the *Geschichte des Dreißigjährigen Kriegs*, was published between 1791 and 1793 in Göschen's *Historischer Kalender für Damen*. It was written at a time when Schiller was struggling against illness, while at the same time holding the post of professor of history at Jena, from which as such he received virtually no income.

The purpose of this chapter is not to give an extensive survey of all of Schiller's historiography, but rather, bearing in mind the focus of this study, i.e. Schiller's presentation of character and action in the historical world, to concentrate on the two large-scale works and to draw on the various minor essays where they throw additional or special light on his development. For this reason there will be no detailed discussion of Schiller's university lectures nor of his miscellaneous sketches for the *Allgemeine Sammlung Historischer Memoires*.

Because Schiller's historiography was produced under great pressure of time for immediate publication in journals of the day, it is tempting to assume that he was not seriously interested in history for its own sake, but only in stocking his poetic imagination

and in publishing what would bring him much-needed money.
Schiller seems, at least superficially, to have lent support to the
former idea in his much quoted words to Körner: 'Wenn ich aber
auch nicht Historiker werde, so ist dieses gewiß, daß die *Historie*
das Magazin seyn wird woraus ich schöpfe, oder mir die Gegenstände hergeben wird, in denen ich meine Feder und zuweilen auch
meinen Geist übe' (J2, 295), and to Caroline von Beulwitz: 'Die
Geschichte ist überhaupt nur ein Magazin für meine Phantasie, und
die Gegenstände müssen sich gefallen lassen, was sie unter meinen
Händen werden' (J2, 350). Certainly the critics and historians of
the nineteenth century took him at face value. Gervinus said, for
example:

Sachverständige, wie Niebuhr, haben sich über die Nichtigkeit seiner
Geschichten schonungslos ausgesprochen, und wir würden dies Urtheil
hier wiederholen, wenn nicht Schiller selbst eben so streng darüber geurtheilt
hätte, und wenn es nicht überall eine Pflicht der Gerechtigkeit wäre,
treffenden Tadel dort zunächst zu suchen, wo er zugleich ein löbliches
Zeugniß der Selbsterkenntniß ist.[1]

Janssen,[2] while giving detailed critical attention to Schiller's
achievement as a historian, starts out from the assumption that
Schiller's historical work was not a serious venture, and quotes on
the title-page from Hoffmeister's biography, *Schillers Leben*:

Es wäre doch sehr unbillig, wenn wir außer Acht lassen wollten, daß Schiller
sich nur eine kurze Zeit seines Lebens, gleichsam im Vorübergehen, und
eigentlich, um sich selbst zu bilden, und die ihm mangelnde unmittelbare
Erfahrung durch eine mittelbare zu ersetzen, mit der Geschichte beschäf-
tigte.[3]

Schiller's words to Körner (as Regin[4] points out) are probably more
correctly understood as a reassurance to an anxious friend about
Schiller's apparent turning away from poetry.

While Schiller's achievement as a historian was easily overshadowed by the great German historians of the nineteenth century,
it is false to assume from the disdain of such as Niebuhr that
Schiller was not genuinely interested in the subject. In fact Hoffmeister's words indicate another important reason for Schiller's
turning to history, apart from the financial advantages of journal-
ism, which emerged only after his first period of intensive historical
reading in 1785/6. Schiller turned to history in the first instance
'um sich selbst zu bilden', to make good what he felt he lacked in
general education. History was a particular gap in his knowledge.

From the Karlsschule he was acquainted with Plutarch, to whose presentation of ancient heroes Karl Moor alludes in his opening speech in *Die Räuber*: 'Mir ekelt vor diesem Tintengleksenden Sekulum, wenn ich in meinem Plutarch lese von grossen Menschen' (NA3, 20). History as an independent discipline was not studied at the Karlsschule.[5] There was, however, considerable emphasis on philosophical reading, in particular Enlightenment philosophy, in which Schiller was given guidance and encouragement by his teacher Abel.[6] It was his friendship with Körner and Huber which encouraged him to catch up on the historical reading he felt he had missed, and gave him the opportunity to do so. Schiller's words in a letter to Körner (J1, 158), 'täglich wird mir die Geschichte theurer', are frequently quoted as an indication of Schiller's enthusiasm at this stage for historical reading. He goes on to say: 'Ich wollte, daß ich zehen Jahre hintereinander nichts als die Geschichte studiert hätte. Ich glaube ich würde ein ganz anderer Kerl seyn. Meinst Du, daß ich es noch werde nachholen können?' and so indicates his sense of inadequate knowledge. It was during this first period of historical reading that he became acquainted with French and English historians, particularly Watson and Voltaire.

There is obvious truth in the argument that Schiller at least made use of his historical interests to make money. Historiography was a popular form of reading at the time. The reading public had not yet overcome a certain moral resistance to works of fiction, and the records of sales at the Leipzig Book Fairs, quoted by Ward,[7] indicate the taste for works of history and theology, which were still felt to be intrinsically improving. Schiller was not writing for the academic world, in so far as it existed, but his histories were nevertheless aimed at the well-informed general reader. Against the obvious financial incentives in the work we have to set the interest which Schiller plainly showed in it, the pains he took over it in spite of poor health, and the fact that he was offered a chair at the University of Jena on the strength of the *Abfall der Niederlande*. Although easier financial circumstances made it possible for Schiller after the completion of the *Geschichte des Dreißigjährigen Kriegs* to follow his own interests more freely and to devote himself to philosophy and aesthetics, he nevertheless maintained until his death his interest in history, not only in his own reading and research for his dramas, but also in the further production of the *Allgemeine Sammlung Historischer Memoires*, a venture begun in 1786 and revived in 1795, over which Schiller maintained a general supervision.

The first of Schiller's historiographical works is a translation of Louis Sébastien Mercier's introduction to his *Portrait de Philippe II Roi d'Espagne*, a play written in the form of a series of tableaux. The introduction gives a short biographical sketch of Philip II, which Schiller translated and published under the title *Philipp der Zweite, König von Spanien* in the second number of his *Thalia* in 1786. The translation was prompted by Schiller's work on *Don Carlos*, for which he was beginning in 1785 to read source material beyond the Abbé de St. Réal's 'nouvelle historique'. This piece is frequently termed a free translation. Koopmann, for example, calls it 'eine recht freie Übertragung'.[8] In fact it is fairly accurate and only slightly abridged. Schiller has preserved in translation Mercier's rather shrill and polemical narrative style, as the following extracts show:

Ce despotisme honteux gâta la législation dans toutes ses branches, la rendit à la fois atroce et minutieuse. Le formel de la religion, semblable à une etiquette fatigante, engendra, par ses gênes perpétuelles, l'hypocrisie, source de tant de vices; les préjugés les plus cruels et les plus déraisonnables s'accrûrent en raison inverse des lumières de la liberté. Tel fut le déplorable sort de l'Espagne.[9]

Dieser schändliche Despotismus verunstaltete bald alle Zweige der Gesetzgebung und machte sie zugleich kleingeistisch und grausam. Die Form des Gottesdiensts glich einer abgeschmackten lästigen Etikette, und dieser ewige Zwang mußte endlich die Heuchelei, eine Mutter so vieler Laster, gebären. Ein finstrer und grausamer Aberglauben verschlang das Licht der Vernunft und errichtete seinen Thron auf den Trümmern der Gewissensfreiheit. Dieses traurige Los traf alle spanische Reiche.

(SA 14, 395)

Mercier's piece is a work of undisguised prejudice. The author flits from one incident to another in Philip's reign, piecing together the major events with anecdotes of doubtful reliability. He draws on every scrap of evidence to support his view that Philip was an unenlightened tyrant. From this negative example the reader/audience should learn to appreciate the Enlightenment values of tolerance and respect for civil liberties. His interest in Mercier highlights an often neglected aspect of the early Schiller, his commitment to the 'Aufklärung', a commitment dating back no doubt to his schooldays and which is evident in *Don Carlos* and later in the *Abfall der Niederlande*.

There is some similarity between Mercier's Philip and Schiller's Philipp of the first two acts of *Don Carlos* as they appeared in 1785/6 in the *Rheinische Thalia/Thalia*. As we noted in Chapter 1, the original Philipp of *Don Carlos* is considerably less sympathetically presented than the Philipp of the final version, despite Schiller's awareness of the danger to the aesthetic impact of his play of making him a mere stage villain. The newer conception of Philipp which emerges in the second half of the play had to be written back into the earlier part. This similarity between Mercier's Philip and Schiller's early conception of his Philipp seems to suggest that the reading of Watson's *History of the Reign of Philip II of Spain*, dating from about the same time, did not radically alter Schiller's presentation of Philipp, in spite of Schiller's much-quoted remark to Huber: 'Ich lese jezt stark im *Watson* und meinem Philipp und Alba drohen wichtige Reformen' (J1, 144). It was rather in the course of the composition of the final three acts that a deeper dimension to Philipp emerges, from the demands of the dramatic action, rather than from source study in itself.

As a work of historiography the Mercier translation occupies an interesting position in Schiller's career because it overlaps in time with his work as a dramatist. Although it is unimportant in isolation, it nevertheless indicates that he was showing greater interest in source material for his dramas, an interest which is not evident in *Fiesco*. The work on the *Abfall der Niederlande* was obviously a much more demanding exercise and it is here that the reading of Watson seems to show its impact. Schiller explicitly states this in his 'Vorrede': 'Als ich vor einigen Jahren die Geschichte der niederlandischen Revolution unter Philipp II. in Watsons vortreflicher Beschreibung las, fühlte ich mich dadurch in eine Begeisterung gesetzt, zu welcher Staatsactionen nur selten erheben' (NA 17, 7). Watson must also have given Schiller a sense of historical breadth as background to *Don Carlos*. Certainly this was the last occasion on which he used anecdotal history as the basis for a play. In future he would invent and shape historical material for his dramatic purposes only when he had thoroughly assimilated the material. Indeed Schiller's later departures from history in his plays, such as the death of Johanna on the battlefield and the meeting of Maria and Elisabeth were made only after extensive reading, as though he wished to reassure himself about his proper study of the sources.

During the period between 1785 and 1787, before the completion of *Don Carlos*, Schiller read and enjoyed not only Watson but also Robertson and Voltaire. He was particularly impressed with the latter's vivid narrative style and writes to Körner: 'Dein Charles XII. entzückt mich. Ich finde ihn mit mehr Genie sogar geschrieben, als das *Siècle de Louis XIV*. Er verbindet das Interesse einer Robinsonade mit dem philosophischen Geiste und der kräftigen Schreibart des letzteren' (J1, 195). He retained his admiration for French historiographers and comparing them with the English, especially Gibbon, he said in 1789: 'im historischen Stil liebe ich doch mehr die schöne Leichtigkeit der Franzosen' (J2, 377).

If Schiller first turned to history in an attempt to extend his range of reading, his later concentration on historiography to the exclusion of the drama cannot be explained fully in terms either of his enjoyment of the work or in terms of financial pressure. *Don Carlos* had been and remained an unsatisfactory work for Schiller. The play had its dramatically effective moments, but taken as an artistic whole it was flawed. Schiller himself had changed radically over the years when it was in progress. More than that, however, he had not yet developed a clear idea of how certain dramatic effects were to be achieved. The tableau/intrigue dramatic structure, which he had chosen at first for *Don Carlos*, had proved unmanageable, and the *Briefe über Don Carlos* indicated that he himself had not yet fully realized what had happened in the course of the play. So in the realm of drama a certain impasse had been reached. In *Don Carlos* Schiller had begun by disregarding historical sources and then had discovered a need to interpret the historical moment. He not only had to extend his knowledge of the historical period, he also had to develop skills of historical judgement. Beyond this, however, was yet another need, that for greater objectivity and for more positive and substantial achievement than he felt he had attained in the field of poetry. We noted in the previous chapter the development of greater objectivity in *Don Carlos*. Schiller himself justifies to Körner his turning to history as a discipline and a means of producing something of substance:

Alles macht mir hier seine Glückwünsche, daß ich mich in die Geschichte geworfen, und am Ende bin ich ein solcher Narr, es selbst für vernünftig zu halten. Wenigstens versichere ich Dir, daß es mir ungemein viel Genuß bei der Arbeit giebt, und daß auch die Idee von etwas *Solidem* (das heißt, etwas, das ohne Erleuchtung des Verstandes dafür gehalten wird) mich dabei sehr unterstützt, denn bis hierher war ich doch fast immer mit dem

Fluche belastet, den die Meinung der Welt über diese Libertinage des
Geistes, die Dichtkunst, verhängt hat.

(J1, 234)

This was also a time of experiment for Schiller. While working on
the *Abfall der Niederlande* he was also experimenting with prose
narrative in *Der Geisterseher*. Storz[10] notes this and suggests how
Schiller was trying at the time to gain experience of various forms
of writing. This can be restated as a quest for greater objectivity
and greater powers of evaluation of material, historical or philosophical.

The *Geschichte des Abfalls der Niederlande* was at first planned
as part of a larger project to produce a series of histories of famous
rebellions and conspiracies—*Geschichte der merkwürdigsten
Rebellionen und Verschwörungen*. Wieland, however, persuaded
Schiller to concentrate on expanding his work on the revolt of the
Netherlands independently of the series (J1, 230). While the work
was aimed at bringing in money, it appears that Schiller greatly
enjoyed this new form of writing, and testifies to this in a number
of letters, a typical example being one to Körner, in which he says:
'Ich bin voll von meiner Materie und arbeite mit Lust' (J1, 211).
Even when the work dragged on, proving to be more demanding
than he had at first anticipated, he still gains pleasure from it: 'Es
ist ungeheuer was sie mich Arbeit kostet ... aber sie gewährt mir
Vergnügen, und ich halte auch die Zeit nicht für verloren' (J2, 248).
The publication was promised to Crusius. Schiller wrote to him
concerning the title of the work, revealing at the same time the
type of public he first anticipates for the book: 'Da diese Materie
jezt gleichsam Mode und Waare für den Plaz ist, so war anfangs
meine Idee, sie auch mit einem besonderen Titel zu versehen und
allein in die Welt zu schicken' (J1, 223). Schiller expects a large
public for his book, and his words 'Mode und Waare für den
Platz' may indicate that the work has a certain propagandist aim.
Regin[11] explicitly states that Schiller turned to historiography in an
attempt to propagate his views on freedom and despotism. W. M.
Simon,[12] speculating on the abrupt finish to the work, suggests that
it was published in incomplete form in order to increase its chance
of influencing contemporary events. While there seems to be no
external evidence for this view, Simon is at least right in identifying
the strong appeal Schiller makes to his readers in his 'Einleitung' to

believe that freedom from oppression can be won in the eighteenth century as it was in the sixteenth.

Schiller's work was so commended in private readings to Wieland and others that he felt it was worth more considerable treatment and wrote again to Crusius:

Soviel ist übrigens gewiß, daß ich keine Mühe geschont habe und schonen werde, ihm Vollständigkeit und Werth zu geben. Denn ich muß Ihnen ... gestehen, daß ich mich durch diese Schrift in dem Neuen Fach der Geschichte, zu dem ich mich angefangen habe zu bestimmen, beim Publikum etwas gut ankündigen möchte. Aus vielen Gründen ... ligt mir äuserst viel daran, daß dieses Buch auch selbst in der *Form* sich von Schriften der Mode, die bloß für die neugierige Lesewelt sind, unterscheiden und im Äuserlichen wie innern, ein mehr solides Ansehen erhalte

(J1, 230)

He has grown in confidence in his ability to produce a valuable work of historiography, an art which was in its infancy in Germany at that time. He is also careful for his reputation as a serious writer as well as ambitious for his work.

As a work of historiography, the *Abfall der Niederlande* tends to leave the modern reader unimpressed. It was, however, widely read in its own day and represents a considerable stride forward in German historiography, which was lagging behind the historiography of England, Scotland, and France, countries which could point to Gibbon and Voltaire, Hume, Robertson, and Montesquieu.[13] Compared with the products of these countries, German historiography was dull and over-simplified. Historians had not on the whole developed a technique of writing beyond the simple cataloguing of events, producing enormous compendia of facts with little or no critical evaluation of the data. Such a work is M. I. Schmidt's *Geschichte der Teutschen*, a huge work in 24 volumes. At the time of writing the *Abfall der Niederlande* Schiller was comparatively unfamiliar with German historians, several of whom (Spittler, Schmidt, and Pütter) he read only after the *Abfall der Niederlande* was completed and his appointment to the chair at Jena was almost certain. One German historian with whom Schiller was familiar from his days at the Karlsschule was Schlözer, whose *Vorstellung einer Universalhistorie* Schiller read under the guidance of his teacher Abel.[14] In the spirit of the eighteenth-century quest for a universal survey Schlözer attempts to get away from the simple catalogue of facts and tries instead to bind the events of history into patterns. However, he is unable to test his sources and has neither the scepticism of the French historians nor the empirical approach of the English. Two notable exceptions to the undistinguished record of German historiography were Möser and Johannes von Müller, the former because he attempted in his *Osnabrückische Geschichte* to relate the movement of local history to principles of land ownership and so evaluate the factors involved in change, and the latter because he brought narrative talents to his works, such as the *Geschichte Schweyzerischer Eydgenossenschaft*, even though he was not a rigorous researcher.

As a work of German historiography of the period Schiller's *Abfall der Niederlande* stands out not only on account of its vivid narration but also by its relative sophistication. Schiller showed a gift in both of his historiographical works for surveying large quantities of facts and working them into a whole. He aimed not only to compile facts into a narrative sequence but to shape his material according to certain unifying ideas, the result of his attempt to perceive patterns or laws in history. Indeed the mere recording of facts was far from his purpose, as Überweg points out:

Nicht die empirischen Einzelheiten fesselten ihn; er suchte sich ihrer durch ein ziemlich sorgfältiges Studium von Quellen und Hülfsmitteln zu bemächtigen; aber sie hatten für ihn doch nur ein secundäres Interesse; ihm lag vornehmlich an dem idealen Gehalt der Geschichte.[15]

Schiller attempted to combine philosophy with the recording of facts. In view of the absence of native models his achievement as a historian was not negligible. According to W. M. Simon his efforts were 'revelations, in the Germany of his day, of the fact that a historical narrative could avoid being dull without becoming inaccurate, that it could be "philosophical" in Schiller's sense without becoming wholly speculative.'[16] Simon is considerably kinder to Schiller than the historians of the nineteenth century,[17] who criticize his inaccuracy especially in the presentation of characters such as William the Silent, the result of his organization of his material according to a speculative principle of freedom. Überweg, however, gives Schiller credit where he feels it is due:

Den Blick für das Wesentliche in dem Gange der Ereignisse, für die Ideen und die psychologischen Motive, für die Bedeutung der Conflicte, für die Mächte, die den Sieg oder die Niederlage bedingten, bekundet Schiller trotz mancher unleugbaren Irrthümer doch in einem ausgezeichneten Maaße.[18]

Historians such as Überweg and Janssen criticize Schiller's approach to the revolt of the Netherlands because it depends on a preconceived notion of mankind's progress towards freedom. More than this, however, it lacks consistency. There is a marked lack of unity of conception in the work and the reader soon detects Schiller's failure to digest his material fully and to give a well-developed and mature view of it. The work is unfinished, having grown out of all proportion to the original plan. It is unnecessary to look far for reasons why Schiller did not complete the work. Janssen's view is as follows:

Daß er die niederländische Geschichte nicht weiter ausführte, lag in der ganzen Art seiner rhapsodischen Thätigkeit auf dem Gebiete der Geschichte begründet, und erklärt sich zugleich aus den verschiedenartigen Arbeiten, die er bald nach Vollendung des ersten Theils seines Werkes für seine Jenaer Professur unternehmen mußte.[19]

Janssen, though assuming only a fleeting interest in history on Schiller's part, is certainly right in indicating the pressure Schiller was under to fit himself for his professorship and the desire he felt to experiment with various forms of writing. Another reason, which complements the first one, lies in Schiller's discovery that his material no longer corresponded to his original conception of it and his beginning to realize how his approach was bound to do violence to the facts. Kurt May, for example, sees in the work evidence that a more pragmatic view of men and events began to assert itself, against Schiller's original impulse to idealize: 'solcher Rückgang der Begeisterung für die Arbeit im geplanten Geist, als Darstellung des Ideals ... hing mit einem Schwachwerden des eigenen Glaubens [zusammen], und zwar von einem damals wieder auf-tauchenden entgegengesetzten Bild von Welt und Menschen her.'[20]

Schiller's original thesis is that by united effort freedom can be won from oppression, and he announces this in his 'Einleitung'. The example of the people of the Netherlands shows 'was Menschen wagen dürfen für die gute Sache und ausrichten mögen durch Vereinigung' (NA 17, 10). The readers are to make a direct compari-son between the possibility of successful rebellion in the sixteenth and eighteenth centuries. Indeed, an explicit statement to that effect was included in the 'Einleitung' as it first appeared in the *Teutscher Merkur*, though Schiller later struck it out of the book edition of the whole work: 'die Kraft also, womit es [das niederländische Volk] handelte, ist unter uns nicht verschwunden; der glückliche

Erfolg, der sein Wagestück krönte, ist auch uns nicht versagt, wenn die Zeitläufte wiederkehren und ähnliche Anlässe uns zu ähnlichen Thaten rufen' (NA 17, 11). Progress towards freedom is seen primarily in political terms. It is possible that Schiller is here appealing to the impact on Germany of the American War of Independence. Ursula Wertheim says of that war: 'Die Frage des gerechten und ungerechten Krieges und die Rolle der Volksmassen als Geschichtsträger treten damit ins historische Bewußtsein der deutschen Intelligenz.'[21] In her article on the subject she concentrates on the references to America in *Kabale und Liebe*. However, it seems not unreasonable to surmise that a revolution which appeared so exemplary to many Germans should either have been in Schiller's mind when he wrote the 'Einleitung', or at least have shaped his historical outlook to some degree. *Don Carlos* and the *Abfall der Niederlande* have it in common that they both suggest a direct link between the turning to Protestantism and the desire for political freedom. In *Don Carlos* Philipp's reaction to Posa's enlightened views of government is to say, 'Ihr seyd/Ein Protestant' (lines 3065/6). Certainly his use of the terms 'Glaubensverbeßerung' and 'neue Wahrheit' to denote the Reformation strongly suggests that, while not necessarily sympathizing fully with its religious standpoint, Schiller believed that the rise of the Protestant faith was a phenomenon directly issuing from, and in turn contributing to, the desire for political liberty:

In der glücklichen Muße des Wohlstands verläßt es [das Volk] der Bedürfnisse ängstlichen Kreis, und lernt nach höherer Befriedigung dürsten. Die neue Wahrheit, deren erfreuender Morgen jetzt über Europa hervorbricht, wirft einen befruchtenden Strahl in diese günstige Zone, und freudig empfängt der freie Bürger das Licht, dem sich gedrückte traurige Sklaven verschließen.

(NA 17, 12)

The tension between the real and the ideal, which became evident in *Don Carlos*, is notably absent from the introduction to the *Abfall der Niederlande*. We noted how the ending of *Don Carlos* created a double perspective on the future. Although Philipp's tyranny will give way to more enlightened government, there is doubt about whether even the most idealistic individual can bring it about. There is evident in the play a tension between Schiller's confidence that progress is a law of history and his more pragmatic insight into the frailty of individuals in the face of the complexity of the world in which it is to be realized. His idealizing tendency has the upper hand as he begins the *Abfall der Niederlande*, but, once again, insight into the complexity of the historical period causes a repetition of that tension evident in *Don Carlos*.

One idealistic preconception which has to be jettisoned is Schiller's belief in the unity of the Netherlanders. One of the noteworthy features of this rebellion, according to the 'Einleitung', was the fact that this people won its freedom through concerted effort. Though not heroic as individuals, they exhibited a communal heroism, in particular in their patience and obstinacy in the face of coercion:

Das Volk, welches wir hier auftreten sehen, war das friedfertigste dieses Welttheils, und weniger als alle seine Nachbarn jenes Heldengeists fähig, der auch der geringfügigsten Handlung einen höheren Schwung giebt. Der Drang der Umstände *überraschte* es mit seiner eigenen Kraft, und nöthigte ihm eine vorübergehende Größe auf, die es nie haben sollte, und vielleicht nie wieder haben wird.

(NA 17, 11)

It is, therefore, the very lack of natural heroism which makes this case significant; it is rather a situation 'wo die Noth das Genie erschuf, und die Zufälle Helden machten' (NA 17, 11). That final comment instantly brings to mind the case of *Wilhelm Tell*. In that play also Schiller depicts the struggle for national liberation of an essentially peaceful, non-heroic community. In the later drama, however, it is evident that he has learnt the dangers of taking popular history at face value. Indeed *Wilhelm Tell* shows how behind the superficial picture of harmonious, altruistic effort, there are many disparate elements and many complex motives at work.

Schiller's efforts in his 'Einleitung' to present the people of the Netherlands as a communal hero turn out, however, to be misleading. Far from being a united and determined people the Netherlanders gradually reveal themselves to be torn by petty quarrels and unable to put aside selfish interests for the sake of a common cause. The Protestant sects show as much hatred towards one another as they themselves are shown by the Catholics. The nobles gradually emerge as being motivated by various impulses, often quite private and selfish. This was a phenomenon of which Schiller was quite aware when he wrote *Fiesco*, but somehow it did not shape his initial judgement in the *Abfall der Niederlande*. Whereas Schiller claims he would show a united people asserting its will, in fact the mass of the people has no role to play in his account, except in his description of the 'Bildersturm'. Janssen explicitly criticizes Schiller's failure to show any connection between the nobles' conspiracy and the 'Bildersturm', which he presents purely as a popular movement.[22] Certainly the belief he states at the beginning of the work—that united effort secured liberty—is not demonstrated by the work itself.

The same tension between the real and the ideal emerges in Schiller's presentation of the leading personalities in the struggle. Schiller was already aware as a dramatist and writer of prose fiction that gripping narrative requires strong characters. In spite of his stated belief in the communal strength of the Netherlanders, his interest in the personalities in the conflict is apparent. In the 'Einleitung' he directs the reader's attention first to the people as a whole and then to William the Silent, whom he calls 'ein zweyter Brutus', despite his earlier insistence that this is not an account of individual heroism. Oranien cannot, however, live up to the role in which Schiller has cast him. His leadership is not triumphant but frequently frustrated by lack of co-operation from others. Schiller does not admire him any the less for the fact that he is not a stirring leader of men, but he admits finally that there is a certain inscrutability about his motivation which defies any easy characterization and which indeed mystified his contemporaries—'niemand hatte in seiner Seele gelesen' (NA 17, 252). An instance of this is his failure to remove his son from the university of Louvain, when he himself went into exile. This was 'eine Unvorsichtigkeit, die, wenn sie wirklich nicht absichtlich war, mit dem richtigen Urtheile kaum zu vereinigen ist, das er in so viel andern Fällen von dem Gemüthscharakter seines Gegners gefällt hatte' (NA 17, 251). Schiller's own, as well as Oranien's, disillusionment with the common people comes through in Schiller's account of Oranien's reasons for going into exile: 'Eine sehr niederschlagende Erfahrung hatte ihn gelehrt, wie unsicher die Hofnungen sind, die man gezwungen ist, auf den großen Haufen zu gründen, und wie bald dieser vielversprechende Eifer dahin ist, wenn Thaten von ihm gefodert werden' (NA 17, 246).

Schiller's idealized portrait of Oranien was severely criticized by critics of the nineteenth century, who viewed Oranien as a cold and inscrutable opportunist, who used all means to achieve his own ends. Schiller's slow awakening to the mysterious and possibly dubious aspects of Oranien's behaviour was noted as soon as the

work appeared by Körner, who complains of a 'Schein von Inconsequenz'[23] in Schiller's depiction of him and a loss of sympathy as
the work progresses. So where later critics criticize Schiller's early
idealization of Oranien, Körner complains rather that the idealization is not maintained. What appeared as a flaw to Körner was
to later historians a sign of Schiller's sounder grasp of the subject.
Janssen rightly identifies why this inconsistency arises, again for
the same reason that Schiller failed to complete the work:

Dieser 'Schein von Inconsequenz' in Wilhelms Betragen entsteht bloß
dadurch, daß Schiller von vornherein den Revolutionsführer, wie wir
gesehen, im Lichte eines idealen Freiheitshelden hinstellt, und nunmehr,
weil er zu ehrlich war, die in den Quellen vorliegenden Thatsachen zu
verschweigen, mit seiner eigenen Auffassung in Widerspruch geräth.[24]

Schiller's preconception of the point his history is going to prove
leads to a very static type of characterization. He wants to cast the
participants into certain roles, a technique which is reminiscent of
the original dramatic ('Gemälde') approach of *Don Carlos*. As
prominent figures come into the action he gives a thumbnail sketch
of each, so establishing their main traits of character and implying
that these are the characteristics which will become apparent in
action, as the history unfolds. For example, Egmont and Oranien
are introduced thus:

Unter den niederländischen Großen, die auf die Oberstatthalterschaft
Anspruch machen konnten, waren die Erwartungen und Wünsche der
Nation zwischen dem Grafen von Egmont und dem Prinzen von Oranien
getheilt, welche durch ... gleiche Liebe des Volks zu diesem Posten will-
kommen waren ... Da wir in der Folge dieser Geschichte beide Namen oft
werden nennen müssen, so kann die Aufmerksamkeit des Lesers nicht
frühe genug auf sie gezogen werden.

(NA 17, 67)

There follows an account of the life and characteristics of Egmont
and then of Oranien. This mode of character presentation implies
not only that Schiller has made up his mind about these figures in
advance, but also that he sees people as having little interaction
with the events round about them. People shape events according
to what they already are. This proves to be a very static and finally
inadequate way of regarding the movement of events in the rebellion
of the Netherlands, and Schiller must, as we have noted above, re-
assess the role of Oranien and finally present him as he reveals
himself through events.

The case of Egmont is somewhat different. Egmont is presented in Book I in the well-roundedness of his character, with good and bad features all detailed:

Höflichkeit, edler Anstand und Leutseligkeit, die liebenswürdigen Tugenden der Ritterschaft, schmückten mit Grazie sein Verdienst; in einem freund-lichen Gruß oder Händedruck verschrieb sich sein überwallendes Herz jedem Bürger. Auf einer freien Stirn erschien seine freie Seele ...

(NA 17, 72)

However, it is Egmont's lack of insight, stretching almost to the point of gullibility, which emerges predominantly from the action itself. Other qualities may be present, but they do not find scope for expression in the course of the narrative.

From the point of view of comparison of Schiller the dramatist and Schiller the historian a glance at the dramatic Philipp and the historical Philip II of the *Abfall der Niederlande* is very instructive. After the picture of Philipp in *Don Carlos* we might reasonably have expected a sympathetic or at least complex portrait of Philip II in the *Abfall der Niederlande*. This is not the case. Schiller presents Philip as a bigoted monarch, determined in advance not only to crush freedom in the Netherlands but specifically to destroy Oranien, of whom Schiller claims he was jealous (NA 17, 68f). Schiller's portrayal of the historical Philip reveals his inability to project himself by conscious effort as a historian into the spirit of the six-teenth century, in particular through his persistent and erroneous belief that Catholicism was the only oppressive religion. What has often been said of Wallenstein is also true of Philip, that Schiller the dramatist comes nearer to the true personality of that monarch than Schiller the historian, and that this is achieved more by intuition than by source study.

Tensions such as those described above no doubt contributed to Schiller's failure to continue the *Abfall der Niederlande* beyond Book 1. It was not merely that the reality behind events was dif-ferent from his preconception of it, but that his original idea of the interrelation of character and event also proved inadequate for the task of documenting a complex historical situation. Amongst the problems of this mode of character presentation certain observations can be made which show how the *Abfall der Niederlande* relates to Schiller's earlier work as a historical dramatist.

In *Fiesco* character is fixed. The participants in the action are playing roles, mostly familiar and stereotyped ones, and the play

concentrates on portraiture of the hero. It is an essentially unhistorical play, in that what happens to the hero, particularly at the
end, is a matter of relative indifference. *Don Carlos* is in its early
stages also concerned with portraiture. Schiller is exploring in the
first instance the relationship between the Queen, Carlos and the
King. Although they are not so stereotyped as the characters of
Fiesco, yet they are familiar stage figures—the fiery youth, the
tyrannical but jealous husband, the young, lonely wife. Even Posa
in the *Thalia* fragment plays only the stock role of confidant. The
early scenes of *Don Carlos* are therefore unhistorical in the same
way as *Fiesco*. Carlos's love for Elisabeth brings to the surface the
tensions existing between the characters, and the portrayal of certain
characteristic situations, held together by intrigue, constitutes the
drama. Character and event do not seem to interact at all. Once
the Posa plot with the plan for Carlos's involvement in the Netherlands rebellion is in motion we feel that characters act less out of
fixed personalities and more in response to a changing situation
in which they both reveal and discover themselves. In the process of
this change, however, Schiller could not control his play and so had
to finish it off with rather surprising and unsatisfactory *coups de
théâtre*.

We can detect a similar development in the *Abfall der Niederlande*.
Schiller tries to control his material at first by casting Oranien,
Philipp, Egmont, and the collective people of the Netherlands into
prearranged roles. Hence there is a static relationship between them
and we are unable to infer from the work any sense of how people
interact with what goes on around them. Further exploration of his
subject matter shows him that the complexity of the situation
cannot be contained in such an over-simplified presentation. So
Schiller abandoned the *Abfall der Niederlande* perhaps because,
pressed as he was with other commitments, there was less he could
do to remedy the situation than in the case of *Don Carlos*. In both
cases the final product far exceeds in length the original plan. In
Don Carlos the changes of scheme and dramatic conception presented Schiller with problems of length which could only be solved
by sudden denouements. Such manipulation of the work is not
possible in historiography and so the rest of the *Abfall der Niederlande* never appeared.

It is interesting and significant that Schiller should twice have
made the same kind of experiment—that of casting characters into

preconceived roles—and twice found in the two works concerned, the *Abfall der Niederlande* and *Don Carlos*, that his original approach was inadequate for the complexity of the material. The fact that he carried over the original method of *Don Carlos* into the *Abfall der Niederlande* may suggest that Schiller did not realize how the experience gained in *Don Carlos* was relevant to the work of the historiographer, who is writing about characters with hindsight. Another explanation is that he had not yet fully decided what had happened during the composition of *Don Carlos*. Certainly the *Briefe über Don Carlos*, written at the time of the *Abfall der Niederlande*, suggest that he was not fully aware of how interaction of character and event had replaced his earlier method of portraiture.

The conflict which is visible in the *Abfall der Niederlande* between the dramatist's desire to present strong, dominant characters and the historian's growing perception of their dependence on circumstances was a matter for further thought and comment by Schiller immediately after the completion of the *Abfall der Niederlande*. Goethe's *Egmont* was first published in the spring of 1788, while Schiller was still hard at work. By the end of May, with the *Abfall der Niederlande* just completed, Schiller began his review *Über Egmont, Trauerspiel von Goethe*, which was to appear in the *Allgemeine Literatur-Zeitung* in September 1788. Obviously this was a valuable opportunity for Schiller the journalist, already well versed in the subject matter of Goethe's play, to comment on the presentation of Egmont and on the use of historical characters in drama. Schiller certainly turned his journalistic skills fully to the task of the review, as well as his knowledge as a historian and experience as a dramatist. A number of critics have tended to dismiss his criticisms of the play on the grounds that he did not understand Goethe's approach to the drama, being himself fundamentally different in his attitude to life and conception of human behaviour.[25] Whether Schiller did indeed fail to grasp the nature of 'das Dämonische' and was judging the play by the wrong criteria is not of primary interest here, but rather what his criticisms indicate about his own conception of historical drama at the time.

Schiller's basic criticism of *Egmont* is not that Goethe's hero enjoys himself at the expense of matters of state, as Ellis,[26] perpetuating this misinterpretation, has recently stated. Schiller certainly does suggest that Egmont does not gain the audience's sympathy by blotting out of his mind all thoughts of the developing crisis. This, however, is not the root of his objection. Rightly or wrongly Schiller is trying to account for the lack of tragic emotion generated by Goethe's *Egmont*. He begins his review by stating that tragedies tend to focus on one of three things—events or situations, passions, or characters. The former two categories are exemplified by Ancient Greek drama, while the third, the character tragedy, was developed by Shakespeare. *Egmont* belongs to the third. The idea that Shakespeare created character tragedy became prominent during the 'Sturm und Drang' period. It is suggested by Goethe himself in the *Rede zum Shäkespears Tag* and by Lenz in his *Anmerkungen übers Theater*. Lenz concludes his critique of Aristotle's stress on 'Handlung' in tragedy by pointing to Shakespeare's portrayal of tragic character and implying that German drama is closer in spirit to such drama:

Das Trauerspiel bei uns war also nie wie bei den Griechen das Mittel, merkwürdige Begebenheiten auf die Nachwelt zu bringen, sondern merkwürdige Personen ... Denn der Held allein ist der Schlüssel zu seinen Schicksalen ... Im Trauerspiele ... sind die Handlungen um der Person willen da.[27]

These statements, particularly the second ('Denn der Held ...') are true of Schiller's own early heroes. The seeds of disaster are in their own personalities, and actions issue from them which are explicable as expressions of those personalities. However, while in *Über Egmont* Schiller acknowledges the existence of the category of 'character tragedy', he seems to cast doubt on whether it can arouse tragic emotion: 'Es ist hier nicht der Ort zu untersuchen, wie viel oder wie wenig sich diese neue Gattung mit dem letzten Zwecke der Tragödie, Furcht und Mitleid zu erregen, verträgt; genug, sie ist einmal vorhanden, und ihre Regeln sind bestimmt' (NA 22, 200).

Schiller sees Egmont as representative of 'schöne Humanität' rather than being in himself an extraordinary personality. His criticism of the play hinges not on Egmont's neglect of political realities, nor on the idea 'daß nur ein heroischer Charakter ein wirklich tragisches Schicksal erfährt',[28] but rather on the conception of how the individual's behaviour is affected by circumstances. Indeed for Schiller it is not character as such, but the presentation of a character in particular circumstances, which calls forth a tragic response. Schiller is therefore not saying that Egmont is not a tragic character because he is unheroic, but rather that Goethe has not put him in circumstances in which his death appears as tragic.

This is emphasized by the fact that Egmont does not respond to what is going on around him. This is what Schiller is referring to when he says: 'Wenn es Euch zu beschwerlich ist, Euch Eurer eignen Rettung anzunehmen, so mögt Ihrs haben, wenn sich die Schlinge über Euch zusammenzieht. Wir sind nicht gewohnt, unser Mitleid zu verschenken' (NA 22, 203). In other words, it is the response of the tragic character to his circumstances, not the character himself, that calls forth the pity associated with tragedy. The argument is crystallized in Schiller's comments on Goethe's substitution of Klärchen for the real Egmont's wife and numerous children. Schiller is neither being pedantic about the changing of historical fact nor moralistic about the substitution of a mistress for a wife. Rather he sees the historical Egmont's behaviour up to his death as the direct consequence of the circumstances of his life. He has been used to living in comparative luxury. His wife and numerous children are not accustomed to deprivation. If they were all to flee the country, Egmont's whole estate would pass to the Crown and he and his family would be as good as destitute. So he was forced to rely on the favour of Philip II, and live in the hope that the storm would not, after all, break over him. In other words, the historical Egmont was a figure with tragic potential for the dramatist who could exploit those circumstances. So when Schiller says that Goethe robs us of 'das rührende Bild eines Vaters' he is not thinking of a sentimental family scene but of a potentially tragic entanglement. Schiller complains, therefore, that Goethe has attempted to sustain a tragedy through the presentation of a character who does not respond to circumstances, as though the character himself and his downfall were capable in themselves of arousing a tragic response.

Schiller may indeed have lacked appreciation of 'das Dämonische', but even so his observations on the nature of tragedy and on the use of historical data by the dramatist are illuminating as far as his own development is concerned. Schiller shows that he has learned that the circumstances surrounding a historical character are not a matter of indifference to the dramatist if he wishes to transmute the historical situation into poetry. Tragic effects are to be achieved through the presentation of human beings in the entanglements of their lives. Ellis is therefore misleading when he says that Schiller wanted 'the inspiring spectacles, great figures and moving events of dramatized history'.[29] Certainly Schiller had the ability to present great dramatic encounters in his plays, such as Elisabeth's meeting

with Maria and Wallenstein's encounters with Max. However,
Wallenstein himself is not heroic. If Egmont fails to live up to his
reputation, if his great deeds all lie in the past, the same is equally
true of Wallenstein. The difference is that Schiller presents
Wallenstein as caught in a complex web of circumstances of which
he is a complete prisoner, and yet able to assert just enough dignity
to evoke a tragic response.[30]

Über Egmont was published in September 1788. A few months
later Schiller published a biographical sketch entitled *Des Grafen
Lamoral von Egmont Leben und Tod*. He later cut this essay by
half for the 1802 edition of his works and called it *Prozeß und
Hinrichtung der Grafen von Egmont und von Hoorne*. Koopmann
aptly calls this sketch 'ein Gegenbild' to Goethe's Egmont.[31] In it
he demonstrates what he had stated in *Über Egmont*—'Seine
Gefangennehmung und Verurteilung hat nichts Außerordentliches,
und sie selbst ist auch nicht die Folge irgendeiner einzelnen interes-
santen Handlung, sondern vieler kleinern' (NA 22, 200). It is as
though Schiller were at pains to show just how far the historical
Egmont was caught up in events beyond his control. In death, far
from seeing a glorious liberation for his country, he gives the impression of a man who cannot believe, even at the last moment,
that Philip seriously means to have him executed. All heroic gestures,
such as addressing the crowd from the scaffold, are ill advised at
that political moment and so Egmont is dissuaded from them for
fear of repercussions to his friends. So Egmont appears as a victim,
not without dignity, but without the power to influence his fate.

II. SCHILLER'S HISTORIOGRAPHY 1789-1792

On the strength of the *Abfall der Niederlande* and Goethe's recom-
mendation Schiller was appointed to a chair of history at Jena
university in January 1789. This appointment made necessary a
period of intensive historical study. It was during this period that
Schiller set out to read some of the standard works of German
historiography, such as Schmidt's *Geschichte der Teutschen* and
Pütter's *Historische Entwicklung der heutigen Staatsverfassung des
teutschen Reichs*. At the same time he also began his reading of
Gibbon's *Decline and Fall of the Roman Empire* and Condorcet's
Esquisse d'un tableau historique des progrès de l'esprit humain.
During this period Schiller was under great pressure to master his
new subject. Because he received as such no fixed salary as professor,

but only occasional tuition fees, his financial circumstances were straitened. In addition, his new post demanded that he reduce drastically his journalistic work, which was a vital source of income. The degree of pressure under which he was working and the seriousness with which he approached his task are shown by a letter to his sister Christophine, explaining why he cannot leave Jena to visit Swabia:

Jezt würde eine so weite und kostbare Reise nach Schwaben nicht nur mein Vermögen übersteigen, sondern auch auf den Anfang meiner neuen academischen Laufbahn einen sehr nachtheiligen Einfluß haben. In den ersten 2 Jahren muß ich alle meine Zeit und Kräfte zusammen nehmen, mich in den Mittelpunkt meines neuen Fachs zu setzen und soviel möglich damit vertraut zu werden. Außerdem rauben mir schriftstellerische Arbeiten, die jezt allein meine Einkünfte ausmachen alle Augenblicke, die mir von Berufsgeschäften übrig bleiben.

(J2, 420)

On 26 and 27 May, a few months after his appointment, Schiller delivered his inaugural lecture, later published under the title *Was heißt und zu welchem Ende studiert man Universalgeschichte?* Schiller's appointment was extremely popular among the students, for his reputation as the creator of Karl Moor and the Marquis Posa had gone before him. On 28 May Schiller wrote at length to Körner (J2, 408) of the tumultuous reception which he had received, of the overflowing auditorium and the stir in Jena afterwards. Schiller's enthusiasm is, however, tempered by his acquaintance with the academics at Jena—'Es ist hier ein solcher Geist des Neides, daß dieses kleine Geräusch das mein erster Auftritt machte, die Zahl meiner Freunde wohl schwerlich vermehrt hat.' The inaugural lecture was later revised and published as one piece in the November 1789 issue of the *Teutscher Merkur*. In writing to ask Körner's comments on the revised form Schiller already shows the disillusionment with his post which soon set in: 'Von Jena aus will ich Dir meine Antrittsrede vom vorigen Sommer schicken ... So wie Du sie lesen wirst habe ich sie freilich nicht gehalten. Ich glaubte dem Publikum etwas mehr ausgearbeitetes schuldig zu seyn, als einem Haufen unreifer Studenten' (J2, 434). The final remark not only indicates Schiller's private disillusionment with his work but also illustrates the fact that German universities and their professors did not yet enjoy the status which they acquired after Wilhelm von Humboldt's reforms. There was as yet no such thing as the production of academic works for an academic audience. Indeed Schiller credits his general readership with greater knowledge and discernment than his students.

Although the inaugural lecture occupies chronologically a position between the two major historiographical works, in spirit it belongs more to the period when Schiller was setting out to write the *Abfall der Niederlande*, for in it he formulates an idea of history which he implicitly rejects in the process of writing that work. He expounds the idea, firmly rooted in Enlightenment thought, that the past shows the pattern and purpose of the development of human faculties, and shows men how to achieve happiness. Unchanging human nature links past to present. These ideas may indeed have informed Schiller's approach to the writing of the *Abfall der Niederlande*, as a demonstration of how history is moving in the direction of freedom, but the lecture presents a more simplified view of history than the one implied at the close of the *Abfall der Niederlande*, where Schiller has to face the reality of history being made not by far-seeing idealists but by a complex process without any obvious guiding force.

Schiller was, of course, bound to give his audience what they wanted to hear on this occasion. Jena was a stronghold of Kantian philosophy and, as Collingwood[32] has indicated, the inaugural lecture bears a resemblance in thought to Kant's historical outlook as expressed in his *Idee zu einer allgemeinen Geschichte in weltbürgerlicher Absicht*. Schiller read and admired this essay in 1785 (J1, 214), and it may indeed have influenced his approach to the *Abfall der Niederlande*. Certain points of contact between Kant's essay and the inaugural lecture are apparent. Kant first uses the term 'philosophischer Kopf' to denote the man who tries to see patterns in history. Schiller takes up this term and contrasts it with the 'Brotgelehrter', the professional who takes a narrow and unimaginative view of his very restricted field of study. Considering that Schiller was as yet untried as a university professor, his distinctions may have seemed rather tactless to the academics at Jena. As well as Kant's *Idee zu einer allgemeinen Geschichte* Regin[33] suggests also the influence on the inaugural lecture of his *Muthmaßlicher Anfang der Menschengeschichte*, an essay in which Kant stresses the necessity of conjecture in historical thought in the many instances where documentation or other concrete evidence is scarce. Another influence suggested by Regin is Herder's essay *Auch eine*

Philosophie der Geschichte zur Bildung der Menschheit, which Schiller had read and which may show its influence in the breadth of interest in the lecture, in civilization in general, rather than simply in politics, which was Kant's main concern.[34] (The influence of Kant can be traced also in Schiller's lecture *Etwas über die erste Menschengesellschaft*. It appeared in print in the *Thalia* II (1790), and the connection with Kant's *Muthmaßlicher Anfang der Menschengeschichte* was alluded to in the *Thalia*. A note to the title read: 'Es ist wohl bei den wenigsten Lesern nötig, zu erinnern, daß diese Ideen auf Veranlassung eines *Kantischen* Aufsatzes in der Berliner Monatsschrift entstanden sind.')

The second of Schiller's major historiographical works, the *Geschichte des Dreißigjährigen Kriegs*, was first published in three parts in Göschen's *Historischer Kalender für Damen* between 1791 and 1793. Schiller's efforts were to be rewarded with an attractive honorarium, and it is possible, as Buchwald suggests, [35] that he imagined this would be a dainty, light-weight work for his genteel readership. However, as in the case of the *Abfall der Niederlande*, the task grew, and although the end product was to be for popular consumption, Schiller took his work very seriously, as his correspondence with Göschen at the time illustrates. His letters to the publisher show his awareness of the tastes of his readership; he considers where the narrative should be broken off and the need to keep the readers' interest for the next publication. He is also protective towards his work, being fearful of censorship and of the possibility that Göschen might make cuts without his approval: 'Wird mir eine Hauptsache *alterirt*, oder kommt etwas fremdes hinein, so muß ich öffentlich meine Sache vertheidigen, denn über *mich* urtheilt das Publikum, weil mein Nahme vor dem Buche steht' (J3, 528). So it seems that Schiller, though very ill during much of the time the book was in progress, could not bear to be thought the author of a slipshod work. His reputation was at stake. After completing the first instalment he writes to Körner: 'Es galt bei dieser Arbeit mehr, meinen guten Namen nicht zu verscherzen, als ihn zu vermehren, und bei der Kürze der Zeit, bei der Ungelehrigkeit des Stoffs war diese Aufgabe wirklich schwer' (J3, 544). Despite Schiller's modesty the work was extremely successful. A book edition appeared in 1793 and a second revised edition in 1802. For the 1802 edition Schiller made a number of alterations and cuts, most of them small and mainly in Book I. For example, some of the most explicit denunciations of the Habsburgs are cut. Speaking of Habsburg ambition, the original version runs: 'Selbst in den kleinsten Geistern aus Habsburgs Geschlechte war diese Leidenschaft groß; dieser Trieb grenzenlos in seinen beschränktesten Köpfen; dieser einzige Charakterzug schlimm in der kleinen Zahl seiner vortrefflichen' (NA 18, 52). This is omitted in the 1802 version.[36] None of these revisions, however, substantially affects our impression of Schiller's basic approach to his material.

The *Geschichte des Dreißigjährigen Kriegs* suffers as a whole from an abrupt ending. As a result it is somewhat uneven; four books deal with events up to 1634, the year of the death of Wallenstein, and only one book with the whole of the remaining period from 1634 to 1648. Schiller apologizes at the end of the work for his failure to discuss the intricacies of the Peace of Westphalia, admitting that it is so complex as to require another major piece of work. His haste to finish the work results in a fifth book which is a headlong rush of events with little comment on their significance. There is no final survey and analysis of the war period and its effects on the Empire and on Europe. The ideas put forward by Schiller at the beginning of the work about the fundamental issues involved in the war are lost from view at the end. It must be noted, however, that he had already suggested that he might give a mere sketch of events after the Battle of Lützen and the death of Gustavus Adolphus. To Göschen he writes:

hier erhält die Geschichte einen sehr glänzenden Schluß, und endigt wie ein Episches Gedicht für den Leser. Die ganze darauf folgende Periode biß zum Westphälischen Frieden fasse ich in Einen kurzen Prospekt zusammen, ohne Details, bloß Resultate. Am Ende sage ich, daß es von Der Aufnahme dieses ersten Versuchs abhängen werde, ob die Ausführlichere Darstellung der 2ten Periode in dem nächsten Kalender nachfolgen solle.

(J3, 528)

Before even the first part of the history was published, however, Schiller extended his plan, intending now to break after the Battle of Leipzig.[37] The death of the Swedish king was to follow. The fact that he so extended the work may be explained by his interest in the conflict of the two great military leaders, Gustavus Adolphus and Wallenstein. Possibly Schiller saw in the struggle between these two figures an opportunity for creating an exciting narrative, for until the advent of these two, whose careers seemed so locked together, it had been hard for Schiller to find a focus in his narrative. The enthusiastic response to the first part no doubt contributed to the growth of the work, but frequent changes in plan led to its lack of unity of conception.

Schiller's sources for the *Geschichte des Dreißigjährigen Kriegs* were numerous. Apart from the general sources—Schmidt, Pütter —Schiller had also already read Bougeant's *Histoire des guerres et des négotiations qui précédèrent le traité de Westphalie*. He added to this biographies of Gustavus Adolphus and Wallenstein by Chemnitz and Schirach respectively. A full list of Schiller's probable sources is given by Tomaschek.[38]

As with the *Abfall der Niederlande*, the historians of the nineteenth century were unimpressed with the *Geschichte des Dreißigjährigen Kriegs*. Überweg criticizes Schiller's lack of discernment in his use of sources[39] and Janssen points out a number of basic misconceptions on Schiller's part about the nature of the conflict, in particular the role played by religious differences in the war, and the figures of Gustavus Adolphus and Tilly: 'Schillers Buch hat diesen Wahn (daß der dreißigjährige Krieg ein Religionskrieg gewesen) besonders verbreitet durch die Lichtgestalt, in die seine dichterische Phantasie den Gustav Adolf kleidete, und durch das Nachtbild, welches er von dem General Tilly entworfen hat.'[40] In fact, Überweg goes so far as to commend the *Abfall der Niederlande* above the *Geschichte des Dreißigjährigen Kriegs* on the grounds that it is better researched, if not better written as a whole.

In spite of the inaccuracies of the *Geschichte des Dreißigjährigen Kriegs* as a work of historiography, it nevertheless indicates a considerably more mature Schiller than the one who set out to write the *Geschichte des Abfalls der Niederlande*, and this is apparent through what Überweg calls the 'größere Unbefangenheit des Standpunktes'.[41] One of the ways in which the contrast comes fully to light is in a comparison of Schiller's introduction to the two works. In his 'Einleitung' to the earlier work he had adopted a highly rhetorical style which sprang from his enthusiasm for what his material would demonstrate. By contrast, his introduction to the *Geschichte des Dreißigjährigen Kriegs* is much more sober in tone. A definite thesis, however erroneous, is put forward, namely the centrality of the religious element in the conflict, but this is done without polemics or exaggeration. The two examples below show this difference clearly, in particular because they both refer to the Revolt of the Netherlands.

Es ist also gerade der Mangel an heroischer Größe, was diese Begebenheit eigenthümlich und unterrichtend macht, und wenn sich andre zum Zweck setzen, die Ueberlegenheit des Genies über den Zufall zu zeigen, so stelle ich hier ein Gemählde auf, wo die Noth das Genie erschuf und Zufälle Helden machten.

Abfall der Niederlande (NA 17, 11)

Die Reformation machte den *Niederländern* das Spanische Joch unerträglich, und weckte bey diesem Volk das Verlangen und den Muth, dieses Joch zu zerbrechen, so wie sie ihm größtentheils auch die Kräfte dazu gab.

Geschichte des Dreißigjährigen Kriegs (NA 18, 9)

Whereas the introduction to the *Abfall der Niederlande* was short and vigorous, spurring the reader on to read the main work, the introduction to the *Geschichte des Dreißigjährigen Kriegs* is comparatively long. Schiller took pains over it and defends its length in a letter to Göschen: 'Wenn ich ein Verdienst um diese Geschichte habe, so ist es dieses, daß ich mich bey dieser Einleitung aufgehalten und das allertrockenste wenigstens menschlich auseinandergesetzt habe' (J3, 528). He is aware of the difficulty of presenting such a complex historical period and so wishes to prepare the reader for the approach to the work which he has chosen. He gives the impression that his introduction is the fruit of his study of the whole period and so it awakens the confidence that he will not depart from his original thesis in the way that he did in the *Abfall der Niederlande*. This hope is not fulfilled. Schiller's original thesis of the primacy of the religious element is lost by the end. The introduction to the *Geschichte des Dreißigjährigen Kriegs* is, however, certainly less speculative than that to the *Abfall der Niederlande*. In the earlier work Schiller had adopted a philosophy that history was moving in a certain direction. This was a belief which he had acquired less from study of the period itself than from his general philosophical reading and his own confidence in progress. This belief does not, however, find confirmation in the course of the narrative. The introduction to the *Geschichte des Dreißigjährigen Kriegs* postulates a more modest thesis, founded in historical events rather than in abstract speculation—that the Reformation was the mainspring of the conflict, but that religious changes had wide-ranging social and political implications, so that it is impossible to isolate the religious aspects:

Das Religionsinteresse war es, was diese neue Sympathie der Staaten mit Staaten veranlaßte, aber die Wirkungen derselben wurden bald im politi-

schen gefühlt. Der nehmliche Staatenbund, welcher streitfertig da stand,
dem Religionszwang seiner Glieder zu steuern, sicherte sie eben dadurch
vor politischer Unterdrückung, denn ohne diese war jener nicht möglich.

(NA 18, 17)

This greater grasp from the outset of the complexity of the historical situation shows a marked advance on the *Abfall der Niederlande;*
one of the faults of that work was the way Schiller tended to separate
the political and religious aspects and was not able to draw them
together. The result is that the political struggle is carried on on
the level of the aristocracy, as one would expect, and the religious
on the level of the common people. In the *Geschichte des Dreißigjährigen Kriegs* Schiller has divested himself of illusions about the
single-mindedness of the parties concerned and the purity of their
motives. Not only are the political and religious bound up together,
but in every matter, for the common people as for the influential,
a whole range of private factors come into play:

Die Religion wirkte dieses alles. Durch sie allein wurde möglich, was
geschah, aber es fehlte viel, daß es *für* sie und ihrentwegen unternommen
worden wäre. Hätte nicht der Privatvorteil, nicht das Staatsinteresse sich
schnell damit vereinigt, nie würde die Stimme der Theologen und des Volks
so bereitwillige Fürsten, nie die neue Lehre so zahlreiche, so tapfre, so
beharrliche Verfechter gefunden haben.

(NA 18, 10 f)

The emphasis which Schiller still lays on the Reformation as a
catalyst to the general upheaval in Europe in the late sixteenth and
seventeenth centuries is reminiscent of *Don Carlos* and the *Abfall
der Niederlande*. In the *Geschichte des Dreißigjährigen Kriegs*,
however, Schiller deduces the Reformation's impact on Europe
from his estimation of the causal relationship of events, whereas
in those two earlier works the Reformation itself is seen more in
the light of speculative philosophy, as a manifestation of progress
towards freedom. Schiller's pro-Protestant standpoint is, however,
still obvious in the *Geschichte des Dreißigjährigen Kriegs*. It is, for
example, implicit in his criticism of Ferdinand's piety, which is
contrasted with that of the idealized Gustavus Adolphus, who was
'frey von dem rohen Unglauben ... und von der kriechenden
Andächteley eines Ferdinand' (NA 18, 139). The same pro-
Protestant bias is evident in the *Geschichte der französischen
Unruhen, welche der Regierung Heinrichs IV. vorangingen*, part of
the 'Universalhistorische Übersicht' which Schiller wrote for the

Allgemeine Sammlung Historischer Memoires. The *Geschichte der
französischen Unruhen* was written in 1791-2, at the same time as
the *Geschichte des Dreißigjährigen Kriegs.* Schiller introduces his
account with a description of the spread of Protestantism in France
and opposition to it:

Die Religionsverbeßrer führten bei ihrer Verteidigung und bei ihrem Angriff
auf die herrschende Kirche Waffen, welche weit zuverlässiger wirkten als
alle, die der blinde Eifer der stärkern Zahl ihnen entgegensetzen konnte.
Geschmack und Aufklärung kämpften auf ihrer Seite; Unwissenheit,
Pedanterei waren der Anteil ihrer Verfolger.

(SA 13, 170)

In spite of his Protestant sympathies, however, Schiller shows, as in
the *Geschichte des Dreißigjährigen Kriegs*, that he realizes that
religious differences can only account in part for the ensuing
conflict:

So feurig auch das Interesse war, mit welchem die eine Hälfte Europens die
neuen Meinungen aufnahm und die andre dagegen kämpfte, so eine
mächtige Triebfeder der Religionsfanatismus auch für sich selbst war, so
waren es doch großenteils sehr weltliche Leidenschaften, welche bei dieser
großen Begebenheit geschäftig waren, und größtenteils politische Umstände,
welche den untereinander im Kampfe begriffenen Religionen zu Hülfe
kamen.

(SA 13, 169)

The more complex interaction of character and event suggests
significant parallels with the later dramas. This second work of
historiography shows the re-emergence of Schiller's interest in great
figures. Whereas in the *Abfall der Niederlande* Schiller had tried,
though not very successfully, to make the people the collective hero
of the piece, in the *Geschichte des Dreißigjährigen Kriegs* he sees
that the mass of the people are powerless victims of the war's rav-
ages, and that the soldiers are frequently mercenaries motivated
by gain rather than conviction, and so he turns to the prominent
figures of the war. It is therefore here much more than in the *Abfall
der Niederlande* that Schiller explores the relationship of great men
to events around them. His presentation of Gustavus Adolphus
and Wallenstein answers, in each case from a different perspective,
the question of how far individuals are in control of events and how
far they are themselves shaped by them.

In the *Geschichte des Dreißigjährigen Kriegs* Schiller abandons
his earlier practice of introducing major figures with a detailed

character description. He brings them into the action merely with a sketch so that they can reveal themselves in the course of events. So when a key figure such as Gustavus Adolphus comes on to the scene he is discussed not as a personality but as a political figure:

Der Sohn des neuen Königs, der unter dem Namen Karls IX. regierte war Gustav Adolph, dem aus eben diesem Grunde die Anhänger Sigismunds, als dem Sohn eines Thronräubers, die Anerkennung versagten ... Gustav Adolph hatte das siebzehnte Jahr noch nicht vollendet, als der Schwedische Thron durch den Tod seines Vaters erledigt wurde; aber die frühe Reife seines Geistes vermochte die Stände, den gesetzmäßigen Termin der Minderjährigkeit zu seinem Vortheil zu verkürzen.

(NA 18, 98 f.)

So Schiller places Gustavus Adolphus immediately in his political context, thus implying that it is in this context that he must act and not merely in accord with the traits of his own personality. It is evident quite early that Schiller warms to Gustavus Adolphus. His approbation goes to the point of idealization and Gustavus Adolphus emerges in Book II as the paragon of Christian kingship and military genius:

Gustav Adolph war ohne Widerspruch der erste Feldherr seines Jahrhunderts, und der tapferste Soldat in seinem Heer, das er sich selbst erst geschaffen hatte ... auch in der Trunkenheit seines Glückes (blieb er) noch Mensch und noch Christ, aber auch in seiner Andacht noch Held und noch König.

(NA 18, 138 f.)

The degree of idealization here obscures the undoubted ambiguity of Gustavus Adolphus's involvement in the war. Schiller presents him more as he sees himself, rather than as the world saw him at that time. This is an over-simplification which Schiller later tries to correct.

Wallenstein makes a different kind of first appearance. He emerges quite suddenly in the action but Schiller takes care not to analyse him in the light of his future career. So we catch a glimpse of Wallenstein as he appears to Ferdinand at the particular moment when Wallenstein offers him the very help he needs:

Unter diesen Umständen konnte dem Kaiser nichts willkommner seyn, als der Antrag, womit einer seiner Offiziere ihn überraschte.

Graf Wallenstein war es, ein verdienter Offizier, der reichste Edelmann in Böhmen. Er hatte dem kaiserlichen Hause von früher Jugend an gedient, und sich in mehreren Feldzügen gegen Türken, Venetianer, Böhmen,

Ungarn und Siebenbürger auf das rühmlichste ausgezeichnet ... Im Besitz eines unermeßlichen Vermögens, von ehrgeitzigen Entwürfen erhitzt, voll Zuversicht auf seine glücklichen Sterne und noch mehr auf eine gründliche Berechnung der Zeitumstände, erboth er sich, für den Kaiser, auf eigne und seiner Freunde Kosten eine Armee aus zu rüsten und völlig zu bekleiden.

(NA 18, 113)

Schiller, therefore, is moving in this work towards a presentation of characters as they appear in the circumstances surrounding them.

As part of this new method of presentation Schiller likes to survey the careers of his major figures when they have left the scene. This is of course the reverse of the method in the *Abfall der Niederlande* where character traits are fixed in advance and Schiller sums people up *before* they act. Here he attempts to make plain all the factors involved in forming a final judgement on historical figures. It has frequently been noted that Schiller's final judgements on Wallenstein and Gustavus Adolphus do not altogether accord with the earlier presentation of these figures. Kurt May,[42] for example, suggests that Schiller may have uncovered new material which caused him to modify his opinion. I feel, however, that such an explanation is unnecessary and that the explanation lies in the work itself.

At the end of Book II Gustavus Adolphus has won his glorious victory at Leipzig. This Schiller sees as an appropriate moment for a reappraisal of the Swedish king, which forms the opening of Book III. Gustavus Adolphus has been changed by his victories into a self-assured leader. Schiller's account, viewed superficially, suggests whole-hearted approval but seems on closer inspection to imply reservations:

Seinem naturlichen Muth kam der andächtige Schwung seiner Einbildung zu Hülfe; gern verwechselte er *seine* Sache mit der Sache des Himmels, erblickte in Tillys Niederlage ein entscheidendes Urtheil Gottes zum Nachtheil seiner Gegner, in sich selbst aber ein Werkzeug der göttlichen Rache.

(NA 18, 185)

The king may wish to give an interpretation to events which is above and beyond natural causality. We as the readers can, however, see in advance how fortunes change in the course of the war and there is an inevitable tinge of irony in the above passage, particularly on second reading. Schiller himself points out shortly afterwards in Book III that Gustavus Adolphus had many advantages to add to his own gifts: 'Wenn Gustav Adolph seinem eigenen Genie das meiste zu danken hatte, so darf man doch nicht in Abrede seyn, daß das Glück und die Lage der Umstände ihn nicht wenig begünstigten' (NA 18, 187). Gustavus Adolphus's success is part and parcel of the circumstances, and his sudden death, apparently at the height of his career, indicates the futility of seeing oneself in a position of control where Fortune's wheel is constantly turning.

Schiller's review of Gustavus Adolphus's career at the end of Book III seems suddenly and surprisingly reserved. It is probably true to say that in the case of Gustavus Adolphus and of Wallenstein Schiller never fully resolved the tension between his personal response to the man, positive or negative, and his recognition that all men, however great, are caught up in a chain of events and circumstances. As indicated above, however, Schiller's sudden reservations about Gustavus Adolphus come not altogether out of the blue, for they are hinted at at the beginning of Book III. What Schiller shows he recognizes in his final appraisal of Gustavus Adolphus is the ambiguity which besets even the apparently most unambiguous figure, for he is caught up in the entanglements of the historical world and there can be no absolute certainty in judgement on him. Even purity of motive and a belief in the justice of one's cause are no guarantee against moral compromise. The case of Posa had already brought this to light. Schiller points out that Gustavus Adolphus's continued power necessarily prevented the German estates from asserting themselves independently until after his death: 'der zweydeutige Beystand eines übermächtigen Beschützers macht der rühmlichern Selbsthülfe der Stände Platz, und vorher nur die Werkzeuge zu Seiner Vergrößerung, fangen sie erst jetzt an, für sich selbst zu arbeiten' (NA 18, 280). Here Schiller points out that the ambiguity lies not necessarily in Gustavus Adolphus himself but is a necessary corollary to all action. An issue which preoccupies Schiller in the later drama is the problem of guilt and innocence; his appraisal of the career of Gustavus Adolphus shows how he recognized at that time that in the historical world innocence cannot exist even in the most exemplary. If they take public action their motives will always be open to conflicting interpretations and they themselves may not even be aware of the ambiguous light in which they appear. This theme comes to prominence several times in the later dramas, but most notably in *Die Jungfrau von Orleans*.

Schiller's final review of Gustavus Adolphus indicates also his awareness of the problem of reputation in history, in particular how we view historical figures in the light of a particular moment or event. Gustavus Adolphus dies at the perfect moment, before he can outlive his reputation as a liberator. Yet, as Schiller says, this would surely have disappeared if he had lived:

> Die wohlthätige Hälfte seiner Laufbahn hatte Gustav Adolph geendigt, und der größte Dienst, den er der Freyheit des Deutschen Reichs noch erzeigen kann, ist—zu sterben ... sein schneller Abschied von der Welt sicherte dem Deutschen Reiche die Freyheit, und ihm selbst seinen schönsten Ruhm.

(NA 18, 280-1)

How tenuous were the alliances forged between France and the Protestant powers was shown by their almost immediate breakdown after his death. The quotation above shows Schiller's recognition of the fact that what we call 'good' or 'bad' with regard to historical figures is in part a matter of perspective and in part the result of circumstances. Gustavus Adolphus died before it could become indisputably apparent that he aimed to seize the Imperial Crown. Chance saved him from being known as a tyrant or oppressor.

These same problems are treated in the case of Wallenstein. Wallenstein is reassessed at the end of his career, after Schiller has tended to give a negative interpretation of his actions. In the earlier part of the history he adopts with regard to Wallenstein the stance of the omniscient narrator, seeing into the mind of his subject. In discussing Wallenstein's removal from power after the Diet of Regensburg he seems quite transported by the dramatic potential of the situation, but in giving a vivid picture of Wallenstein's reaction he also assumes a full knowledge of his motives: 'In dieser prahlerischen Dunkelheit erwartete Wallenstein still, doch nicht müßig, seine glänzende Stunde, und der Rache aufgehenden Tag' (NA 18, 134). Later, when Wallenstein returns to power, Schiller is assured in his own interpretation of Wallenstein's behaviour. He reports a conference held between Wallenstein and the Swedes and claims that in it Wallenstein requested as his part of the deal the Bohemian crown: 'Jetzt aber war die Decke von dem Plan weggezogen, worüber er schon Jahre lang in geheimnisvoller Stille gebrütet hatte' (NA 18, 304). Again, in discussing the apparent contradictions in Wallenstein's behaviour, Schiller is quite definite: 'Alle diese Widersprüche flossen aus dem doppelten und ganz unvereinbaren Entwurf, den Kaiser und die Schweden zugleich zu verderben, und mit Sachsen einen besondern Frieden zu schließen' (NA 18, 308). It is evident that he has no time for Wallenstein's belief in astrology. In his introduction to Wallenstein he says that Wallenstein was 'voll Zuversicht auf seine glücklichen Sterne und noch mehr auf eine gründliche Berechnung der Zeitumstände', so implying that Wallenstein's real confidence was in his ability to seize the moment. The same implication emerges from his account of Wallenstein's dismissal: 'Man brauchte die Sterne nicht zu bemühen, um mit Wahrscheinlichkeit vorher zu sagen, daß ein Feind wie Gustav Adolph, einen General wie Wallenstein nicht lange entbehrlich lassen würde' (NA 18, 133). In this matter Schiller the dramatist probes more deeply than Schiller the historian, although the astrological motif caused him problems during composition. Whereas astrology is presented in the *Geschichte des Dreißigjährigen Kriegs* merely as unenlightened superstition, one which belonged to the times and was practised by Wallenstein throughout his career, in the trilogy Schiller uses it to probe into his hero's attitude to the problem of decision and action and the individual's control over external circumstances.

Despite the tone of censure in his presentation of Wallenstein, when Schiller comes to sum up his career he shows much greater reserve and admits that Wallenstein's behaviour and motives are essentially a mystery to us: 'unter seinen öffentlichen allgemein beglaubigten Thaten ist keine, die nicht endlich aus einer unschuldigen Quelle könnte geflossen seyn' (NA 18, 329). We have no unbiased account of his actions. Here the historian admits the unreliability of his sources and the fact that a man's reputation is in the hands of those who outlive him. Gustavus Adolphus expired at the ideal moment, before his critics could speak out against him; Wallenstein made enemies of the very people who could control his reputation: 'Ein Unglück für den Lebenden, daß er eine siegende Partey sich zum Feinde gemacht hatte—ein Unglück für den Todten, daß ihn dieser Feind überlebte und seine Geschichte schrieb' (NA 18, 329). Schiller's apparent volte-face at the end of Wallenstein's career may not be so hard to explain as it seems. What we see in the closing stages of Wallenstein's life is Schiller's ability to project himself into the experience of his subject and feel the irony of his position as traitor betrayed by those whom he trusted. Whereas earlier Schiller had seemed to be the omniscient narrator, viewing his subject as from above and with emotional detachment, now in the final stages of his life Schiller seems to be 'menschlich näher' to Wallenstein and to bring him closer to the reader as he hoped later to do in the *Wallenstein* trilogy. Schiller obviously responds to the idea of a great man showing greatness of spirit when his back is to the wall:

Einsam steht er da, verlassen von allen, denen er Gutes that, verrathen von allen, auf die er baute. Aber solche Lagen sind es, die den großen Charakter erproben. In allen seinen Erwartungen hintergangen, entsagt er keinem einzigen seiner Entwürfe; nichts giebt er verloren, weil er sich selbst noch übrig bleibt.

(NA 18, 321)

It may be that once Schiller had given sympathetic, rather than aloof, critical appraisal to his subject, he was able to give a more incisive and yet equitable view of Wallenstein's career. Indeed, Golo Mann's essay, 'Schiller als Historiker', brings to prominence the fact that it was in the *Wallenstein* trilogy, more than in the *Geschichte des Dreißigjährigen Kriegs*, that Schiller came close to the conclusions of twentieth-century research on Wallenstein's motives and personality. Mann considers that Schiller the dramatist's requirements of the material coincide with modern, and, he implies, sound historical judgement. Though he had access to no new information after 1793, Schiller showed in the trilogy a sure sense of the vital factors in Wallenstein's behaviour, in particular his confidence in the army and the impact of Regensburg: 'Es war die Intuition des Dichters, die aus dürftigen Fragmenten ein Ganzes schuf: ein Ganzes der Kunst und der Wahrheit.'[43] This is the second time such a process occurred. In the case of Philip II, Schiller comes closer in *Don Carlos* than in the *Abfall der Niederlande*, and again more by intuition and discovery of the political world than by source work, to the modern appraisal of that monarch.

What we find in Schiller's appraisal of Wallenstein is his recognition that men in the historical world are not free to act as they would choose but rather are themselves confined by their circumstances. Indeed circumstances thrust roles upon them which they might never have chosen. This insight is summed up in the well-known verdict on Wallenstein:

Wenn endlich Noth und Verzweiflung ihn antreiben, das Urtheil wirklich zu verdienen, das gegen den Unschuldigen gefällt war, so kann dieses dem

Urtheil selbst nicht zur Rechtfertigung gereichen; so fiel Wallenstein, nicht
weil er Rebell war, sondern er rebellirte, weil er fiel.

(NA 18, 329)

This method of character presentation is quite the opposite of that
in the *Abfall der Niederlande*. In the earlier work events were frequently confused but political leaders such as Alba, Philipp, and
Oranien were essentially in charge of them. In the *Geschichte des
Dreißigjährigen Kriegs* Schiller presents an epoch which is in any
case confused, but his depiction of it suggests strongly just how
little the individual can control history, being rather controlled
by it and locked into its causality. And yet Schiller is drawn to
concentrate on great figures as a way of imparting some kind of
unity and focus of attention to the material. So he says after the
deaths of Gustavus Adolphus and Wallenstein: 'Gustav Adolph
und Wallenstein, die Helden dieses kriegerischen Dramas, sind von
der Bühne verschwunden, und mit ihnen verläßt uns die Einheit
der Handlung, welche die Uebersicht der Begebenheiten bisher
erleichterte' (NA 18, 328). Gustavus Adolphus and Wallenstein,
though both named 'Helden' above, illustrate in separate ways the
limitations of any one individual in the face of the complexities
of history and its unpredictability. Gustavus Adolphus is felt by
Schiller to be an extraordinary figure, a kind of bolt from the blue
which disturbs the usual course of events:

Die Geschichte, so oft nur auf das freudenlose Geschäft eingeschränkt, das
einförmige Spiel der menschlichen Leidenschaft aus einander zu legen,
sieht sich zuweilen durch Erscheinungen belohnt, die gleich einem kühnen
Griff aus den Wolken in das berechnete Uhrwerk der menschlichen
Unternehmungen fallen.

(NA 18, 279)

Even so, history reasserts its control over individuals and Gustavus
Adolphus's sudden death demonstrates how the normal process of
life can be disrupted only for so long. Schiller presents Sweden's
allies as simply waiting to move in other directions. France, for
example, wishes to restore the balance of power in Europe, which
Gustavus Adolphus's sudden ascendancy has disrupted.

Wallenstein's position is somewhat different. He must struggle
continually to maintain his authority while enemies at court are
trying to undermine it. It is clear from his actions that he is brooding
on some sort of extraordinary plan and looking to the stars for
confirmation that the right moment has come. He cannot, however,

prevent circumstances from forcing him into a line of action which may or may not have been his choice.

The last of Schiller's historiographical works to merit special mention here is another appendix to the *Abfall der Niederlande*, called *Merkwürdige Belagerung von Antwerpen in den Jahren 1584 und 1585*. Schiller prepared this piece in 1795 for *Die Horen*. It is hard to imagine why Schiller should have produced this piece if he had not some interest in the subject matter and yet he writes to Goethe: 'Freilich gibt sie [die Arbeit] mir auch nur einen magern Genuß' (J6, 832). It seems probable, since the piece was written specifically for *Die Horen*, that he wished to add some historical material to the literary and philosophical contributions. The essay adds to the argument of this chapter because it was written shortly before Schiller turned his mind to the theatre and his plans for *Wallenstein* and also because it provides another example of his understanding of how great men are the product of the circumstances of history. This latter aspect is doubly interesting because of the distance at which the essay stands from the work which it is supposed to supplement. The contrast with the *Abfall der Niederlande* is very striking. Whereas in the major work Schiller was obviously partisan, in the *Belagerung von Antwerpen* this partisanship has virtually disappeared. What Schiller is attracted by is the extraordinary nature of this incident, that which makes it 'merkwürdig'. And what makes it so is not so much the victory of the good cause through genius, determination and perseverance; it is rather the combination of that with its opposite: 'das Schauspiel des Gegentheils, wo der Mangel jener Eigenschaften alle Anstrengungen des Genies vereitelt, alle Gunst der Zufälle fruchtlos macht, und weil er ihn nicht zu benutzen weiß, einen schon entschiednen Erfolg vernichtet' (NA 17, 312). The account tells how the people of Antwerp were eventually defeated, not so much by force of arms as by their own unwillingness to take the risks necessary to save themselves. These were the very circumstances in which Alexander von Parma could shine as a general, and Antwerp's decline marked his ascendancy. Schiller obviously admires Parma's vigorous and determined leadership, but recognizes how, in spite of his gifts, he would not have made his name at Antwerp if it had not been for the narrow and selfish outlook of the people of Antwerp. One cannot talk of a philosophy of history in this short account, but it contains at the least Schiller's recognition of the haphazard nature of historical events and the lack of any force of justice operating in history. The presentation of Parma recalls the latter half of the *Geschichte des Dreißigjährigen Kriegs*. Parma is not idealized like Gustavus Adolphus, but he is admired for his bravery, acumen, and generous spirit. He is, however, at the mercy of circumstances beyond his control, facing difficulties which simple genius cannot solve.

CHAPTER 3

WALLENSTEIN

The essential character ... of all dramatic poetry must depend on the poet's religious or philosophical sentiments, on the light in which he contemplates history and life, on the belief he entertains as to the unseen hand that regulates their events.

These words are found in an essay, 'On the Irony of Sophocles', by Connop Thirlwall.[1] In order to make clear what he means by the term 'irony' in his essay (and indeed Thirlwall was one of the first commentators to take over the term and apply it not to word-play but to certain dramatic situations, especially in tragedy)[2] Thirlwall explains how he envisages the way the dramatist must stand in relation to his play if such dramatic effects are to be created. These words are an appropriate introduction to Schiller's *Wallenstein*, because they bring into focus the importance of his ten years' dramatic silence and the value of his study of history during that period. Between 1787 and 1797 Schiller had obviously amassed ten years' more experience of life, had held an academic post, married, and formed friendships with members of the Weimar circle, Goethe above all. After spending some five years as a historiographer and professor of history he was able to devote himself more fully to philosophy and aesthetics. The study of history had forced Schiller to reconsider his former assumptions about the 'unseen hand' which regulates life and history. It had forced him also to take a more objective view of human behaviour and involvements and to see the danger of looking to history for confirmation of his preconceptions. It was a training in the examination of how human personality interacts with the world outside itself and how human action is part of a complex causal chain.

In addition to his own study and immediate experience of life during those years, an important factor in the development of Schiller's outlook on life and history was the course taken by the French Revolution.[3] Up to 1793, Schiller's recorded comments on the events in France are sparse in spite of the fact that in 1792 he was made a citizen of France on the strength of *Die Räuber*. The abolition of the monarchy and subsequent execution of Louis XVI filled him with repugnance for the revolutionaries and their extreme measures, and destroyed once and for all any lingering belief he may have had about the ability of political change to effect any moral regeneration in a people. Schiller's considered reflections in the mid-1790s on the French Revolution are probably to be found in the *Ästhetische Briefe*. In Letter 2 in particular he justifies the fact that in such times of political upheaval, when contemporary events seem to demand everyone's attention, he is dealing with the subject of aesthetic education. Far from being irrelevant, he says, the subject is at this time of all times most pressing; when the bankruptcy of political solutions to the problem of freedom is quite manifest, it is proper to consider how mankind can progress towards truly moral behaviour, and that progress is to be achieved through art:

Erwartungsvoll sind die Blicke des Philosophen wie des Weltmanns auf den politischen Schauplatz geheftet, wo jetzt, wie man glaubt, das große Schicksal der Menschheit verhandelt wird. Verräth es nicht eine tadelns-werthe Gleichgültigkeit gegen das Wohl der Gesellschaft, dieses allgemeine Gespräch nicht zu theilen? ... Ich hoffe, Sie zu überzeugen, daß diese Materie weit weniger dem Bedürfniß als dem Geschmack des Zeitalters fremd ist, ja daß man, um jenes politische Problem in der Erfahrung zu lösen, durch das ästhetische den Weg nehmen muß, weil es die Schönheit ist, durch welche man zu der Freyheit wandert.

(NA 20, 311 f.)

Apart from demonstrating the ineffectiveness of political change to bring mankind to freedom and true humanity, the course of the French Revolution demonstrated also the inability of individuals to exert any lasting control over the movement of events. By the time Schiller actually received the official document conferring on him his French citizenship it was 1798, and the men whose signatures were on it, men such as Danton, had long since gone themselves to the guillotine.[4] Certainly Schiller's observation of the course of the Revolution confirmed the view of historical figures which we noted towards the end of Chapter 2, the view that even the most apparently powerful are ultimately shown to be subject to circumstances and to the tide of events. Such observations on the Thirty Years War, coupled with confirmation in contemporary events, were parti-cularly appropriate to Schiller's preparation for a play about a hero of the seventeenth century, for in them is echoed the typically

Baroque theme of 'Wandelbarkeit'. Great stress is often laid on Schiller's writings on aesthetics during this period between 1787 and 1797 as a key to his later dramas. It is, however, important to acknowledge also the role played by the general maturing of his outlook, to which his historical study bears witness, and to which it, along with contemporary events and his own broadened experience, contributed.

It is difficult to speak of Schiller's historical dramas in general terms, if only because Schiller's boldness in attempting new forms of drama demands that each play should be read first of all on its own terms. It is, however, possible, without violating the individual plays, to trace the influence of Schiller's experience as a historian and to see how some of the insights, sharpened between 1787 and 1792, re-emerge through varying subject matter and treatments. Having stated that, it is also important to see the later dramas as works of art, in which Schiller was above all concerned with aesthetic effects, rather than the mere dramatization of history. From *Wallenstein* onwards he transforms his historical subject matter into what he called 'eine reine poetische Fabel' (cf. J5, 1176; 1184; 1260), so that its symbolic nature is apparent. Even so, as Thirlwall says, the dramatist's perception of history and life penetrates his plays. The more this is realized, the more vital Schiller's study of history appears to have been, but the more elusive its actual influence is.

The *Geschichte des Dreißigjährigen Kriegs* not only created in Schiller the urge to turn to poetry—'Ich bin jetzt voll Ungeduld, etwas poetisches vor die Hand zu nehmen, besonders juckt mir die Feder nach dem Wallenstein' (J4, 608)— it also provided him with possible subject matter. He had contemplated but rejected the idea of composing an epic poem on the subject of Gustavus Adolphus and finally settled on Wallenstein. Even so, it was some four years after the letter above, written in May 1792, before Schiller in fact set to work on his project. In March 1796 he wrote to Körner, 'In meinen Arbeiten, wo ich seit Neujahr zu keiner Entscheidung kommen konnte, bin ich nun endlich ernstlich bestimmt, und zwar für den *Wallenstein*' (J4, 1022). One specific spur to new dramatic work came when Goethe invited him to adapt his *Egmont* for the Weimar stage. Schiller went about the task vigorously and with great concern for dramatic effects. Anton Genast records how Schiller involved himself even in the rehearsals: 'Schiller rezitierte und spielte zuweilen in den Proben den Schauspielern einzelne Stellen vor ... Daß Alba im *Egmont* im fünften Akt als Henker mit großem roten Mantel und tief ins Gesicht gedrücktem Hut erscheinen mußte, geschah auf seine Anordnung.'[5] Not all of Schiller's suggestions were acceptable to Goethe, who felt that Schiller retained 'ein gewisser Sinn für das Grausame'.[6] Whatever the merits and demerits of Schiller's adaptation of the play, he himself took it to be a useful reintroduction to dramatic work and to Wallenstein in particular, as he wrote to Körner: 'der Egmont hat mich doch interessirt, und ist mir für meinen Wallenstein keine unnützliche Vorbereitung gewesen' (J5, 1027).

Some of the points of contact between Goethe's Egmont and Schiller's Wallenstein as dramatic characters provide an interesting insight into Schiller's dramatic presentation after his long silence as a dramatist. One of the central themes of his later historical dramas is the examination of the phenomenon of greatness. As we observed in the previous chapter, Schiller's presentation of Wallenstein was uneven, as a result of his lack of sympathy for Wallenstein at the beginning of the narrative but increased sympathy towards the end. In the final analysis Wallenstein's career was intriguing because of its scope, and because of the questions it raised about the ability of the individual to show greatness while caught up in the contingencies of life. The historical Wallenstein is somewhat glamorized in the final stages of his life and here the idealising tendency in Schiller is intervening: 'Einsam steht er da, verlassen von allen, denen er Gutes that, verrathen von allen, auf die er baute' (NA 18, 321). In his summing up, Schiller takes a more sober view of Wallenstein's involvements with the Church and the Emperor. In the trilogy he does justice to both impulses, his perception of Wallenstein's greatness and his insight as a historian into the limitations of the individual participant, however extraordinary, who acts on the stage of history. Wallenstein offered the dramatist a hero who combined in one person extreme moral ambiguity and loss of self-determination, with some kind of greatness. Schiller deploys all his dramatic skills in the ending of *Wallensteins Tod* to provoke in the audience a tragic response to the downfall of a man who in the course of the action has actively *done* virtually nothing, who, though inactive himself, has brought disaster on family and friends, who has in fact used them without consideration of them as independent beings.

In some respects Wallenstein is close to Schiller's impression of

Goethe's *Egmont*, in that he fails to live up to the audience's expectations of him. In *Wallensteins Lager* we are encouraged to expect a dominant, larger than life figure; he is a man so adulated by his men and about whom so many legends circulate that we cannot but expect an impressive figure to emerge eventually. In *Die Piccolomini* the process of creating curiosity about Wallenstein continues, especially when we see the obvious devotion of Buttler and Max. When Wallenstein finally arrives his appearance is an anti-climax. His is not a larger than life figure at all, though he is jealous of his power and ruthless in his manipulation of others to maintain it. He is, however, powerless to control his own destiny, though he believes he is specially favoured by destiny, and it is only when his back is to the wall that Schiller creates a sense of his dignity in the face of disillusionment and desertion.

Neither Wallenstein nor Egmont lives up to his reputation. For both of them the days of action lie already in the past. There is, however, a very significant difference in dramatic technique. Egmont is created from the beginning of the play as an attractive character, representative in Schiller's words of 'schöne Humanität'. We see the many facets of his personality illustrated in the encounters with other characters but finally he stands as a definable character with certain characteristics which contribute to his eventual arrest and execution. Wallenstein, by contrast, seems to have no definable character. He thinks and behaves in certain ways but his personality is highly elusive, and this is, of course, Schiller's design. This elusiveness has been pinpointed by Alfons Glück, who says: 'Wallensteins Charakter könnte durch eine Beschreibung (statisch) nicht dargestellt werden. Das Geschehen bringt ihn zum Vorschein.'[7] In other words, Schiller bases his drama not on a conception of tragic personality but on a conception of tragic situation, and on a tragic view of the nature of the world of action. One of the problems he complained about to Goethe when he was planning his material was that 'Das eigentliche Schicksal thut noch zu wenig, und der eigne Fehler des Helden noch zu viel zu seinem Unglück' (J5, 1133). Circumstances, what the 'Prolog' calls 'die unglückseligen Gestirne' (110), in the finished play prevent personality from showing itself unambiguously in action. What Wallenstein is, is an unanswerable question. It is only what he becomes that slowly reveals itself to us.

This new emphasis in Schiller's later drama on tragic situation rather than tragic character presupposes a far greater degree of objectivity of presentation than was characteristic of the earlier dramas, where he depicted what he felt to be inherently tragic personalities, figures such as Ferdinand and Karl Moor. Paradoxically, the ability of Schiller in *Wallenstein* to maintain a greater distance from his drama results in a much stronger impression of the tragedy of Wallenstein's downfall. This increased aloofness can be explained, and frequently is, in terms of his lack of involvement in his subject matter, a complaint which he makes himself a number of times during composition (cf. J5, 1133; 1134; 1221). However, it is more fully explained as a developing attitude on Schiller's part, which was at least fostered by his study of history and his growing awareness of 'der Doppelsinn des Lebens'. Staiger says of the later historiographical works: 'Die späteren Schriften zeichnen sich durch einen gewissen Gleichmut, eine souveränere Haltung aus.'[8] This is true as much also of *Wallenstein*, if not of all of the later dramas. Since this new objectivity is so fundamental to the dramatic effectiveness of *Wallenstein*, and to the later historical dramas also, it is valuable at this point to examine it both in Schiller's terms and in the light of recent discussions of irony in the drama.

In the 'Prolog' to *Wallenstein* Schiller discusses the nature of drama and its relation to contemporary events. He also discusses the audience's position in relation to the play, in other words the nature of the play as a theatrical experience. The sense of aloofness in *Wallenstein* is closely bound up with the fact that the play is a theatrical event. Heselhaus amongst others has pointed out how Schiller's return to the drama was also a return to the theatre.[9] The 'Prolog', rather than making the audience forget it is in a theatre, in fact begins by pointing out that the Weimar theatre has been restored. It is also a place where the actor performs, however transient his art. Schiller then reminds his audience of the 'real world' outside the theatre—

> Und jetzt an des Jahrunderts ernstem Ende,
> Wo selbst die Wirklichkeit zur Dichtung wird
>
> (61-2)

—and the theatre's obligation to rise to the challenge of such events, before reminding them of the historical context of his play. Sixteen years of war have ravaged the country. Against this background we see a bold enterprise, led by a man familiar to the audience ('Ihr

kennet ihn'), though still an enigma to the historian. Then come
the famous lines which bring to light something of Schiller's view
of the relationship between art and life and art and history:

> Doch euren Augen soll ihn jetzt die Kunst,
> Auch eurem Herzen, menschlich näher bringen.
> Denn jedes Äußerste führt *sie*, die alles
> Begrenzt und bindet, zur Natur zurück,
> Sie sieht den Menschen in des Lebens Drang
> Und wälzt die größre Hälfte seiner Schuld
> Den unglückseligen Gestirnen zu.
>
> (104-10)

As Heselhaus rightly points out, Schiller is not concerned with the
facts of history: 'Es geht ihm nicht um Darstellung der Geschichte,
sondern um Darstellung der Welt und besonders der politischen
Welt.'[10] He is, in his own words, concerned with 'den Menschen in
des Lebens Drang'—man in his historical and political context,
subject to the pressures of public life. While this is an authentic
presentation of human involvements, it is not, however, a naturalistic one; it is life presented within the confines of art. Connop
Thirlwall, in 'On the Irony of Sophocles', virtually restates lines
106-7 above when he says of the dramatist:

Nothing that rouses the feelings in the history of mankind is foreign to his
scene, but as he is confined by artificial limits, he must hasten the march of
events, and compress within a narrow compass what is commonly found
diffused over a large space, so that a faithful image of human existence
may be concentrated in his mimic sphere.[11]

Towards the end of the 'Prolog' Schiller offers an apology for
his use of 'Knittelvers' in *Wallensteins Lager*. He explains that its
function is to give us a proper sense of the play as an artistic creation which is not raw reality but a transmutation of it, and we are
made aware of this transmutation by the operation of stylizing
devices. He concludes with his famous dictum 'Ernst ist das Leben,
heiter ist die Kunst' (138). This line is not only a pointer to major
themes of the play, but also has important implications for how
Schiller sees the relationship of artist (and audience) to the play.
The idea contained in the words 'heiter ist die Kunst' can, of course,
be discussed in terms of the *Ästhetische Briefe* as another statement
of art as 'Spiel'. There is, however, another dimension to this; the
artist and the audience are aware of the theatrical illusion for they
have a sense of being outside the drama. The drama is a different

world and the awareness that the action takes place in another realm gives the audience a certain detachment and ability to view the action as from above. This detachment is a balance of the sense of involvement and yet pleasure at the skill of the work of art. The dramatist himself also stands aloof from the world he creates. A number of critics have identified this objectivity in *Wallenstein*, sometimes referring to it as 'realism'. Witte says for example, 'Instead of frankly identifying himself with the hero ... he now seeks to proceed with a realist's detachment',[12] and Marleyn, 'The greatness of Wallenstein appears ... to be indeed inseparable from its "realism".'[13]

If the study of history contributed to Schiller's aloofness from the world of his drama, it also developed in him an increased insight into the ambiguity of life. Wallenstein, the historical character, is himself an ambiguous figure and Schiller realizes that there is no point in trying to answer in his drama the question of Wallenstein's guilt or innocence. In any case it is not the task of the dramatist to solve the mysteries of the historical world. But by the time Schiller comes to write his *Wallenstein* he has realized that the question of Wallenstein's guilt or innocence is essentially unanswerable. Indeed this insight lies behind the famous verdict on Wallenstein at the end of Book IV of the *Geschichte des Dreißigjährigen Kriegs*—'so fiel Wallenstein, nicht weil er Rebell war, sondern er rebellirte weil er fiel' (NA 18, 329). In accepting this mystery Schiller uses it to explore the relationship of personality and action and to question the whole notion of guilt and innocence. He does so by that mode of character presentation where personality reveals itself through, and is shaped by, action. Since, however, action is not free, but the product of external pressure, there is a constant discrepancy between what people think and what they do, between what they intend and what happens, between what they are and what they seem.

A failure to grasp this fundamental issue in Schiller's presentation of Wallenstein is evident in some interpretations of the play. Some critics who lean heavily on Schiller's theoretical writings find Wallenstein hard to define in terms of those writings. Schiller has been strongly associated with the creation of 'idealist' heroes, characters such as the Marquis Posa, Karl Moor, Ferdinand, Johanna, and Max. For critics who draw heavily on the theoretical writings Wallenstein presents a problem because he is something of

a realist, a 'Machtpolitiker'. While a number of critics[14] call Wallenstein a realist, if we look at the essay *Über naive und sentimentalische
Dichtung*, where Schiller establishes his own definition of these
terms 'idealist' and 'realist', we see that Wallenstein is somewhere
between the two, with Octavio the thoroughgoing realist. Wallenstein may, like the realist, look at ends rather than means, but
rather than finally losing his personal dignity, in the end he in fact
regains it. However, he does not fall into the category of hero who
recognizes his guilt and transcends present suffering, as Maria
Stuart does. A character cannot be 'erhaben' without a degree of
insight into his position, particularly into his own guilt, and a
willingness to admit his failure. Wallenstein does not embrace his
own death willingly and, in spite of his lament for Max, has only
limited insight into the nature of the events of which he has been
part. For Strich Wallenstein is so far from moral self-determination
that he cannot be heroic:

Wallenstein, der Realist, dem es nur nach dem Erfolg, der Macht und
schließlich nur noch nach der Rettung des Lebens verlangt, kann die
sittliche und also die menschliche Entscheidung nicht treffen. Er ist im
Schillerschen Sinn kein Held, und sein Untergang ist nicht heroisch.[15]

This approach to *Wallenstein* springs from an exaggerated view of
Schiller the idealist and from the consequent neglect of that strand
of his development (the historiography is one indication of it)
which counterbalances the idealist image. It emerges from a glance
at *Don Carlos* that Schiller needed to study both history and tragedy
to be in a position to execute a play according to his mental picture
of it. So while the theoretical works are considerations of how tragic
drama is to be created, the period of historical writing and study
was also a training ground, a consideration of 'den Menschen in
des Lebens Drang', equally vital to Schiller's growth as a dramatist. If one accepts the importance of this aspect of Schiller's
development, then Wallenstein does not appear oddly out of line as
a 'Schillerian' hero, but rather the necessary product of those years
of contemplating history and drama.

The combination of a perception of the ambiguity of life and the
ability of Schiller to stand aloof from his drama produces a specific
type of irony, not only in *Wallenstein* but in the later dramas in
general. The word 'irony' requires some discussion because of the
variety of uses it has acquired, some of them through a line of

development in English criticism which may not be immediately familiar in European criticism. It also requires definition because certain instances of dramatic irony are immediately obvious in *Wallenstein* and may not seem to require special discussion. However, we are at the moment dealing with the ironic standpoint of the dramatist himself. Most of the types of irony which are now familiar and accepted would not have been called irony by Schiller himself, though of course the dramatic effects long predated the extension of the term to denote them. In fact the need to give a name to such dramatic effects has caused the extension of the use of the term 'irony'. Up to the beginning of the nineteenth century in England the term irony referred to a verbal device, roughly that of saying one thing but conveying the opposite meaning. Towards the end of the eighteenth and at the beginning of the nineteenth century, the Schlegels in Germany were beginning to use the term 'Ironie' to refer to situations as well as word-play, and also to the detachment or objectivity of the artist in relation to his work.[16]

In 1833 Connop Thirlwall published the essay referred to at the very beginning of this chapter, called 'On the Irony of Sophocles'. It was a significant essay because in it Thirlwall, who was familiar with the Schlegels' ideas, extended the sense of the word irony to apply to certain dramatic situations, especially those which involve superior knowledge on the part of the audience, knowledge which is shared by one or more of the characters, but not by the character who would benefit by it most. This is tragic irony. Thirlwall, however, distinguished another form of irony which springs from the conflict of two irreconcilable attitudes:

There is always a slight cast of irony in the grave, calm, respectful attention impartially bestowed by an intelligent judge on two contending parties ... Here the irony lies not in the demeanour of the judge but is deeply seated in the case itself, which seems to favour each of the litigants, but really eludes them both ... the liveliest interest arises when by inevitable circumstances characters, motives and principles are brought into hostile collision, in which good and evil are so inextricably blended on each side, that we are compelled to give an equal share of our sympathy to each, while we perceive that no earthly power can reconcile them.[17]

Thirlwall recognizes as potentially ironic a basic human situation (potentially, because the irony is apparent only if the dramatist maintains his aloofness). Inherent in human behaviour is a complexity of motive and a limitation of insight which make certain problems insoluble, indeed impenetrable. It is impossible to make absolute judgements about them because the issue defies judgement at all. The contending parties cited by Thirlwall are Creon and Antigone, who both suffer from this incomplete insight and who are both right in their way. Thirlwall goes on, however, to identify the standpoint from which the dramatist must view the action if this insoluble conflict is going to be seen as having 'a slight cast of irony'. He cannot postulate some higher reconciliation which he may not believe to exist. He must simply present the case of the two parties and allow each its validity. So Thirlwall concludes his essay by describing the dramatist's necessary aloofness from his drama if this irony is to come to light. Because of its interesting applicability to *Wallenstein* this part of the essay will be quoted at length:

The dramatist is the creator of a little world, in which he rules with absolute sway, and may shape the destinies of the imaginary beings to whom he gives life and breath according to any plan that he may choose. Since however they are men whose actions he represents and since it is human sympathy that he claims, he will, if he understands his art, make his administration conform to the laws by which he conceives the course of mortal life to be really governed. Nothing that rouses the feelings in the history of mankind is foreign to his scene, but as he is confined by artificial limits, he must hasten the march of events, and compress within a narrow compass what is commonly found diffused over a large space, so that a faithful image of human existence may be concentrated in his mimic sphere. From this sphere however he himself stands aloof. The eye with which he views his microcosm and the creatures within it will not be one of human friendship, nor of brotherly kindness, nor of parental love; it will be that with which he imagines that the invisible power who orders the destiny of man might regard the world and its doings. The essential character therefore of all dramatic poetry must depend on the poet's religious or philosophical sentiments, on the light in which he contemplates history and life, on the belief he entertains as to the unseen hand that regulates their events.[18]

Not only does the dramatist stand aloof from the world he has created but the audience in some ways also stands aloof. Thirlwall does not stress this but it is an important extension of his idea. The audience becomes aware in the drama of the superior vantage point from which it views the action. While the characters in the drama have only partial insight into events, the audience enjoys a panoramic view. Commentators on irony have returned frequently to this phenomenon, seeing it as one of the central principles of drama and related to the old concept of verbal irony through the idea of discrepancy or distance between what is said and what is understood,

between those who speak and act and those who, from a higher
vantage point, hear and observe.[19] This line of discussion of irony
immediately suggests connections with the remarks above p. 77 on
the 'Prolog' and Schiller's reminder to the audience of their position
as spectators to the theatrical event. Another element in irony is
the mixture of pain and pleasure. An ironical remark is at once
penetrating and jesting. By analogy, the principle of irony in the
presentation of dramatic situation suggests a more complex standpoint on the part of the dramatist and a more complex impression
gained from the drama by the spectators. A. R. Thompson[20] says
of dramatic irony that it 'makes us intellectually conscious of
double meanings', whereas David Worcester says that it furnishes
an alternative scale of values, which prevents the spectator from
being altogether carried away by sympathy with the actors.[21] This
view immediately brings to mind again Schiller's 'Ernst ist das
Leben, heiter ist die Kunst', which suggests the seriousness of the
subject of the play and its consequent engaging of the emotions,
but the effect of the spectator's sense of distance and awareness of
the play as a work of art, which balances the effect of seriousness
and involvement.

Wallenstein is the most obviously ironical of all Schiller's dramas.
Although the presence of irony in the other dramas can be dis-
puted Schiller has made obvious use in *Wallenstein* of the conventional and most widely recognized forms of dramatic irony, where
the victim reveals his ignorance of the real state of affairs by words
or actions. Thus Wallenstein's

> Ich denke einen langen Schlaf zu tun
>
> (*W. T.* 3677)

is an example of the *double entendre* technique, where the speaker
is unaware of the situation and his words betray his ignorance to
the audience and make them aware of their superior insight. The
irony is the more striking in the situations where a person on stage
perceives the irony along with the audience, as Gordon does just
before Wallenstein's murder. The potential for irony of the Wallenstein material was at least spotted before Schiller's *Wallenstein*.
Among the several known subliterary Wallenstein plays was one
regularly performed during the early part of the eighteenth century
called *Der verratene Verräter oder der durch Hochmut gestürzte
Wallensteiner*, author unknown.[22] For ironic vision it is necessary

to look deeper to the standpoint which Schiller adopts towards his characters and to the presentation of the central issues of the play.

We have seen in the previous chapter how keenly he encountered the problem of the conflict of motive and reputation with regard to the historical Wallenstein. In fact it is a problem treated by him even some time before he wrote the *Geschichte des Dreißigjährigen Kriegs*, in his short story, *Der Verbrecher aus verlorener Ehre*, published in 1786. The story is one of a number written by Schiller between 1782 and 1786, and they are largely anecdotes with some kind of surprise or twist, which gives them a quality of strangeness. These short stories form an interesting line of development, culminating in Schiller's historiography. They are stories taken from life, in which he consciously cultivates the role of the impartial narrator. This is particularly true of *Der Verbrecher aus verlorener Ehre*, which is based on a true story told to him by Abel at the Karlsschule. Schiller, the omniscient narrator, wishes to present us with an inner core of fact, which will help us to give unbiased attention to the life of the criminal Christian Wolf: 'wir müssen ihn seine Handlung nicht bloss *vollbringen* sondern auch *wollen* sehen. An seinen Gedanken liegt uns unendlich mehr als an seinen Taten, und noch weit mehr an den Quellen seiner Gedanken als an den Folgen jener Taten' (NA 16, 8 f.). We are given insight into the natural disadvantages and pressure of circumstances working in Wolf's case. He is unattractive and susceptible to personal injury. The prejudice of his community and his defiant reaction to that prejudice spark off a chain of events which reduces him to the life of an outlaw. The irony of the story is that Wolf gains some standing as a leader of an outlaw band, beyond the pale of that society which rejected him. A deeper irony lies, however, in the mystery surrounding the Sonnenwirt's guilt. Certainly he is guilty of minor misdemeanours, and nature has made him susceptible to slights both real and imaginary. The harshness of his punishment for these minor offences, however, convinces his community that their original prejudice against him was justified. The result is that the loss of Wolf's 'Ehre' comes *before* his real life as a criminal. He is forced finally to become what others have already judged him to be. Yet beyond the specific instance of Wolf is the final mystery of what a man could be in different circumstances, and the insoluble problem of the cause and effect relationship between motive and external circumstances.

The case of Wolf brings to mind Schiller's later summing up of the Wallenstein enigma: 'so fiel Wallenstein, nicht weil er Rebell war, sondern er rebellirte weil er fiel' (NA 18, 329). In the story of the Sonnenwirt Schiller's psychology is very similar to that in *Wallenstein* in that he conceives of the human personality as being very uniform in composition from one person to another, but capable of infinite variety of action, according to the different circumstances which influence a personality's development:

Es ist etwas so Einförmiges und doch wieder so Zusammengesetztes das menschliche Herz. Eine und eben dieselbe Fertigkeit oder Begierde kann in tausenderlei Formen und Richtungen spielen, kann tausend widersprechende Phänomene bewirken, kann in tausend Charakteren anders gemischt erscheinen, und tausend ungleiche Charaktere und Handlungen können wieder aus einerlei Neigung gesponnen sein, wenn auch der Mensch, von welchem die Rede ist, nichts weniger denn eine solche Verwandtschaft ahndet.

(NA 16, 7)

The psychology of *Der Verbrecher aus verlorener Ehre* is similar to that of *Wallenstein* in the sense that pressure of circumstances plays a vital part in determining how people's personalities will emerge. However, at bottom Schiller sees character at that time as being composed of a number of potential traits which are brought out by circumstances. By the time he is writing *Wallenstein* the psychology of *Der Verbrecher aus verlorener Ehre* is taken a stage further. There is a sense in which character as such no longer exists. Max Kommerell identified this phenomenon when he said, 'Es gibt also strenggenommen für Schiller keinen Charakter. Er ist der Dramatiker ohne Charaktere.'[23] Hence the extreme elusiveness of Wallenstein's personality. Schiller's later characters are not limited and somehow programmed by predisposition, a kind of psychological determinism, but rather by the path in life which they either choose or have forced upon them. They stand ready to turn one way or another until obliged to act. Their deeds in this sense create what they are, or as Max Kommerell puts it: 'daß die Tat den Charakter schafft, und nicht der Charakter die Tat. Genau dies ist aber die Ansicht, die Schiller über den Charakter gehabt haben muß.'[24] In *Der Verbrecher aus verlorener Ehre* we see Schiller working towards this concept of character, although it is not fully articulated until *Wallenstein*.

Another insight of *Der Verbrecher aus verlorener Ehre* which re-emerges in *Don Carlos*, in the historiography, and in *Wallenstein,* is the problem of the limited insight of participants in any action into the true nature of their circumstances. The Sonnenwirt continually feels himself to be disadvantaged and so reacts with heightened sensitivity to those around him. He is constantly at odds with his community and so feeds the prejudice against him. Even his admission of his true identity to the magistrate at the end of the story is possibly made as a result of mistaken appearances. The magistrate suspects Wolf but realizes he will be intractable if treated high-handedly: 'es wäre vielleicht besser getan, ihm mit Anstand und Mäßigung zu begegnen' (NA 16, 28). Wolf takes this, possibly erroneously, as the sign that the magistrate has not approached him with the usual prejudice. To the magistrate it was, of course, simply a ploy. So Wolf's apparent moral rebirth is based on a mistaken perception of the situation.

Mistaken perceptions are a basic element in the world of Schiller's drama from *Wallenstein* onwards, but not in the way that they were in the earlier dramas. The plots of *Die Räuber* and *Kabale und Liebe*, for example, are based on deliberate deception. In *Don Carlos*, however, this has been refined to the stage where the true state of affairs becomes increasingly hard to discover. Posa gives false impressions because he is caught between the King and Carlos, not because he deliberately sets out to deceive; his deception of the King, however, undermines the latter's sense that he can ever trust anyone again and forces him back into his withdrawal from human affections. This develops in the historiography and in *Wallenstein* into the idea that it is virtually impossible to gain any objective or true perception of the world.

As a result of this increasing awareness on Schiller's part of the impenetrability of other people's motives and the unpredictability of their reactions, the world takes on a hostile aspect in *Wallenstein*. Wallenstein himself is only too aware of the hostile nature of the world, referring to 'jenen tückischen Mächten' (*W. T.* 190). It is a world in which appearance and reality are confused because people judge according to their own preconceptions. Not only that, people are aware of the danger of exposing their true motives and so constantly resort to the playing of roles and the wearing of masks. Wallenstein becomes painfully aware of the discrepancy between reality and appearance in his monologue (*W. T.* I, 4) after the capture of Sesina. Allowing for some whitewashing on his part,

one can still say that he realizes that the world is a place where the
process of action and reaction continues beyond the control of any
one person. He tried to control the process by giving false appearances, but false appearances are as committing as real ones:

> Strafbar erschein ich, und ich kann die Schuld,
> Wie ichs versuchen mag! nicht von mir wälzen;
> Denn mich verklagt der Doppelsinn des Lebens
> (*W. T.* 159-61)

Up to this point in the action Wallenstein has merely toyed with
ideas, preferring to enjoy the sense of possible action. What he
has not realized is that no one can escape the burden of participation in action. Simply seeming is an action with its own consequences, since that appearance is perceived by others, by those such
as Octavio, who bring their own interpretation to it. The masks
adopted for protection are finally forced upon the wearers, as
Wallenstein realizes when he exclaims to Illo:

> Wie? Sollt ichs nun im Ernst erfüllen müssen,
> Weil ich zu frei gescherzt mit dem Gedanken?
> Verflucht, wer mit dem Teufel spielt!—
> (*W. T.* 112-14)

Schiller's treatment of the astrological motif is closely linked
to this problem, indeed the astrological motif expresses it in concentrated form. The historical Wallenstein, as depicted in the
Geschichte des Dreißigjährigen Kriegs, is from the start of his
career a believer in astrology. In his opening description of the
historical Wallenstein Schiller briefly mentions that Wallenstein
was 'voll Zuversicht auf seine glücklichen Sterne und noch mehr
auf eine gründliche Berechnung der Zeitumstände' (NA 18, 113).
Schiller does not attempt to project himself into the spirit of the
times and explain Wallenstein's superstition. In a later and more
critical reference to the stars Schiller again suggests that Wallenstein's astrology was also very much bound up with his own judgement of the propitious moment for action: 'Man brauchte die Sterne
nicht zu bemühen, um mit Wahrscheinlichkeit vorher zu sagen, daß
ein Feind wie Gustav Adolph einen General wie Wallenstein nicht
lange entbehrlich lassen würde' (NA 18, 133). The dramatic Wallenstein begins his study of the stars only after his removal from the
command of the army after Regensburg, as we learn from the
Herzogin in Act III Sc. 3 of *Wallensteins Tod*:

> ... seit dem Unglückstag zu Regenspurg,
> Der ihn von seiner Höh herunter stürzte,
> Ist ein unsteter, ungesellger Geist
> Argwöhnisch, finster, über ihn gekommen.
> Ihn floh die Ruhe, und dem alten Glück,
> Der eignen Kraft nicht fröhlich mehr vertrauend,
> Wandt er sein Herz den dunkeln Künsten zu,
> Die keinen, der sie pflegte, noch beglückt.
>
> (*W.T.* 1402-9)

In composing the *Wallenstein* trilogy Schiller was at first at a loss to know how to incorporate the astrological element, calling it 'eine Fratze' (J5, 1412). It was a superstition for which he had little sympathy, the inner essence of which he felt he could not grasp. It was, of course, the subject of correspondence between Goethe and Schiller, in which Goethe suggested how the believer in astrology had a sense of the whole system of the universe and attempted to perceive the world as governed by patterns.[25] The astrological motif has received a certain amount of critical attention. Witte sees it as an indication of Wallenstein's hybris.[26] In similar vein Wells sees it as a token of Wallenstein's confidence in himself and his superior judgement.[27] Seidlin sees the astrological motif as bound up with the presentation of action in history,[28] a theme implied by Böckmann[29]—astrology as a means of robbing fate of its power. Glück[30] and, even more recently, Hinderer,[31] rightly point to the impact of Wallenstein's removal from power at Regensburg as a key to the astrological motif.

Before discussing the impact of Regensburg, however, it is necessary to take note of another key we are given to the astrological motif, this time by Gordon in *W.T.* IV, 2. Buttler repeats to Gordon a popular story of how Wallenstein once fell from a high window and stood up again unscathed. This anecdote has a number of functions, not the least of which is to help recreate the mystique surrounding Wallenstein in the closing stages of the play. It is in fact Gordon who confirms and amplifies this story and in doing so he performs a parallel function to some of the characters of the *Lager*, who also create the myth of Wallenstein before his appearance. Gordon comments on the effect of his miraculous escape on Wallenstein:

> Wunderbar hatt ihn das Wunder
> Der Rettung umgekehrt. Er hielt sich nun

Für ein begünstigt und befreites Wesen,
Und keck wie einer, der nicht straucheln kann,
Lief er auf schwankem Seil des Lebens hin.

(*W. T.* 2566-70)

In other words, Wallenstein felt himself after that incident to enjoy
a special destiny, indeed to enjoy a special position in the naturai
world. He was no longer bound by the same iron rule of cause and
effect which governs the world in general. He had once and for all
been freed from its restrictions. He could act without consequences,
without regard for the laws which govern events. However, his
removal from power at Regensburg created in him a brooding spirit,
as the Herzogin says:

Ihn floh die Ruhe, und dem alten Glück,
Der eignen Kraft nicht fröhlich mehr vertrauend,
Wandt er sein Herz den dunkeln Künsten zu,
Die keinen, der sie pflegte, noch beglückt.

(*W. T.* 1406-9)

His belief in the stars is certainly, as critics have said, a projection
of his belief in himself, an attempt to link his success and good
fortune with the designs of a higher authority: 'Sie [die Sterne] sind
das Glück, das in den Weltlauf ausgestrahlte Vermögen der Person,
das ihn solange zwingt, bis ihre Bannkraft erschöpft ist.'[32] Yet the
fact that Wallenstein took up astrology only when felt that his
destiny was not being fulfilled suggests something more. Wallenstein is deeply shocked by the intervention in his life of events
beyond his control, events like his sudden loss of authority. His
study of the stars therefore suggests a new anxiety about his ability
to choose the proper moment for action. He still believes in his
great destiny but is aware that the unforeseen can break in at any
moment. The only way to guard against that is to gain a superior
vantage point and have some higher confirmation that the correct
moment has come, so that he will not be caught out again, as at
Regensburg. Glück says: 'Machtgier und Rache treiben ihn an, sich
wieder in das Spiel einzuschalten, in dem Königreiche zu gewinnen
sind. Aber unsicher geworden, wagt er nicht mehr, den Zeitpunkt
des Einsatzes zu bestimmen. Er schiebt die Entscheidung den
Sternen zu.'[33]

It is in these terms that we must understand Wallenstein's reluctance to act. His reluctance springs not from an indecisive personality, as some critics have suggested, nor does it spring solely from

an enjoyment of his sense of power, as Ilse Graham tends to suggest.[34] It springs from a keen awareness of the incalculability of the effects of action and an unwillingness to unleash a chain of events over which he has no control. Böckmann identifies this:

Man wird das Hinausschieben des Entschlusses nicht als ein psychologisches Problem verstehen dürfen, als wäre Wallenstein eine zögernde Natur ... Viel eher unterstreicht dieses Zögern die Doppelgesichtigkeit der schließlich gefallenen Entscheidung, sofern sie den Handelnden bindet.[35]

So Wallenstein somehow believes it possible to remove himself from the causal chain, to stand outside history until the perfect moment for action arrives and he can stride on to the 'Welttheater' and take control. Ironically, of course, the more he looks to the stars for confirmation of the right moment, the more removed his judgement becomes from the actual circumstances. Until that moment arrives he can spend his time manipulating the participants in the action, which he attempts to survey as from above. To those people, characters such as Buttler, Wallenstein appears as a cold manipulator, ready to move people round his chessboard with no regard to their individual lives. Buttler, resenting this reduction of his significance, says to Gordon:

> Ein großer Rechenkünstler war der Fürst
> Von jeher, alles wußt er zu berechnen,
> Die Menschen wußt er, gleich des Brettspiels Steinen,
> Nach seinem Zweck zu setzen und zu schieben
> (*W.T.* 2853-6)

It is not until the opening of the final part of the trilogy that Wallenstein discovers that he cannot stand outside history. He can control neither people nor events. While he thinks he is holding himself apart from the movement of events he is in fact being carried along by it. The capture of Sesina is the first occasion in the drama when Wallenstein has to admit that, despite his precautions, the unexpected can break in at any moment and thus he says, 'Es ist ein böser Zufall!' (*W.T.* 92). This line appears to be in direct contradiction to Wallenstein's later words to Illo, 'Es gibt keinen Zufall' (*W.T.* 943) but to Illo Wallenstein is asserting his faith in his remarkable destiny, his faith in himself as one to whom heaven gives special signs, as before the Battle of Lützen, to which he refers. After the capture of Sesina Wallenstein slowly discovers, though only through tragic disillusionment, that that confidence was false and that he is as susceptible as everyone else to the intervention of chance. His soliloquy (*W.T.* I, 4) as he considers the implications of Sesina's capture and the pressure of time which is forcing him to act promptly, shows the dawning of his sense of 'Verstricktheit' in the events from which he thought to hold aloof:

So hab ich
Mit eignem Netz verderblich mich umstrickt
(*W.T.* 177-8)

Wallenstein's belief in destiny is oddly paralleled in the final two acts by Buttler's attitude to the murder of the man who had so abused his loyalty. Buttler refers on several occasions to Wallenstein's evil destiny which has brought him within Buttler's grasp and which has ordained his fall from power and his death. For example, in the soliloquy with which he opens Act IV of *Wallensteins Tod* he claims that fate has brought Wallenstein inside the walls of Eger:

Er ist herein. Ihn führte sein Verhängnis.
. . . .
Bis hieher, Friedland und nicht weiter! sagt
Die Schicksalsgöttin.
(*W.T.* 2424, 2433-4)

Later he says the same to Gordon, possibly in an attempt to convince Gordon that there is no point in attempting to resist the murder rather than in order to justify himself:

Doch nicht mein Haß macht mich zu seinem Mörder.
Sein böses Schicksal ists. Das Unglück treibt mich,
Die feindliche Zusammenkunft der Dinge.
(*W.T.* 2873-5)

Far from being a commentary by Schiller on the action, as some critics (Ludwig,[36] Garland,[37] Silz[38]) have suggested, Buttler's words are virtually a conscious parody of Wallenstein's own attitude to action, where Wallenstein himself appeals to fate and necessity to justify his behaviour (cf. *Die Picc.* 701-2, *W.T.* 883-5). Buttler's argument is weak, for he wishes to kill Wallenstein for revenge and yet derives satisfaction from the idea that he is appointed by the ministers of a higher justice to give Wallenstein his deserts. After Octavio has won Buttler over, Buttler sets out to beat Wallenstein at his own game of manipulation. He realizes that he can make himself arbiter of the general's fate and appreciates the irony of the situation:

> Nimm dich in acht! dich treibt der böse Geist
> Der Rache—daß dich Rache nicht verderbe!
> (*W.T.* 2443-4)

Buttler fails in his attempt to give his actions dignity, for his motives of revenge are all too apparent. However, he is at least prepared, unlike Octavio, to take responsibility for what he has done, and finally leaves for Vienna to claim his reward.

Wallenstein's principle of behaviour is a belief in his special destiny. Other characters have their own standards and criteria of judgment. All, however, suffer a loss of integrity through involvement in action in the historical world. It is characteristic of Schiller's tragic vision that all action, morally justified (within the terms of the play) or not, involves loss of integrity. Characters must act with only limited insight into their circumstances; they are driven by necessity rather than by free choice and so their actions are frequently uncharacteristic and take on an ambiguity from the world around them. This was already true in *Don Carlos*, where we observed the phenomenon of the character (Posa) whose actions were somehow less noble than he himself seemed intrinsically to be, and certainly less noble than his own words and ideals. There it became obvious that the ambiguity lay not so much in Posa as a personality as in the complexity of the historical world. In a world where actions are presented as part of causal chains, it is inevitable that characters are caught in a web of relationships and circumstances, in which every move they make must have a double aspect. In *Wallenstein*, where Schiller's presentation of the interlocking of the tragic action is much tighter than in *Don Carlos*, this ambiguity in action is the more striking. Thus Kommerell, adapting Goethe, can say of Schiller's world, 'der Handelnde ist unrein'.[39] Pressure from 'des Lebens Drang' inevitably results in forced decisions, and the lack of a sure perspective from which to view events inevitably leads to misinterpretation and false assumptions. What people appear to be is almost by definition not what they are unless, like Max, they have not discovered the nature of the political world. (This is a problem which comes again to prominence in *Maria Stuart*.)

This painful realization dawns on Max Piccolomini in the course

of the drama. Up to this time life has been easy for Max and free
from difficult choices, as Wallenstein points out to him:

> Sanft wiegte dich bis heute dein Geschick,
> Du konntest spielend deine Pflichten üben,
> Jedwedem schönen Trieb Genüge tun,
> Mit ungeteiltem Herzen immer handeln.
>
> (*W.T.* 719-22)

Max is appalled at the idea of his father's own treachery against
his general and friend and cannot accept the rather sententious
defence which Octavio makes of his course of action:

> Mein bester Sohn! Es ist nicht immer möglich,
> Im Leben sich so kinderrein zu halten,
> Wie's uns die Stimme lehrt im Innersten.
>
> (*Die Picc.* 2447-9)

We lose respect for Octavio because he can so readily accept this
sacrifice both of his friend and of the principle of upright behaviour,
to the point of deceiving a man who has implicit trust in him. He
seems to suggest in this dialogue with Max that his own guilt is
somehow expunged by Wallenstein's and by the demands of the
situation. Hence he can say:

> Das eben ist der Fluch der bösen Tat,
> Daß sie, fortzeugend, immer Böses muß gebären.
> Ich klügle nicht, ich tue meine Pflicht.
>
> (*Die Picc.* 2452-4)

Max, on the other hand, has never yet had to face the implications
of involvement in the political world. He has not yet realized that
the private and the public are inextricably linked. The inner voice
which he has followed up to now falls silent, unable to judge unequivocally between the claims on either side. The only solution
which Max can find is to opt out of history, to jump off the great
wheel, for he cannot bear the violation of his sense of integrity
which allegiance to the Emperor at the expense of his dearest friend
will entail. Max then deliberately embraces this line of action. An
interesting parallel to this is to be found in the death of Maria in
Maria Stuart. At the meeting of the two queens Maria gives vent
to her long-restrained grievances against Elisabeth and so condemns
herself to death. She does not deliberately choose this path as a
solution to her problems but rather acts in the heat of the moment.
Having done so, however, she too has removed herself from the

sphere of historical and political action. She can piece together before her death the fragments of her personality and rediscover her integrity, which was forfeit in the world of politics.

While critics have frequently made much of the 'sublimity' of the deaths of Max and Maria, they have often failed to notice their ambiguity. Maria's death is forced upon her; she comes to terms with it and can leave the scene of history but others have to live on in the shadow of her 'martyrdom'. Their lives will be changed by her death. Max chooses to die but his death is in a sense a luxury which few can afford; most actors on the 'Welttheater' are obliged to accept the consequences of their actions and to discharge their responsibilities. Max indeed warns his men:

> Wer mit mir geht, der sei bereit zu sterben!
> (*W.T.* 2427)

His warning is horribly fulfilled and all are killed. Indeed, while Max's death removes him from the scene of history, at the same time his deliberate death is an action *in* history, which therefore has its own consequences and its own 'Doppelsinn'. Max's death in fact hastens Wallenstein's. The news of the defeat of the Pappenheimer and the victorious advance of the Swedes give Buttler the excuse he needs for insisting on the prompt murder of Wallenstein. The fact that Max's death is a historical event (i.e. an event within the historical world of the play) with repercussions is reinforced in the final act of the drama when Gordon and Seni both implore Wallenstein to reverse his plans. Wallenstein points to Max's death:

> —Blut ist geflossen, Gordon. Nimmer kann
> Der Kaiser mir vergeben. Könnt ers, ich,
> Ich könnte nimmer mir vergeben lassen.
> (*W.T.* 3654-6)

Max's death stands now between Wallenstein and the Emperor, almost as a token of Wallenstein's 'Ernst'; any appearance of innocence or 'Spiel' has now been eradicated by the fact that blood has been shed. Wallenstein may be a moral pragmatist, but his grief at Max's death makes him realize that it cannot be made insignificant by an easy reconciliation. Perhaps there is a hint of this in his words:

> Zu ernsthaft
> Hats angefangen, um in nichts zu enden.
> (*W.T.* 3661-2)

The problems confronting Max are echoed in a minor key in the final two acts of *Wallensteins Tod* by Gordon. In certain respects Gordon's role is parallel to Max's. It is he who assumes Max's role of reflecting Wallenstein's noble qualities and his great prestige. So Gordon can listen to Buttler's plans for assassinating Illo and Terzky without regret but feels that Wallenstein himself deserves the regard due to a prince:

> O seiner Fehler nicht gedenket jetzt!
> An seine Größe denkt, an seine Milde,
> An seines Herzens liebenswerte Züge,
> An alle Edeltaten seines Lebens
>
> (*W. T.* 2863-6)

With Wallenstein's entry into Eger, Gordon, a modest man with no ambition, suddenly finds himself in the thick of the action and obliged to dissemble, to adopt an ambiguous role, doing his duty as keeper of the fortress but aware of the danger into which Wallenstein has walked. He tries to make excuses for himself and to Buttler, with typical efforts at self-justification, to quieten his own conscience as he perceives the invidious role he must play. He laments to Buttler:

> Wir Subalternen haben keinen Willen,
> Der freie Mann, der mächtige allein
> Gehorcht dem schönen menschlichen Gefühl.
> Wir aber sind nur Schergen des Gesetzes,
> Des grausamen, Gehorsam heißt die Tugend,
> Um die der Niedre sich bewerben darf.
>
> (*W. T.* 2507-12)

Gordon, who, like Max, feels obliged to follow his heart, soon finds himself confused and anguished as he discovers that a mental assent to the idea of duty does not rule out a deeper sense of the moral acceptability of certain courses of action. Though in the speech above he bewails his lack of freedom to follow his own judgement he finds that this lack of freedom does not free him from a sense of responsibility.

Gordon's sense of anguish mounts as Buttler moves inexorably towards his goal and he finds that he must choose either to be for Buttler or against him. Buttler perceives the timidity and sensitivity of the man and is brutal in securing his loyalty by instilling in him fear of the consequences of letting Wallenstein escape:

Nehmt Ihrs auf Euch. Steht für die Folgen ein!
Mag werden draus was will! Ich legs auf Euch.

(*W.T.* 2733-4)

As Buttler draws near with Wallenstein's murderers Gordon considers leaving the whole matter to providence, hoping that passivity will be a means of removing himself from the scene of action. With Buttler's arrival and refusal to put off the murder even by an hour he feels obliged to make some sort of stand and places himself somewhat ineffectually in Buttler's way. He is immediately pushed aside and has to endure the appearance of Octavio in the fortress. Having discovered Wallenstein's murder Octavio appeals both to Buttler and Gordon for a denial of the fact:

Es darf nicht sein! Es ist nicht moglich! Buttler!
Gordon! Ich wills nicht glauben. Saget nein.

(*W.T.* 3777-8)

Gordon cannot answer and dumbly points to the back of the stage where Wallenstein's body is lying. It is in trying to effect a compromise that Gordon fails to rescue either his convictions or his stature in the sight of others. He discovers that a line of action has to be chosen unreservedly. Unlike Max, he cannot step outside history and in a sense he is right to attribute this to his humble station. His death would be in no way significant and would not alter the course of events. It is the prerogative of the makers of history to make the grand gestures which are absurd in the insignificant. So Gordon remains at the end with Octavio, both representatives of a bankrupt order, greatness and integrity having left the stage.

The use of the word 'stage' is very appropriate to *Wallenstein* because it is a drama which involves the characters themselves in so much conscious and unconscious role-playing. This role-playing and the use made of the motif of 'Spiel' in the play are in a sense particularly appropriate to a play set in the Baroque period, a time when the *theatrum mundi* motif was so popular. Schiller was, of course, not acquainted with the plays of the German Baroque.[40] He uses the motif to illuminate the problem of the discrepancy between will and action, between inner personality and public deeds. Yet at the same time one detects in *Wallenstein* a secularized treatment of a typically Baroque theme, that of the irredeemable corruption of the world. Schiller uses the motif to bring to light the

corrupt state of the world, which violates the individual's integrity
by forcing a discrepancy between will and action, such that a man
can keep his conscience pure only by leaving the world altogether.
It is again the 'Prolog' which points to the theme of role-playing
and the *theatrum mundi* motif. In the 'Prolog' Schiller is at pains
to establish connections between the stage and the real world. He
reminds the audience first of all of the building in which they are
sitting and of previous events which have taken place there. Before
he introduces his own play he makes the audience think of the
world in which they are living, a time of crisis for Europe:

> Wo selbst die Wirklichkeit zur Dichtung wird.
>
> (62)

In view of the import of contemporary events in the real world
Schiller states the need for the stage to take up the challenge to
broaden its horizons and not to shy away from subject matter of
similar magnitude. The theatre will never achieve that kind of
dynamic relationship with life which Schiller envisaged for it
(e.g. in the *Ästhetische Briefe*) if it does not concern itself with
the basic and vital preoccupations of the age:

> Jetzt darf die Kunst auf ihrer Schattenbühne
> Auch höhern Flug versuchen, ja sie muß,
> Soll nicht des Lebens Bühne sie beschämen.
>
> (67-9)

Schiller takes up the idea of the world as a stage and connects
it with that significant line at the end of the 'Prolog', already discussed in connection with irony, 'Ernst ist das Leben, heiter ist
die Kunst' (138). There is continual reference in the play to the
problem of Wallenstein's 'Ernst', which stands in contrast to his
taste for 'Spiel'. The word 'Spiel' has, as in English, the sense of
play either as a game or a stage play. There are numerous examples
of the use of the word in the former sense, notably Terzky's exasperated words to Wallenstein:

> So hast du stets dein Spiel mit uns getrieben!
>
> (*Die Picc.* 871)

There are many instances, often more implicit, of the awareness of
the characters of their playing roles and their participation in some
kind of grand play. Wallenstein is obviously the most consummate
role-player but the tendency for other characters to do the same is

very marked. A partial explanation for this is in the nature of action as depicted in the play, where decision and involvement are thrust upon the characters, often against their own wishes. Often characters, such as Wallenstein himself, feel the need to preserve appearances in the eyes of the world. Whereas the will is private, action is public and characters experience a discrepancy between the private realm of their will and the public realm of action. In the world of historical event action takes place on a 'Schauplatz', where one not only acts but one is seen to act. Role-playing is therefore a universal phenomenon in the world of *Wallenstein* and the degree of awareness of it and the type of reaction to it are indicative of the various characters' mode of moral judgement. The more sensitive and scrupulous characters in the play, such as Max, become painfully aware of this discrepancy, whereas the more thoroughgoing pragmatists like Gräfin Terzky are able to turn it to their advantage.

Gräfin Terzky, for example, impresses on Wallenstein the unsatisfactory role he will have to play if he retires into private life:

> Auf seinen Schlössern wird es nun lebendig,
> Dort wird er jagen, baun, Gestüte halten,
> Sich eine Hofstatt gründen, goldne Schlüssel
> Austeilen, gastfrei große Tafel geben,
> Und kurz ein großer König sein—im Kleinen!
>   (*W. T.* 507-11)

She realizes that to Wallenstein it is very important what role he plays. She knows that he has a need to feel significant and admired by others and that if she presents to him at this critical moment an unsatisfactory role for the future he will be bound to reject it. He must always play the role which he envisages for himself and nothing is worse than having no public for one's performances. The audience of course knows that Gräfin Terzky is herself playing a role. She is too shrewd really to believe that Wallenstein would simply be allowed to go into retirement but she is rising to the occasion when she can be in the spotlight of attention and demonstrate her powers of persuasion.

Octavio, on the other hand, plays roles without even realizing it. He assures Questenberg that he never actually deceived Wallenstein:

> Befiehlt mir gleich die Klugheit und die Pflicht,
> Die ich dem Reich, dem Kaiser schuldig bin,

Daß ich mein wahres Herz vor ihm verberge,
Ein falsches hab ich niemals ihm geheuchelt!
(*Die Picc.* 350-3)

These words betray the fact that he has not the imagination to contemplate his actions. His watchword is:

Ich klügle nicht, ich tue meine Pflicht.
(*Die Picc.* 2454)

Although he claims never to have deceived Wallenstein actively his language in the opening scenes of *Die Piccolomini* when he appears before the assembled generals with Questenberg has a loftiness and formality which betray the dissembler, who is not prepared to speak his mind like the other generals.[41] It is because Octavio is completely oblivious to the wider implications of his actions and insensitive to the discrepancy between the end he pursues and the means he employs that he can press on so implacably.

Role-playing extends even to Max, the most guileless and transparently honest person in the play. Although he has no wish to dissemble Max is still aware of the public nature of the life he leads and the sense in which it is acted out in full view of the world. Thus he says when he confronts Wallenstein:

Geh vom Schauplatz. (*W. T.* 824)

He also offers to go to Vienna to plead Wallenstein's case before the Emperor. He does not intend to falsify the case but wishes all the same to portray Wallenstein to the Emperor in the light of his own knowledge of him, almost as an actor would portray a character whose personality he mediates to the audience:

Er kennt dich nicht, ich aber kenne dich,
Er soll dich sehn mit meinem reinen Auge.
(*W. T.* 817-8)

Even Max becomes aware during the course of the drama that the world demands a sacrifice of the individual's integrity. People cannot simply express their whole will and personality in action. They are forced to do things to which they do not give their full assent. Hence the sense of acting out a part from which the actor can stand back because less than his whole will and personality are engaged in it.

Buttler is much more conscious of his role-playing than

Octavio, even though they are allies and both working towards the same end through deception of Wallenstein. Buttler, as we have already noted, sees himself as an agent of retribution. Some critics have seen Buttler's speech at the opening of *Wallensteins Tod* Act IV, beginning 'Er ist herein' (2428) as being in the tradition of the Greek chorus. Garland[42] and Silz[43] both see Buttler as stepping out of his own character for a short time, in order that Schiller might speak through him and indicate to the audience that Nemesis is at work in the drama, and that this is how we are to view the ensuing action. This analysis is risky, in that it implies the direct intrusion by Schiller into the play. Certainly Buttler's sudden poetic outburst is surprising from someone normally so laconic and brooding. We have, however, already seen him show the same kind of eloquence in front of Questenberg in *Die Piccolomini* (I, 2) and it seems that indignation is capable of producing this reaction in him. Another reason for being wary of this view of Buttler's role as suggesting the principle of Nemesis, is that the play itself tends to run counter to this idea.

There has been a limited amount of critical examination of the question of Nemesis in *Wallenstein*. Schiller himself has lent some force to the notion that *Wallenstein* is a Nemesis tragedy, first through his admiration at the time of composition for Shakespeare's *Richard III*, of which he said, 'Eine hohe Nemesis wandelt durch das Stück, in allen Gestalten, man kommt nicht aus dieser Empfindung heraus von Anfang bis zu Ende' (J5, 1277); secondly, because he suggested that he would like on the title-page of the book edition of *Wallenstein* a vignette of Nemesis (J5, 1135; 1152). The question, however, remains unanswered of what Schiller understood by the concept of Nemesis, and here the play itself must be paramount.

In a letter to Goethe Schiller discusses the nature of moral judgement on Wallenstein himself and the problems involved in producing a satisfactory synthesis of the moral and the poetic:

Ich lege doch jetzt ganz unvermerkt eine Strecke nach der andern in meinem Pensum zurück und finde mich so recht in dem tiefsten Wirbel der Handlung. Besonders bin ich froh, eine Situation hinter mir zu haben, wo die Aufgabe war, das ganz gemeine moralische Urtheil über das Wallensteinische Verbrechen auszusprechen und eine solche in sich triviale und unpoetische Materie poetisch und geistreich zu behandeln, ohne die Natur des moralischen zu vertilgen. Ich bin zufrieden mit der Ausführung und hoffe unserm lieben moralischen Publikum nicht weniger zu gefallen, ob ich gleich keine Predigt daraus gemacht habe. Bei dieser Gelegenheit habe ich aber recht gefühlt, wie leer das eigentlich moralische ist, und wieviel daher das Subjekt leisten mußte, um das Objekt in der poetischen Höhe zu erhalten.

(J5, 1319)

It seems from his remark, 'Ich bin zufrieden ... gemacht habe', that Schiller did not have in mind any sort of morality play, where the one who is guilty of hybris is pursued by Nemesis. Certainly the moral aspects of Wallenstein's treachery and the behaviour of others towards him had to be manipulated by the dramatist, in order that moral objections would not destroy the desired aesthetic effect. As Schiller's words would suggest, the play offers a more complex perspective on justice, retribution, and morality than the simple term 'Nemesis tragedy' would suggest.

That more complex perspective emerges at least in part from the nature of action as we have seen it emerge in *Wallenstein*. The immediate implication of the word Nemesis is a system of justice, often a higher justice than human, which operates in human affairs. However, in a world where people are prevented, by the very nature of action, from following not only their innermost desires but also their highest ideals, there can scarcely be a system of just rewards and punishments. While Wallenstein's frequent appeals to the pressure of circumstances are attempts to escape responsibility, the world in which he lives is nevertheless hostile. This point of view is contested. R. D. Miller says, for example:

The references to 'Notwendigkeit,' 'Geschick', Doppelsinn des Lebens' and 'des Lebens Fremde' are to be interpreted as the utterances of a man who either does not comprehend his moral failure, or else seeks to exonerate himself by appealing to some impersonal factor indicated by these terms.[44]

Miller's comment suggests that the world of *Wallenstein* is a place where the righteous and the unrighteous reap the rewards of their actions and where Wallenstein falls because he fails to recognize his guilt. But this is not the view of life which prevails within the play, otherwise how would Thekla bewail the cruelty and injustice of a world where Max is trampled under the hooves of his horses? In one sense justice is done to Wallenstein, in that the betrayer is betrayed. In the *Geschichte des Dreißigjährigen Kriegs* Schiller succumbs for a moment to the temptation of using the term Nemesis with regard to the historical Wallenstein—'die rächende Nemesis wollte, daß der *Undankbare* unter den Streichen des *Undanks* erliegen sollte' (NA 18, 323). This is not, however, characteristic

of his view of history in the work as a whole, and certainly not of
the view of history in the play.

Schiller's dramatic sense told him early in the composition of
Wallenstein that he could not set against Wallenstein an antagonist
of great stature, in case that antagonist overshadowed Wallenstein
himself—'Um ihn nicht zu erdrücken, darf ich ihm nichts großes
gegenüberstellen; er hält mich dadurch nothwendig nieder' (J5, 1134).
Octavio is not a villain, as Schiller was at pains to point out to the
critic Böttiger (J6, 1438). He is 'ein ziemlich rechtlicher Mann' but
he is a man who rejects, or perhaps is incapable of, any disturbing
insights into his own treachery against the man who trusts him
implicitly. He exemplifies fully what Schiller had in mind when in
Über naive und sentimentalische Dichtung he described the realist's
lack of moral awareness: 'Der Realist büßt die Mängel (seines
Systems) mit seiner persönlichen Würde, aber er erfährt nichts von
diesem Opfer' (NA 20, 498). In pursuit of his 'Zweck' he closes his
mind to his loss of integrity. Wallenstein grows in stature, as Octavio
gains the ascendancy in the play and towards his death shows a
nobility of which Octavio seems incapable. But Octavio has a
double role. He is, artistically speaking, the character whose
treachery creates sympathy for Wallenstein. At the same time he
is the representative of legitimate government, i.e. the Emperor.
The Emperor himself, of course, never appears, but is constantly
in the background. He has shown himself unreliable in his dismissal
of Wallenstein at Regensburg, and although he is the legitimate
ruler, our sense of his legitimacy is undermined by the treachery of
his representatives. Morally speaking, Octavio's betrayal of Wallenstein seems more reprehensible than Wallenstein's betrayal of the
Emperor. Wallenstein himself says of Octavio:

> —Wär ich dem *Ferdinand* gewesen, was
> Octavio *mir* war—Ich hätt ihm nie
> Krieg angekündigt—nie hätt ichs vermocht.
> Er war mein strenger Herr nur, nicht mein Freund
> (*W.T.* 2119-22)

Our sense of Ferdinand's legitimacy is further undermined by the
fact that Max takes seriously the proposition that the Viennese
party is not seriously interested in peace, but motivated by terri-
torial ambition. He says this roundly to Questenberg:

> Ihr seid es, die den Frieden hindern, ihr!
> (*Die Picc.* 565)

In the *Geschichte des Dreißigjährigen Kriegs* Schiller had already stressed the Habsburg 'Länderdurst' (see p. 58). He had also said of Wallenstein's dubious negotiations and movements: 'Viele seiner getadeltsten Schritte beweisen bloß seine ernstliche Neigung zum Frieden' (NA 18, 329). This possibility emerges again in the play when Wallenstein meets Questenberg:

> Vom Kaiser freilich hab ich diesen Stab,
> Doch führ ich jetzt ihn als des Reiches Feldherr,
> Zur Wohlfahrt aller, zu des *Ganzen* Heil,
> Und nicht mehr zur Vergrößerung des *Einen*!
> (*Die Picc.* 1180-3)

The suggestion of Habsburg ambition, combined with the possibility that Wallenstein's manoeuvres are in part aimed at peace, in spite of the Emperor, further undermines our sense of the Emperor's authority as legitimate.

So at the end of the drama we see legitimate authority restored and the usurper defeated, but the agents of the legitimate order are themselves tainted. The legitimate authority they represent has no greatness, no nobility, no moral integrity. Heselhaus, in considering the question of *Wallenstein* as a Nemesis tragedy, a view he retracted in his later article, 'Wallensteinisches Welttheater' (see n. 9), is of the opinion that Octavio has a more noble role than Buttler: 'Gegenüber dem Rache-Instinkt bei Buttler erscheint in Octavio mehr die strenge Gerechtigkeit der Nemesis.'[45] Heselhaus bases his view on the idea that Octavio is ennobled by being the agent of a higher justice: 'In dem Wissen darum, daß Octavio als Werkzeug ein höheres Schicksal zu vollziehen hat, liegt eine gewisse Rechtfertigung für seine Gegenverschwörung und liegt der zweideutige Lohn seines Erfolgs.'[46] The 'gewisse Rechtfertigung' for his conspiracy would seem to lie not in any idea of Octavio's that he is fulfilling a higher purpose. He says himself to Max:

> Ich klügle nicht, ich tue meine Pflicht,
> Der Kaiser schreibt mir mein Betragen vor.
> (*Die Picc.* 2454-5)

The second of the two lines removes from the word 'Pflicht' any abstract moral connotations. It is simply the obedience demanded by those held to be in legitimate authority over him, whom he is told to safeguard from a usurper. Heselhaus's distinction between Buttler and Octavio would seem to be a distinction in Buttler's favour rather than Octavio's. Buttler certainly has taken the opportunity to murder Wallenstein, using pressure of circumstances as justification, but having done so he does not waste time in self-justification. So when Octavio says:

> Ich bin an dieser ungeheuren Tat
> Nicht schuldig   (*W.T.* 3784-5)

Buttler replies:

> Eure Hand ist rein. Ihr habt
> Die meinige dazu gebraucht.
>   (*W.T.* 3785-6)

This shows Buttler's ability, however ruthlessly expressed, to look facts in the eye and not to shy away, as Octavio does, from admitting responsibility.

While Buttler's ruthlessness is appalling, it is at least more honest than Octavio's attempt to whitewash himself. So when Octavio is made 'Fürst' at the closing moment of the play we are painfully aware of his inadequacy to fill the gap left by the real 'Fürst'. Kurt May sums up the final scene of Wallenstein by saying: 'Der Große ist in den Abgrund gestoßen worden, um der Geltung des sittlichen Gesetzes unter den Menschen willen. Aber von so unzulänglichen Kräften, daß nun der Tag der Edlen auch nicht kommen kann.'[47] In other words, the legitimate authority is restored but morally it is a bankrupt order which can accommodate neither the greatness of Wallenstein nor the integrity of Max. We cannot therefore agree with Benno von Wiese, who says of the spectator at the end of the drama:

Er wird ... das Theater verlassen, angerührt vom Schauder der Tragödie, über alle verständigen Maßstäbe der Erkenntnis hinaus nunmehr eingeweiht in eine umfassendere Ordnung der Dinge, die zwar unserem Zugriff entzogen ist, aber mit der ewigen Gerechtigkeit auf eine für uns unbegreifbare Weise im Bunde steht.[48]

Rather than being filled with the sense of a higher order of justice operating in the play, we have a deep sense of the lack of justice and vindication in the course of history. It was the pessimism of this view of history in the play which so appalled Hegel. In his essay 'Über Wallenstein'[49] Hegel analysed the drama as showing the process by which Wallenstein is forced to make a decision ('das Schicksal des Bestimmtwerdens eines Entschlusses') and the reper-

cussions of that decision once taken ('das Schicksal dieses Entschlusses und der Gegenwirkung auf ihn').[50] Hegel considers
Schiller's treatment of the first masterful and consistent, but is
appalled by the fact that there is no life and vigour in the opposing
force which crushes Wallenstein. So life is defeated by death: 'Wenn
das Stück endigt, so ist Alles aus, das Reich des Nichts, des Todes
hat den Sieg behalten; es endigt nicht als eine Theodizee.'[51]

The extreme pessimism of Schiller's view of history in *Wallenstein*
may be surprising to those who are accustomed to the image of
Schiller the idealist. It was certainly not true of him in the first
period of dramatic work up to 1787, where justice prevailed to
a great extent. The early idealistic heroes realized finally that they
could not change the world and were reconciled to it. This early
confidence, already disappearing in *Don Carlos*, has now quite
disappeared. Schiller's theoretical works of the period shortly
before *Wallenstein*—the *Ästhetische Briefe* and *Über naive und
sentimentalische Dichtung*—reflect a certain historical optimism
about the capacities of the human race for education to fuller
humanity through art. However, his historical dramas, being rooted
in the world of experience and reflection on the past, express a
profoundly pessimistic view of a hostile world.

CHAPTER 4

MARIA STUART

In *Maria Stuart* Schiller abandons the broad historical canvas of *Wallenstein* to experiment with the closely structured analytic form of tragedy which he admired in the Greeks, particularly Euripides. The play has enjoyed a mixed reception from critics since its appearance. In recent years there have been those who consider it to be Schiller's masterpiece. Steiner, for example, says, '*Maria Stuart* is an incomparable work ... It is, with Boris Godunov, the one instance in which romanticism rose fully to the occasion of tragedy.'[1] Steiner sees in the play a double tragedy. Melitta Gerhard, however, suggests that the play is contrived in its concentration on theatrical effects and remote from Schiller's normal voice—'Weniger aber als in irgendeinem seiner anderen Dramen vernehmen wir hier Schillers wahren Herzton.'[2] Whereas Melitta Gerhard and Sengle[3] deprecate this concentration on form (Sengle suggests that formal considerations have made the play too black and white) other critics such as Storz[4] and Beck[5] have shown the many critical insights which can be gained from a close look at this concentrated structure. Storz, for example, points to the discrepancy between the initial objectives of the two queens and what they finally achieve, a point echoed recently by Sautermeister.[6] *Maria Stuart* certainly is a very theatrical play, and the reasons for and results of this theatricality will be discussed in this chapter.

Maria Stuart has at times been taken as representing a move by Schiller away from the historical drama. This assumption also lies behind the comments of critics who give prime place in the drama to Maria as an example of tragic sublimity. Helmut Koopmann explicitly states, 'Mit dem *Wallenstein* begann und endete zugleich Schillers Geschichtsdrama.'[7] Koopmann refers to a letter from Schiller to Goethe, written during the period of work on *Maria Stuart* (20 August 1799), though not specifically about *Maria Stuart*. In fact it is in that letter that Schiller first discusses his discovery of the Warbeck material. Schiller says:

Überhaupt glaube ich, daß man wohl thun würde, immer nur die allgemeine
Situation, die Zeit und die Personen aus der Geschichte zu nehmen und
alles übrige poetisch frey zu erfinden, wodurch eine mittlere Gattung von
Stoffen entstünde welche die Vortheile des historischen Dramas mit dem
erdichteten vereinigte.

(J6, 1490)

Schiller is speaking in the first instance about the Warbeck material
and not about *Maria Stuart* but his words give an indication of his
attitude to historical drama at the time. He seems to imply that
he feels less tied by the material than he was in *Wallenstein*, more
willing to interpret the characters according to the aesthetic effects
he wished to create.[8] Sengle sees the willingness on Schiller's part
to develop the idea of the heroine's private guilt and regeneration
as a move away from historical drama.[9] Schiller's reference to
'Situation' is significant, however, for situations recorded in history
are the product of historical forces and if they are to be used in
drama the dramatist has to interpret those forces. When we look
at *Maria Stuart* we realize that if Schiller had moved away from
any feeling of being tied by the historical data, he had not moved
away from his interest in the depiction of the world of politics. His
research for *Maria Stuart*, as for all his later dramas, was extremely
thorough, as though to disarm in advance any criticism of his free
use of history as stemming from ignorance or lack of historical
awareness. What seems not to bother him greatly in the drama is his
possibly anachronistic interpretation of the political issues, particularly of the nature of rulership.[10]

The need to stress that Schiller's presentation of the historical
and political world was vital to the play's conception springs from
a tradition of over-emphasis of one aspect of the drama, namely
the tragic suffering and final sublimity of Maria. In this chapter
we will attempt to show how a more balanced perspective on that
and on the play in general can be gained from recognizing Schiller's
starting-point as being a tragic situation, rather than individual
tragic characters. (This may, of course, be partly what Schiller had
in mind when he spoke of the 'allgemeine Situation' in the letter to
Goethe above.)

The idea that Schiller may have been interested more in exploit-
ing situation than in presenting Maria as an inherently tragic figure
tends to be overlooked by critics who take Schiller's philosophy
and aesthetics to apply very closely to the drama. R. D. Miller says,

for example: 'In *Maria Stuart* (1800) are reflected both Schiller's philosophy of moral freedom and his philosophy of harmony. The characters of Maria Stuart and Queen Elizabeth illustrate these two main branches of Schiller's philosophy.'[11] This approach to interpretation naturally encourages the view that Schiller was concerned in his drama with moral issues in themselves rather than with aesthetic effects. Some other critics adopt a similar approach, though with stronger apparent emphasis on the aesthetic:

> These three plays (*Maria Stuart, Die Jungfrau von Orleans, Die Braut von Messina*) embody and illustrate Schiller's idea of the tragically sublime—the triumph of man's higher moral self over the limitations of his material existence ... While the essence of the tragedy is to be found in the inward crisis, the external conflict between Mary and Elizabeth provides the play with its main structural principle.[12]

Witte's stress on the tragically sublime—'the triumph of man's higher moral self over the limitations of his material existence'—neglects the fact that Schiller gives equal time to the court at Westminster. In Chapter 3 it was pointed out that Schiller's return to the drama was also a return to the theatre. The theory of the tragically sublime has to be understood primarily as a dramatic concept, as an answer offered to the vexed issue of whether tragic effects could still be created in the drama of Schiller's own day. So the drama was not to be created in order to supply a morally edifying spectacle but to serve to arouse the emotions associated with high tragedy. Certainly the tragic sublimity of Maria is an indisputable element in the play, its climax even, but that sublimity has to be understood in its proper context. That context is the historical world, or 'des Lebens Drang', as the 'Prolog' to *Wallenstein* puts it. In *Über das Erhabene* Schiller stresses that an appreciation of the nature of the sublime rests on a proper understanding of the world of action, described thus: 'Die Welt, als historischer Gegenstand, ist im Grunde nichts andres als der Konflikt der Naturkräfte unter einander selbst und mit der Freyheit des Menschen, und den Erfolg dieses Kampfs berichtet uns die Geschichte' (NA 21, 49). Maria's solution to the problem of how to face death triumphantly can be understood only if the conflicts of the world of action are brought fully to light.

One of the results of the approach to the play described above is that it leads to a comparative neglect of half of the action, the half which concerns Elisabeth. If the play is primarily designed to give

Maria the role of tragic heroine, then the Elisabeth action can be regarded merely as a framework, a 'structural principle', to use Witte's term. The drastic conclusions to which this line of argument can lead are demonstrated in Otto Ludwig's judgements on the play. Ludwig in any case took an unsympathetic view of what he considered Schiller's dramas to be, contrasting them unfavourably with Shakespeare and the Greeks, whom he took Schiller to be emulating unsuccessfully. On the subject of *Maria Stuart* he expressed two closely related opinions. First he criticizes the dramatic structure which he charges with being essentially undramatic; the central character is passive, more acted upon than acting; her death is certain from the outset and there is therefore no dramatic conflict. There is, in other words, no drama: 'Man könnte ganz gut von da, wo Maria erfährt, daß ihr Urteil gefällt sei, bis zur Vollendung und nach dieser alles streichen, ohne daß etwas Wesentliches fehlte.'[13] Ludwig holds that the intrigues of the court are extraneous to the main character and comes to the surprising conclusion that the play is really an epic, since it consists of loosely connected episodes of intrigue. The second opinion is on the figure of Elisabeth, whom he calls 'ein Scheusal', 'einen platten Theaterbösewicht'.[14] These two opinions are closely connected, in that the second issues from the first. If Maria is pushed into the position of unequivocal tragic heroine, then Elisabeth is seen merely as a foil to her, part of an action which simply provides the necessary plot before Maria's sublime death. Ludwig obviously is almost deliberately mistaking Schiller's dramatic method and drawing extreme conclusions from his observations. However, the imbalance in criticism of the drama, the over-emphasis on Maria's role, lays the play open to charges similar to Ludwig's, namely that much of the action is irrelevant and that Elisabeth is simply a more or less crude foil to Maria. Seen in the light of such an approach the play's plot does indeed seem contrived, and the private aspect of Maria's guilt and the political aspect of the play's action seem brought together in an artificial manner, as Melitta Gerhard observes:

Wie die Vorgänge, die zu ihrer Verurteilung führen, mit dem frühen Gattenmord in keinerlei Zusammenhang stehen, so erscheint die Bezugnahme darauf als eine künstliche und nachträgliche, Marias Los aber als das Ergebnis politischer Verknüpfungen und höfischer Intriguen, deren unverschuldetes Opfer sie wird.[15]

George Steiner, who approaches the play without preconceptions about its philosophical content, comes closer to seeing the two halves of the play in some relationship to one another when he writes, 'The tragedy of Elisabeth matches that of her victim, and the action dramatizes at every moment the exact balance of doom'.[16] Steiner sees Elisabeth as experiencing a tragedy of her own. This is open to question, but what Steiner has achieved is a demonstration that the sphere and activity of Elisabeth are not simply a foil to the action at Fotheringhay, but rather that the one modifies and supplements our view of the other. Ilse Graham has highlighted another aspect of the dependence of the two strands of action on each other by pointing to how the two queens each embody the repressed aspects of the other's personality.[17]

If we look at Schiller's own accounts of his choice of the material and the advantages he felt it afforded, it is clear that he settled on neither Maria nor Elisabeth as a tragic personality but rather on the situation in which they found themselves as extremely suitable for dramatic treatment. Before he begins work Schiller writes to Goethe:

Indessen habe ich mich an eine Regierungsgeschichte der Königin Elisabeth gemacht und den Prozeß der Maria Stuart zu studieren angefangen. Ein paar tragische Hauptmotive haben sich mir gleich dargeboten und mir großen Glauben an diesen Stoff gegeben, der unstreitig sehr viele dankbare Seiten hat. Besonders scheint er sich zu der Euripidischen Methode, welche in der vollständigsten Darstellung des Zustandes besteht, zu qualifizieren, denn ich sehe eine Möglichkeit, den ganzen Gerichtsgang zugleich mit allem Politischen auf die Seite zu bringen und die Tragödie mit der Verurtheilung anzufangen.

(J6, 1452)

This letter shows Schiller's interest at the time in form and his appreciation that tragic effects are bound up not with personalities but with the dramatic form which he gives to his subject matter. Shortly afterwards he writes again to Goethe:

Die Idee, aus diesem Stoff ein Drama zu machen, gefällt mir nicht übel. Er hat schon den wesentlichen Vortheil bei sich, daß die Handlung in einem thatvollen Moment konzentriert ist und zwischen Furcht und Hoffnung rasch zum Ende eilen muß. Auch sind vortreffliche Charaktere darin schon von der Geschichte her gegeben.

(J6, 1466)

Again Schiller mentions the advantage of the pace and momentum which can be gained by starting the action at a critical moment, as well as the powerful personalities which history gives him. Again slightly later Schiller writes:

Ich fange schon jetzt an, bei der Ausführung mich von der eigentlich *tragischen* Qualität meines Stoffs immer mehr zu überzeugen und darunter gehört besonders, daß man die Catastrophe gleich in den ersten Scenen sieht, und indem die Handlung des Stücks sich davon wegzubewegen scheint, ihr immer näher und näher geführt wird.

(J6, 1469)

All of Schiller's comments above on his treatment of the material point to his concern with poetic form and structure, with a closely interlocking dramatic movement. The basis of this interlocking structure is a potentially tragic situation, concentrated into its critical moment. Even Maria herself is to arouse tragic emotion not through the audience's identification specifically with her but rather through the whole situation: 'Meine Maria wird keine weiche Stimmung erregen, es ist meine Absicht nicht, ich will sie immer als ein physisches Wesen halten, und das Pathetische muß mehr eine allgemeine tiefe Rührung als ein persönliches und individuelles Mitgefühl seyn' (J6, 1469).

If, then, we were to try to identify that tragic situation, in which Schiller saw the dramatic possibilities of his material, we could look at two moments in the action, one in Act II and the other in Act IV. In Act II, 3 Burleigh tries to press decision on Elisabeth by saying:

Ihr Leben ist dein Tod! Ihr Tod dein Leben!

(1294)

Act IV, 9 shows a recapitulation of the argument of Talbot and Burleigh, though intensified, in which Elisabeth, exasperated by the pressure of Maria's presence and the threat it poses, exclaims:

Muß eine von uns Königinnen fallen,
Damit die andre lebe [...]?

(3146-7)

Schiller, then, has seen in his material a situation where two queens have been so brought together by historical circumstances that the life and freedom of the one seem necessarily to exclude the life and freedom of the other. And yet, even though these two monarchs have been so joined by historical circumstances and family ties that their futures depend on each other (for Elisabeth's depends on

Maria, no less than Maria's on Elisabeth), they are personalities whose thoughts, preoccupations, perceptions of the world are so fundamentally different that there is, in spite of all political and dynastic ties, virtually no sphere in which their minds overlap.

In such a situation it is impossible to see one as right and the other as wrong. The complexity of the situation, the limitations of both of the women, make such a judgement impossible. The two queens are separated from each other not only by the fact that one holds the other prisoner. The gulf between them is created also by different training and different traditions. Mainland groups the differing backgrounds, moral values and political outlook under the headings of tradition and experiment.[18] Maria belongs within an old and fixed system of government, a system within which she is rightly monarch and Elisabeth a bastard. Maria has a strong network of church and family ties with European ruling houses, and within her own church she stands in the position of a sinner who can nevertheless expect forgiveness. Elisabeth, by contrast, has been brought up in turbulent times to exercise power without the comfort of established structures behind her. She has no assurance of her right to rule and is to some degree at the mercy of public opinion, which holds her on the throne in spite of the quarrel over her legitimacy. She can expect no comforting counsel from a priest, no unequivocal word of guidance. She has to listen to separate and conflicting voices and resort in the end to her own conscience, in which an internal war is being waged between her prudence and shrewdness as a monarch, and her envy, malice, and resentment as a woman.

In this complexity of situation it is possible again to point to Schiller's ability to stand back from his work to allow the two areas of action to speak for themselves and to reflect those different aspects of human involvement with which they are concerned. The one does not invalidate the other. This is an essential part of Schiller's art as a dramatist in these later plays, as we have already observed with *Wallenstein.* Sautermeister has recently pointed out in connection with Schiller's letters, quoted above, on the subject of *Maria Stuart,* how he is unashamedly direct in assessing its value for the theatre.[19] *Wallenstein* was a theatrical experience and *Maria Stuart* was to be also. Sautermeister also stresses the function of the work of art of reminding the audience through its own stylization that they are witnessing not life in the raw but a poetic transmutation of it. The political world is made transparent through the medium of art but not by naturalistic techniques. This was made explicit in the 'Prolog' to *Wallenstein* ('Ernst ist das Leben, heiter ist die Kunst') but is implicit in all Schiller's later dramas. Sauter-meister recalls Schiller's own concept of 'Gemütsfreiheit', explored in *Über naive und sentimentalische Dichtung*, to denote that sense of balance and a certain distance which should proceed from the experience of tragic drama and which is bound up with the sense of observing a work of art:

Die dramatische Bühne bildet die Realität nicht ab, sondern überführt sie in den schönen 'Schein'—das ästhetische Gebilde. Dieses raubt allerdings dem Leben nicht seine wahre Bedeutung, sondern erhellt sie, verflüchtigt nicht die Schwerkraft der Wirklichkeit, sondern verleiht ihr Maß, verschönt nicht das empirische Material der Geschichte, sondern macht es auf Grundzüge und Triebkräfte hin durchsichtig.[20]

This idea of the play as a theatrical event from which both the dramatist and the audience maintain a certain aloofness in their knowledge that this is art rather than life, is very close to those concepts of irony discussed in the previous chapter. *Maria Stuart* does not contain the same obvious types of dramatic irony that are found in *Wallenstein*. However, there is an insoluble conflict between the life and good of one queen and the life and good of the other, which in Schiller's presentation approaches irony. Schiller has juxtaposed the worlds of Maria and Elisabeth, letting our view of one modify our view of the other. It is only through seeing the two that we can gain a true perspective on either. This balance in the structure of the play reflects the fact that neither queen has an adequate perception of human involvements and the problems surrounding them. Not only are their problems and preoccupations different, the solutions which they find to their problems are valid only in their own circumstances and sphere of action. By juxta-posing the worlds of private conscience and public action Schiller emphasizes the fact that there is no easy solution to the problem of how to satisfy the demands of either. We cannot, as the audience, simply put the two halves of the drama together and achieve an answer to the question of how to act with integrity in the political world. When, therefore, we see Maria's solution in the final act to her guilty conscience, we are prevented from being completely transported by this sublime spectacle by the change of scene to Westminster. The final scenes at Westminster certainly emphasize,

by contrast with Maria, the lack of authenticity in Elisabeth's
world. On the other hand, they also emphasize the fact that Maria
leaves behind a world, the problems of which are still pressing and
still unsolved for those whose responsibility they are. So the final
scenes can be said to act as a counterpoise to the emotions aroused
by the death of Maria, and prevent us from losing our true perspective on it. In this sense Schiller can be said to have approached
irony in his dramatic presentation. This technique of juxtaposition
is one which Schiller fully develops in *Maria Stuart* through the
balance of the dramatic structure and the shift of location to and
from Fotheringhay to Westminster. It occurs also in *Die Jungfrau
von Orleans* where the dramatist gives a different view of Johanna
through the juxtaposition of certain scenes.

There are, of course, more obvious ironies in the outcome of the
action of *Maria Stuart.* There is the discrepancy between what the
characters aim for and what they finally achieve, in all cases the
exact opposite of their original hope or intention. Maria tries to
gain her freedom both by relying on Leicester and Mortimer and by
pleading with Elisabeth. In each case she finds her means of rescue
leads to disaster. Elisabeth hopes to maintain her freedom of action
and her reputation but loses both. Mortimer only hastens Maria's
end instead of rescuing her, while Leicester, through trying to play
safe, betrays both queens.

The gulf which separates the two queens is nowhere more apparent than in their respective approaches to the political world. Maria
is politically inept, whereas Elisabeth has schooled herself in state-
craft. If we look more closely at Maria's attitude, more significant
things come to light. Maria, it has been observed, maintains in
spite of considerable moral guilt (in the case of Darnley) a certain
perpetual innocence.[21] This is an ingenuousness which becomes
evident early on in the play. An encounter which illustrates this is
in the first act (I, 7), where Burleigh arrives to inform Maria of the
court's verdict on her. Schiller has here made interesting use of
the historical material. The historical Mary, as Robertson,[22]
Schiller's main source, records, used as a defence at her trial the
fact that as a foreign queen she was not subject to English law,
nor to judgement by people who were not her peers. This was, in
fact, probably her best line of argument. Schiller takes up this
theme in the encounter with Burleigh, but it is significant that his

Maria is more ingenuous than her historical original. One of her
speeches to Burleigh illustrates this point:

> Ist mein Gewissen gegen diesen Staat
> Gebunden? Hab ich Pflichten gegen England?
> Ein heilig Zwangsrecht üb ich aus, da ich
> Aus diesen Banden strebe, Macht mit Macht
> Abwende, alle Staaten dieses Weltteils
> Zu meinem Schutz aufrühre und bewege.
> Was irgend nur in einem guten Krieg
> Recht ist und ritterlich, das darf ich üben.
> Den Mord allein, die heimlich blutge Tat,
> Verbietet mir mein Stolz und mein Gewissen,
> Mord würde mich beflecken und entehren.
>
> (944-54)

Maria is proud and spirited in her own defence. At the same time
she is very intent on abstract principle, on concepts of what is
right and honourable, concepts which would hardly impress a
pragmatist like Burleigh. Maria, however, is in some ways invoking
principles which belong to the secure traditions in which her idea
of monarchy has been nurtured. She appeals to 'Recht' and 'Ehre'
and is concerned with religious and ethical principles of conduct.
In her situation, of course, she can only appeal to justice and a
sense of honour in her judges. However, Maria's habitual mode of
thought is to see herself as the natural queen by divine right. The
sort of obligation which Elisabeth feels to rule by pragmatic assessment is foreign to Maria. This is shown by her lack of sense of the
broader issues surrounding her actions. While she concerns herself
with abstract principle she fails to see some of the wider-ranging
effects of these principles. In the opening scenes of the play Maria
is presented as rembering her guilt with regard to Darnley. She is
filled with a sense of personal sin. Yet it is significant that nowhere
does she express regret that she has failed as a monarch, that she
has caused yet more unrest in her country or that her failure has
caused anything other than personal disaster to herself. This can
only partly be explained by the fact that Maria in captivity has
much less political involvement—in fact no personal active involvement at all—and so can give herself over to expiation of her past
sins. This explanation is inadequate, because Maria, even in captivity, continues to regard herself as no less fitted for the task of rulership as a result of her previous poor performance. To her it is a case
of once born a queen, always a queen, the traditional belief.

If we turn to the confession scene (V, 7) with Melvil we hear Maria exculpating herself from involvement in assassination attempts against Elisabeth. The significant words are:

> Ich habe alle Fürsten aufgeboten,
> Mich aus unwürdgen Banden zu befrein,
> Doch nie hab ich durch Vorsatz oder Tat
> Das Leben meiner Feindin angetastet!

(3727-30)

These words have often been taken to show unequivocally that Maria is in fact innocent of political plotting against Elisabeth,[23] and indeed she does deny complicity in the Babington plot. If that is the case then the revelation of Maria's innocence is a rather crude *coup de théâtre*. There is, however, great danger in assuming that any character's pronouncements have objective value rather than simply indicating the belief of that character. Schiller makes Maria feel herself to be innocent with regard to Elisabeth, and indeed as far as intention, 'Vorsatz', and deliberate action, 'Tat', are concerned, she is. Maria fails, however, to grasp that actions are not limited by intention and have consequences which stretch far beyond any effect one could have anticipated. In calling up the rulers of Europe to free her from her imprisonment she may not have intended any harm to come to Elisabeth, but it is highly unlikely that her freedom could have been secured without widespread violence. We have seen in the course of the play itself how Mortimer has taken up Maria's cause, how Maria herself has given him encouragement, hoping to gain her freedom, and how this has led directly to an attempt on Elisabeth's life. There is, therefore, an ingenuousness in Maria's claim to be innocent with regard to Elisabeth. She feels it her right to be free and this is understandable. She knows that she is the victim of a judicial murder and we can certainly feel moved by her ability to come to terms with that by investing it with her own private meaning. However, while she has a conscience about her sins she is not able to interpret the complexities of the political world, and her words to Melvil show that she has not grasped the nature of political involvement. Mainland also casts doubt on Maria's innocence. He believes it is only in the moment of hesitation before receiving the cup from Melvil that Maria dimly perceives that she may be guilty of hitherto unsuspected rancour.[24] It is, however, difficult to see Maria's hesitation as anything other than her doubt and sense of inadequacy about her right as a lay person to enter into the prerogative of the priest. Even so, Mainland's central point is vital, namely that Maria's own perception of her guilt and innocence is not absolute but rather has to be assessed within the context of the play.

To suggest that Maria has an imperfect understanding of how her political involvements have threatened Elisabeth's life is not an invalidation of her final state of sublimity. Rather it is a means of stressing just how private the root of that sublimity is. A great deal of critical emphasis tends to be laid on the link, forged by Schiller's use of historical data, between the anniversary of Darnley's murder and the pronouncement of sentence on Maria, who accepts her death as an expiation of her sin of complicity in the murder.[25] The fact that Maria explicitly says to Melvil

> Gott würdigt mich, durch diesen unverdienten Tod
> Die frühe schwere Blutschuld abzubüßen.
>
> (3735-6)

is occasionally taken as an absolute statement about the play, hence Melitta Gerhard's criticism that it is artificial and Maria the 'unverschuldetes Opfer' of court intrigues. As we have seen above, while Maria is mainly passive in the play, she is nevertheless not entirely 'unverschuldet', not only because of her guilt with regard to Darnley but in her involvements in the political world. Indeed to Elisabeth Maria is hardly powerless and passive. She seems constantly to be touching on Elisabeth's life, to the extent of destroying her French marriage and stealing her lover. Maria indeed is in the odd position of being personally confined and yet somehow making her influence felt time and time again. She may in one sense be passive, but she gives the impression of posing an enormous threat and possessing enormous influence. While she is, however, unaware of her political responsibility, Schiller makes her be oppressed by a sense of guilt which cannot be removed by time or by the observances of the church. She herself forges the link with her past which gives her the capacity for calm and dignity at the end. It is not recognized at all by the other characters, who are unconcerned about guilt or innocence or who, like Maria's retinue, are devoted to her personally. The scene with Melvil reveals at one and the same time the fragility of Maria's perception of the situation, her belief in her own innocence with regard to Elisabeth and yet the process by which she can give herself dignity in the face of judicial murder.

To view Maria in this way is not to see her as deluded. Rather it is a feature of Schiller's presentation of the complexity of the situation that it is for the audience to stand back and view that situation with the greater breadth of vision of which they are capable. Maria herself cannot be credited with greater insight than she possesses for she is necessarily limited, and beyond that, as victim of, above all, the political situation, she cannot be expected to glimpse her own ambiguity where her life is at stake.

Maria's ingenuousness in the field of politics emerges, as we have noted, in Act I. It culminates in her challenge through Burleigh to Elisabeth:

> Und was sie *ist*, das wage sie zu scheinen!
>
> (974)

In one sense Maria's bold challenge to Elisabeth is the only form of attack open to her. She recognizes that Elisabeth is taking refuge in ambiguous appearances and calls on her to show her true colours. Maria knows that her reputation is already tarnished by the past and so is not afraid to be what she seems, as she claims in her encounter with Elisabeth:

> Das Ärgste weiß die Welt von mir und ich
> Kann sagen, ich bin besser als mein Ruf.
>
> (2425-6)

Maria's challenge to Elisabeth in Act I shows that she sees through the latter's anxiety about her reputation. It also embodies a call for authenticity which cannot be fulfilled in the changing world of politics inhabited by Elisabeth. Maria requests the meeting with Elisabeth in the mistaken hope of exerting some human influence over Elisabeth as a woman and as a cousin. Elisabeth knows it is weakness to consent to the meeting and so tries to pretend that others have surprised her with the encounter (2233-4). Elisabeth knows that simple frankness and candour cannot solve the political entanglement in which either she or Maria must eventually be the victim. Maria fails to see that her call to authenticity cannot sweep away those problems. Indeed, Maria herself adopts a mask of submissiveness at the beginning of her encounter, which Elisabeth, by provoking her, forces her to drop ('Jetzt zeigt Ihr Euer wahres/ Gesicht, bis jetzt wars nur die Larve'—2419-20).[26]

Elisabeth is a problematic figure. It is unjust to Schiller's presentation of her to say that his 'treatment of Elisabeth throws the martyrdom of the Catholic Queen into high and unchallenged relief.'[27] Elisabeth's desire to return to the seclusion of Woodstock is genuine. She faces a demanding task, for she has to hold together a new mode of government, while facing continual threats of aggression from abroad. The dangers of violent uprising and assassination are real, as the attempt on her life in the play shows. Even the most trusted friends turn out to be false. Elisabeth knows that her throne is not secure without the approval of the people and so she must retain their support. Elisabeth has a keener eye than Maria for the realities of the political situation into which she has been thrust, as well as in general a greater awareness of the nature of political involvement. Elisabeth knows that the days of divine right are over in England, that monarchs have to prove themselves equal to the task of prosperous government. Being forced to weigh each situation from that point of view, Elisabeth has no absolute standards of judgement, such as those applied by Maria. Even so, it would be unjust to see her debates with her councillors as pure show. She does not know Maria. To Elisabeth Maria has always been a problem, a thorn in her flesh. Shrewsbury himself points out (II, 3) how nothing speaks in Elisabeth for her prisoner. For Elisabeth Maria is the hardest task she has yet had to face—'die erste schwere Königspflicht'—and she senses that much is at stake. The people who cheer her today may suddenly condemn her tomorrow, once the deed is done. Elisabeth in some ways resembles Philipp in *Don Carlos*, in that both depend on others for information and advice but are aware that they may be deceived or misled. The ruthless Burleigh is as devoted to Elisabeth as the gentle Shrewsbury, but who is to say which of them is right in his prediction of the country's reaction to Maria's death? The two men put forward cogent but fundamentally opposing views of the problem, but in the final analysis Elisabeth has to decide for herself and face the fact that she cannot know in advance what the effect of her actions will be. Being aware of this, Elisabeth feels that her only refuge is in ambiguity of conduct. The masks she wears are an attempt to escape the iron causality of events by keeping herself out of the action and playing temporary roles rather than engaging herself fully. This is, however, an illusion; in the world of action masks assume a reality and there is no longer an authentic 'self' beneath them. This is how Elisabeth's masks differ from those of Fiesco. Fiesco's masks could be shed to reveal the true Fiesco; beneath Elisabeth's masks there is no true Elisabeth.

There are a number of significant similarities between Elisabeth's situation and that of Wallenstein. Both are powerful and therefore obliged to make decisions, which they find a difficult process. Both make the painful discovery that when they are forced to act they most acutely experience their own lack of freedom. The most striking parallel in their situations is their full discovery in different ways of the nature of political involvement. Wallenstein mistakenly believes that by remaining undecided he can opt out of the causal chain, into which all others are locked, until he feels that the time is right for him to intervene and take over the initiative. It is when he discovers that there is no choice left to him but to act that he realizes how he has been caught up in the causal chain after all and that pure 'Spiel' without consequences is impossible in the political world. Elisabeth sees her decision concerning her rival as a turning point in her career, the first occasion when she feels conflict between the needs of the moment and her sense of what is acceptable as an action in the political sphere. Both have it in common that they discover the controlling influence of 'Schein'. Wallenstein discovers this only when it is too late. He says:

> Strafbar erschein ich, und ich kann die Schuld,
> Wie ichs versuchen mag! nicht von mir wälzen;
>   (159-60)

Elisabeth, however, is from the outset aware of the importance of appearances and impressions. Yet although she recognizes the need to retain support by favourable appearances she places a distinction between what one is and what one appears to be and so replies to the deliberately ingenuous Mortimer:

> Ihr kennt die Welt nicht, Ritter. Was man *scheint*,
> Hat jedermann zum Richter, was man *ist*, hat keinen.
>   (1601-2)

She seems to suggest that it is possible to preserve the intrinsic self, which is hidden from the world's view, while projecting the image one chooses to the world. Hence she continually wears a mask to conceal her true feelings. Yet this hope turns out to be in vain. Like Wallenstein, Elisabeth finds that the appearance she has given to the world limits her freedom to act. Her just rule has preserved her power yet robbed her of the freedom to use it to anything but overtly just ends. So the external world impinges on this inner self which Elisabeth would like to preserve and robs it of its autonomy. She discovers that in political action it is not just a case of giving deceptive impressions but of being oneself determined by those impressions. As Kommerell puts it, 'Der Handelnde *muß* scheinen: was er scheinen will, steht ein Stück weit in seinem Belieben, vielleicht auch nicht, aber wenn er es einmal zu scheinen begann, wird es ihm unentrinnbarer als was er eigentlich ist.'[28] So Elisabeth's belief that she can preserve an area of freedom in the secret part of herself is found to be mistaken.

As Elisabeth experiences more and more forcefully the implications of involvement in politics, Maria withdraws more and more from the ambiguity of that world. As a prisoner Maria enjoys various benefits which are denied the apparently free agent, Elisabeth. Whereas Maria moves towards absolution, Elisabeth moves ever more towards responsibility, however much she tries to avoid it. In the final act Maria confesses to the full extent of her understanding to Melvil and is assured that she is forgiven and accepted by God. Any consequences of her life are temporal only and she has passed outside the sphere of their influence. Elisabeth, however, realizes that all of her actions will have consequences and that the results for her of Maria's execution are entirely unpredictable. Once her fate is sealed Maria is outside history. None of her actions will have consequences for her, though they will for others. No more decisions are required of her and no human involvements impinge on her any longer. She can concentrate on the purely private matter of guilt and absolution. The process of transformation does not take place on stage but rather we hear of it later from Hannah:

> Gott gewährte meiner Lady
> In diesem Augenblick, der Erde Hoffnung
> Zurückzustoßen mit entschloßner Seele,
> Und glaubenvoll den Himmel zu ergreifen.
> (3405-8)

It is from this moment that Maria can concentrate on gathering together the threads of her personality. She is no longer exposed to the constricting nature of earthly life, where people are the unwilling victims of the appearances and attitudes they betray to others. Maria has herself experienced this most recently in her encounters with Mortimer. Maria's reputation as a sensual and passionate nature makes Mortimer attempt to force that role on her again. At one point the threats from her supposed liberator are as terrible as the fear of execution or murder—'Hier ist Gewalt und drinnen ist der Mord' (2597). Now, in the final act, she is aware of being outside history. Schiller's Maria has no conscious intention of using her death to score a political point, as the historical Mary may have done.[29] She is rather intent on finally being what she intrinsically is. She takes on a clarity and transparency towards her death, while Elisabeth appears more and more fragmented and unsure of herself. Maria is still laden with guilt, and not only with regard to Darnley. Her whole involvement in the world of politics has been a disaster. However, in the final act Schiller achieves something similar to what he achieves in *Wallenstein*. He reduces the audience's perception of the hero's (heroine's) culpability, not so that we are not aware of their failings, but so that the impression of their dignity outweighs the sense of their culpability. If Schiller is to achieve his intended aesthetic effect we must have a sense of Maria's guilt. We are not to experience her death as innocent suffering, and this is what Schiller stressed when he said, 'Meine Maria wird keine weiche Stimmung erregen.' We experience it rather as an assertion of dignity in the face of the death she has to some degree brought upon herself, but now accepts as a kind of freedom.

In spite of that apparent freedom in her death, it must all the same be admitted that martyrdom (or sublimity) is in itself a role, which Maria does not choose but which is forced on her. She is created by external pressures just as much as Elisabeth. In the encounter of the queens we catch a glimpse, in Maria's anger and denunciation of Elisabeth as a bastard, of a quite different Maria. There is a mobility in the impression we gain of her in the play until finally she is trapped by circumstances. Her martyrdom, though an act of stepping outside history, is nevertheless an event *in* the historical world and as such has its own consequences. In this it bears a certain resemblance to the death of Max Piccolomini. In both cases the world threatens the individual's moral integrity. Max preserves his by his death, though it is an act of despair which brings death also to his men. Maria's death is a means for her of regaining her personal integrity. Just as Max's death impinged on Wallenstein's fate, so Maria's death impinges on Elisabeth. It is from the moment of Maria's death that Elisabeth finds herself alone. Her intention to keep her role in Maria's death ambiguous is of no avail and the action which she feels is forced on her in Act IV marks her out in Act V as a tyrant. She has made her decision, for whatever reasons, and its consequences stay with her. Even so, Schiller portrays the process of decision in Elisabeth in a way which does not alienate her from us but rather brings her for a time 'menschlich näher'. In death Maria's legend lives on, we suspect. Her death appears as a martyrdom and she as the victim of political necessity. Yet as the play progresses it is almost as though it were Elisabeth who is the victim. Even in life Maria begins to assume almost mythical proportions because of her ability to impinge on Elisabeth's life. This process reaches its height in Elisabeth's monologue (IV, 6) where Elisabeth, though ostensibly free, is more confined than Maria. Elisabeth describes herself as 'ein wehrlos Weib' in her struggles against the powers of Europe, while Maria is 'Ein Plagegeist vom Schicksal angeheftet' (3231). Everywhere Elisabeth turns she is thwarted by Maria:

> Wo ich mir eine Freude, eine Hoffnung
> Gepflanzt, da liegt die Höllenschlange mir
> Im Wege.

(3232-4)

This is not gratuitous exaggeration by Elisabeth. Maria genuinely has posed a threat not only to Elisabeth's throne but to her life and to her private happiness. Leicester has proved unfaithful and Mortimer too because of her. Certainly personal as well as public motives enter into Elisabeth's decision to sign the death warrant, but this inability to separate the private and the public is characteristic of all decisions in the political world, and exacerbated only by the unhappy decision to meet Maria. Having finally signed the death warrant and heard news of Maria's final removal, however, Elisabeth finds that she is not free, that Maria is as much 'ein Plagegeist' in death as in life. The decision she has made brings her isolation in the shadow of Maria's final transfiguration.

Schiller then has juxtaposed the very different worlds of these two queens, characters who share no common ways of thought and yet whose lives are caught up together in a way which Schiller illuminates through his dramatic structure. The question remains of the relationship of these two worlds which we see juxtaposed. How does the one impinge on the other? We have seen how in physical and political terms Maria and Elisabeth are bound together.

But beyond the dramatic situation which Schiller depicts lies the question of whether one world, the world of Elisabeth, acts merely as a foil to the other, or whether the world of Elisabeth and the world of Maria shed light on each other. This chapter has argued that the world of Elisabeth is not simply a foil to the pure spiritual world of Maria but rather the means by which that world can be fully understood. It is only in seeing the nature of the pressures of the political world that Maria's death can be understood as the act of transcendence that it is. Can the reverse be said, however? Do the death of Maria and the vision of ideal humanity which she reflects at the end in any way illuminate the problems of the political world, in which the majority of the characters are obliged to live? Sammons suggests it does not. He feels that Maria's death transforms the historical tragedy into a private one in which the moral issues push the political ones out of view: 'The issued raised in the fabric of the historical setting are made to matter and not to matter at the same time.'[30] Sautermeister, however, sees Maria's transformation as demonstrating the true goal of history:

So will das Drama dem Zeitgenossen nicht nur die Erfahrung der Totalität, des 'lebendigen Spiels aller seiner Kräfte' ermöglichen, damit er selber ein Bewußtsein vom wahren Ziel der Geschichte gewinne: es will ihm auch die Einsicht in politische Herrschaftsformen vermitteln, die seine Selbstverwirklichung verhindern und jenes Ziel in eine utopische Ferne rücken.[31]

Many problems arise from this interpretation. It suffers from the fact that it takes as its starting-point not so much the play itself as the categories of Schiller's works *Über Anmut und Würde* and the *Ästhetische Briefe* as guidelines to interpretation. The implication is that Maria's world embodies a symbolic portrayal of growth to perfect humanity through art (expressed in the play as religion). Maria is not, in fact, a 'schöne Seele' (though it can be argued that she exhibits 'das Erhabene der Fassung') and the world she inhabits is as much the historical world as Elisabeth's. It is not the world of the ideal but of the real, in which nevertheless certain noble gestures are possible which produce an aesthetic effect which can be called tragic. Sautermeister is right to point out how the change of scene after the execution from Fotheringhay to Westminster gives a certain perspective on Elisabeth's world, and certainly the lack of truth, authenticity, and justice are startlingly evident in those final scenes. But the sort of integration of personality which is evident in Maria is only possible for someone stepping

out of the world of history. It is by definition a state which does not
exist in the world, and so to speak of it as the true goal of history
introduces a criterion of judgement which is foreign to the play,
which itself takes place in history. The death of Maria leaves unanswered those very pressing questions about how one lives *in* the
world.

Superficially, it may seem that those questions are answered in
the figure of Shrewsbury. Shrewsbury combines humanity with
service to his queen, avoiding the ruthless pragmatism of Burleigh
but being no less loyal to Elisabeth for it. His words to Elisabeth at
the end

> Ich habe deinen edlern Teil
> Nicht retten können...
>
> (4028-9)

are more the words of disappointment than of rebuke. He has tried
to guide Elisabeth to follow the dictates of humanity rather than of
pure *raison d'état* but admits failure and withdraws from the world
of politics. However, while Shrewsbury is loyal and humane, he is a
man of very faulty judgement, in a way that the shrewder Burleigh
is not. Rather undiplomatically Shrewsbury betrays to Elisabeth,
through his sympathy for Maria, that he has fallen under the spell
of her charm, so much so that Elisabeth says:

> Das müssen Reize sondergleichen sein,
> Die einen Greis in solches Feuer setzen
>
> (1400-1)

Shrewsbury advocates a meeting between the queens, which
Burleigh, with sounder judgement, absolutely rejects. Burleigh, of
course, turns out to be right, for the tensions between the two
women are too great not to cause a catastrophe. It is true that
Shrewsbury does not know of Leicester's duplicity, which adds a
further dimension to the queens' hostility when they meet. However, he is not shrewd enough to see that two women with such
grievances against each other could not fail to say things which
would only make clear the irreconcilable nature of their conflict.
Shrewsbury, then, can regret Elisabeth's lost humanity, but he is
withdrawing from the world. His involvement in the action has
shown not how humanity and good counsel can be reconciled, but
rather how it is impossible to satisfy the demands of conscience and
the demands of the political moment simply by trying to please

everyone. Shrewsbury has the opportunity to withdraw, a choice
which is not open to Elisabeth, who has to live on with the consequences of a decision made harder and more destructive to her by
the increased personal element introduced by the unfortunate
meeting.

In *Maria Stuart*, no less than in *Wallenstein*, Schiller shows himself to be deeply concerned with this problem of how a human
being can act responsibly and bear the consequences of action in
the world. Oskar Seidlin poses the question in succinct terms:

[Maria] can well afford to insist on man's inner freedom, on his authenticity,
on his exemplary submission to the highest and eternal moral values,
because all that is left to her is to die, and to die nobly. But is dying nobly,
the extreme sacrifice by which we liberate ourselves from the burden of
our earthly existence, an answer to the burning question of how to live
in and with the world, how to act responsibly so that this world will bear
the imprint of our existence as humans?[32]

To suggest, as Sautermeister does, that the world of Elisabeth is
simply portrayed to show how far mankind is from the aesthetic
state is akin to seeing Elisabeth herself merely as a foil to Maria.
Schiller certainly did look forward to a world where people could
realise their full humanity through the educative function of art.
However, his dramas, and specifically his choice of historical
subject matter, show him to be deeply concerned with the portrayal
of man's entanglements in the here and now. Merely to write off
the historical world as wicked and a hindrance to the dawn of utopia
is a travesty of Schiller's concern for the problems of the individual
caught up in that world, as well as an over-simplification of
Schiller's own vision of the future. Yet if we were to ask how man
copes with this fateful involvement with the world, there would, on
the basis of *Maria Stuart*, be no answer.

CHAPTER 5

DIE JUNGFRAU VON ORLEANS

Die Jungfrau von Orleans, Wilhelm Tell, and the *Demetrius* fragment share a number of common features. In all of them Schiller
departs from the closed, analytic form of drama he created in *Maria
Stuart* and adopts a more epic style of drama, with an extended
time-scale and much colour and movement. Another common
feature is that in all three plays the protagonist is not aristocratic
or powerful but of the people. In each case this central figure is
thrust into the limelight from the previous obscurity of his life.
Both Joan of Arc and Wilhelm Tell are remembered for the patriotic
zeal which they exhibited. Both are regarded as having saved their
countries at times of national crisis. The treatment of Johanna's
appearance on the stage of history is, however, very different from
the way Schiller presents the rise of Tell and Demetrius. A great
deal more is known of Joan of Arc than of Wilhelm Tell, who may
never have existed at all; contemporary documents give details of
Joan's career and in particular her trial. However, in Schiller's day
the quest for the historical Joan had not yet begun—that was to be
the work of the nineteenth century—and Quicherat's *Procès de
condamnation et de réhabilitation de Jeanne d'Arc dite la Pucelle*
(1841-9) did not appear until some forty years after Schiller's play.
At the time Schiller was writing, the historical and the legendary
Joan were much harder to disentangle, and so it was much easier at
that time for Voltaire to write his *Pucelle* than it would be now,
when, since her canonization, there is widespread awareness of a
body of historical evidence for Joan's career. Yet in spite of the
fact that Schiller had contemporary source material for his *Jungfrau
von Orleans*, it is in fact in *Wilhelm Tell* that he demonstrates how
a national hero is created, not by his own choice or effort, but by
the force of circumstance. In the case of Joan of Arc Schiller has
not attempted to explain her appearance on the stage of history as
a combination of circumstances. There is no attempt to rationalize
her advent as saviour of her country. Nor does Schiller attempt a
psychological portrayal of the dawn of her sense of mission. She

remains an extraordinary phenomenon, who suddenly changes the historical scene, challenging the assumptions of those who normally consider themselves in authority.

Bernard Shaw's criticism of Schiller's play is well known, that Schiller 'drowned his heroine in a witch's cauldron of raging romance'.[1] It is not merely romantic trappings and historical inaccuracy which Shaw censures, but the fact that Schiller's heroine is so far removed from the common run of humanity, as well as from the specific figure of Joan of Arc, that the play bears little relation to its source: 'Schiller's Joan has not a single point of contact with the real Joan, nor indeed with any mortal woman that ever walked this earth. There is really nothing to be said of his play but that it is not about Joan at all.'[2] Shaw is assuming that Schiller's play has to be, like his, a quest for the historical Joan. Shaw considers that the real Joan is accessible, though one might well object that his own presentation of Joan as an incipient Protestant and a nationalist and his wholesale rationalization of the mystical element is as anachronistic as Schiller's interpretation is romantic, in spite of Shaw's confident 'Preface'.

Shaw is certainly right, however, in indicating that this 'romantische Tragödie' is not a historical drama in the way that *Wallenstein, Maria Stuart,* and even *Don Carlos* are. It is not essentially a drama of politics and though it is nominally set in the late Middle Ages Schiller has not attempted to evoke the epoch with any strong authenticity, save possibly in his emphasis on superstition, the belief in witches, and the power of black magic, and in the presentation of the Dauphin as weak and unwilling to assert himself. Romantic paraphernalia are used such as the 'schwarzer Ritter', the thunderclaps, and the storm, and these evoke a magical atmosphere in which nature and supernature are intermingled. One could even say that Schiller has defeated himself in the play. He has written a play in some sense to vindicate the reputation of someone who has been the butt of ribaldry. As he says in 'Das Mädchen von Orleans':

> Es liebt die Welt, das Strahlende zu schwärzen
> Und das Erhabne in den Staub zu ziehn;
> Doch fürchte nicht! Es gibt noch schöne Herzen,
> Die für das Hohe, Herrliche entglühn
>
> (SA1, 275)

Joan has lived on in the memory and the hearts of her people but
what has made her memorable is arguably her tragic death at the
stake at the age of only nineteen. Sellar and Yeatman aptly sum up
her career:

... the Hundred Years' War was brought to an end by Joan of Ark ... who
after hearing Angel voices ... became inspired, thus unfairly defeating the
English in several battles. Indeed, she might even have made France top
nation if the Church had not decided that she would make an exceptionally
memorable martyr. Thus Joan of Ark was a Good Thing in the end and is
now the only memorable French saint.[3]

On the one hand Schiller has chosen to vindicate someone whose
legend is famous but on the other hand he has robbed her of that
very death by which she *is* memorable. One can go on to argue that
in so doing Schiller has made her whole career quite incomprehensible. By reducing the role of politics in the drama and concentrating
on Joan herself as a phenomenon, Schiller can be said to have
broken the ties which bind his Johanna to her earthly situation and
so has made her inaccessible as a character and, as a result, un-
interesting and unsympathetic as a dramatic creation; she cannot be
understood in the context of the play in the way that Elisabeth can,
as we see the pressures which influence her actions. Even Tell is
very much the product of his society, though also separate from it
as a lonely hunter, and is caught up in a situation which is beyond
his control. Johanna, however, seems not to interact in this way
with the world around her. She is neither product nor victim of her
environment.

Interestingly, Schiller could be accused in the play of falling
himself into the very trap into which, many years before, he accused
Goethe of falling in his *Egmont*. He views *Egmont* from the standpoint of the historian who is aware of the forces acting upon the
historical Egmont. His criticism of the play is not that Goethe has
changed history by substituting Klärchen for the real Egmont's
wife and eleven children, but that in so doing Goethe has removed
a vital set of circumstances and so made his whole 'Schlafwandler'
stance seem incomprehensible. Goethe, of course, was trying to
create a *Sturm und Drang* hero, a great genius, sadly crushed by
meaner men. But Schiller points out the flaw in this; historical
characters act not as *Sturm und Drang* heroes, i.e. with some kind
of detached independence, but as beings forced one way or another

by many pressures and by the contingencies of their situation. The historical dramatist may recreate figures who respond to these pressures without losing their greatness, even though they lose the power to control events, as Schiller himself showed later in *Wallenstein*.

In *Die Jungfrau von Orleans* one could claim that Schiller has made Johanna remote and inexplicable. Having reduced the political pressures on her, and moved the focus of interest away from her death to her life, Schiller has to invent a crisis and resolve it in a way which anticipates Joan's later rehabilitation and which acts as a vindication of her legend. However, it is the real Joan's trial and execution which bring into sharp focus the intricacies of the historical situation, for example the hostility of the French and English to each other as well as the jealousy and intrigue at Charles's court. Without these intricacies Charles's and the other courtiers' treachery and superstition over Thibaut's accusation are not satisfactorily motivated. They seem shallow and ungrateful men, in spite of their reappearance at the moment of Johanna's death. In addition, Johanna seems to have a determination to fulfil some sort of pre-determined mission, her 'Schicksal', as she calls it on numerous occasions. This suggests that some kind of force of destiny is operating in the play over and above the usual cause and effect relationships of history. Indeed Johanna's faith in her destiny seems to be vindicated in the end, when she leads her people to victory one last time and is received back as one of their number. So Johanna's world seems not to be subject to the same sort of natural causality that governs the world in *Wallenstein* and *Maria Stuart*, but rather to a divine will which reveals itself through the virtually mindless action of the heroine, particularly in the early stages of the action.

Schiller, we may take it, was concerned with other aspects of the legend of Joan of Arc than an examination of the historical forces which caused her downfall. This he has suggested in his correspondence from the time of composition, which stresses the appeal the play is to make to the heart and imagination: 'Dieses Stück floß *aus dem Herzen* und *zu dem Herzen* sollte es auch sprechen. Aber dazu gehört, daß man auch ein Herz habe und das ist leider nicht überall der Fall' (J6, 1761). This letter was written to Göschen, Schiller's publisher. An earlier letter to Goethe reveals perhaps more soberly what Schiller's intention was in his recasting of the story: 'Das historische ist überwunden, und doch soviel ich urtheilen kann, in seinem möglichsten Umfang benutzt, die Motive sind alle poetisch und größtentheils von der naiven Gattung' (J6, 1650). Schiller's emphasis is therefore on the freedom from any historical fact which could restrict his own poetic conception of the material.

The fact that Schiller is not bound by history does not mean, however, that he is not interested in certain issues which have been prominent in the later drama, issues which, broadly speaking, are historical. In *Die Jungfrau von Orleans* Schiller's interest in the phenomenon of sainthood, the nature of Johanna's action in the world, as well as in transcendence and commitment are apparent. History is used—'in seinem möglichsten Umfang benutzt'—but no longer to create the world of 'allgewaltige Notwendigkeit' in which Wallenstein and Maria Stuart live.

The figure of Johanna herself has been the subject of much conflicting criticism. Early commentaries on the drama accepted Johanna simply as an ideal figure who embodies dedication to duty, and love of country. Ludwig Bellermann, for example, sees no conflict between Johanna's God-given mission and the ruthlessness with which she shuts out any human feeling: 'Die beiden Seiten des 'furchtbar bindenden Vertrags', Berufung zur Befreiung des Vaterlandes und Entsagung der irdischen Liebe, gehören wirklich innerlich und untrennbar zusammen. Nur ein in sich einiges Wollen kann das Große, das Göttliche vollbringen.'[4] Bellermann here assumes that Johanna is able to perceive the nature of her calling accurately and that it must be understood as objective fact by the audience that she must not be touched by human love. Thus her suppression of mercy, as in the killing of Montgomery, is not questioned or felt to be reprehensible. This view endures and is reflected in R. D. Miller's opinion that Johanna's 'idealism triumphs' in her refusal to spare Montgomery.[5] The questionable morality of Johanna's behaviour in battle, her inability to show mercy and her self-confessed loss of private will and desires have been recognized by a number of critics, who have offered various types of explanation. Gerhard Storz,[6] for example, rejects the idea that the play is an embodiment of an 'Idee' for that 'Idee' can only be the glorification of machine-like action, which Schiller steadfastly rejected. So Storz takes the play as a stylised presentation of events, held together by poetic motifs. Johanna, as part of this

presentation, cannot be properly subjected to psychological interpretation. This same stress on Johanna as a poetic creation is found
also in the comments of Engel and Mainland: 'Examined psycho-
logically, she is an assembly of contradictions ... the coherence and
dignity which she represents are to be found completely in the
poetic structure alone.'[7]

These critics stand therefore in opposition to another development in criticism, which attempts to psychoanalyse Johanna. Such
critics reach the opposite conclusion from Bellermann's, namely
that far from being a person with a united will and purpose,
Johanna is in fact suppressing half of her personality. Timothy
Sellner, for example, suggests that the play is a portrait of ado-
lescence.[8] Johanna is suppressing her sexual drive, fearing that it
will overcome her. Ilse Graham, who is less specific, sees Johanna
as a kind of split personality who has to be forced by a sudden
shock to integrate the side of her nature which she has previously
been unwilling to acknowledge.[9] This form of interpretation raises
the question of the meaning of the word 'Tragödie' when Schiller
subtitles the play 'eine romantische Tragödie', because in Sellner's
and Graham's view the shock and temporary suffering caused by
the encounter with Lionel must be, in the end, good and desirable
for it to lead to the integration of personality, or adulthood quite
simply. It is of course in any case difficult to find truly tragic
feeling and situations, whatever one's interpretation of the play,
for the death of the heroine is a triumph, whichever way one looks at
her development. Perhaps, therefore, it is safest to regard the term
'Tragödie' as denoting nothing more specific than the fact that the
play ends with the death of the heroine, which is a moving spectacle.

These interpretations are not, however, fully conflicting. Johanna
is a dramatic character, from whom we can expect some kind of
psychological consistency, and also a poetic creation whose words
and role in the play form part of the fabric of motifs through which
its meaning should emerge. A point of contact between all the
various interpretations of Johanna is the recognition of some kind
of development in the heroine herself and a change in the way she
perceives and interacts with the world around her. E. L. Stahl
sums this up by saying: 'In the beginning of the drama Johanna is
eine schöne Seele, at the end *ein erhabener Mensch.*'[10] This may be
misleading, in that the activity of a 'schöne Seele' is by definition
laudable, whereas Johanna's early activity in the play is open to

doubt. What Stahl does pinpoint, however, is the progress in the drama from unselfconscious to purposive action, involving the assertion of the will. At the beginning of the play and up to the encounter with Lionel, Johanna is unselfconscious. As Ilse Graham puts it, she regards the world *sub specie aeternitatis*, in spite of the chaos and disintegration around her.[11] This is another way of saying what we have already said of the early Johanna, that she proceeds without letting the various circumstances of the world impinge on her. She is remote from her family and a mystery to them. On the battlefield and at court she can inspire admiration and love but cannot herself form relationships of anything but a purely formal kind with those around her. She stands at one remove from the life of the emotions. Ilse Graham, discussing the scene (III, 4) where Dunois and La Hire sue for Johanna's hand, claims that Johanna is unable to see that her rejection of womanhood and her rather tactless rebuke to the court are out of place.[12] To criticize Johanna for this is perhaps to credit her with a greater capacity for sensitivity to people than we have evidence up to that point that she possesses. We have seen in her so far no ability to change or adapt according to situation at all.

The encounter with Lionel marks the end of this mode of action. To say that Johanna falls instantly in love with Lionel is perhaps overstatement. Certainly any feeling of love is very soon changed into a feeling of guilt. It is the inner change in Johanna which is important. Johanna meets Lionel in an encounter which is the counterpart to her earlier encounter with Montgomery. She is about to sacrifice Lionel as a sort of sacred victim—

> Die heilge Jungfrau opfert dich durch mich!
>
> (2465)

—when she catches sight of his face and instantly the spell is broken and she is no longer impervious to human emotion. Professor Fowler has already noted the importance of the motif of sight and seeing in the play.[13] An instance which he does not mention is in the reconciliation scenes between Karl and Burgund (III, 3/4). A sort of crisis is reached when Johanna asks Burgund to be reconciled also with Du Chatel. Du Chatel appears first at a distance, and then, according to the stage directions:

> *Du Chatel tritt einige Schritte näher und sucht in den Augen des Herzogs zu lesen*
>
> (NA 9, 247)

It is as though Du Chatel wants not only to discern what Burgund is thinking but knows also that to look him in the eye will break down his resistance. Again, in the Lionel scene, as soon as Johanna looks into Lionel's face she loses at once the power of unself-conscious action. It is as though she had never really looked at anyone properly before, for previously she has simply pronounced to people. In the past she was able to stand outside human passions and do only what seemed to fulfil her duty. In one sense there is a conflict between duty and inclination—

> Sollt ich ihn töten? Konnt ichs, da ich ihm
> Ins Auge sah?
>
> (2564-5)

—but it is a conflict made possible only by this change in Johanna, which produces an ability to *have* inclinations at all. Schiller has, of course, been severely criticized for this departure from histori-cal fact, partly because it is such a blatant departure, partly because it is taken to be self-indulgence on his part to want to introduce romantic love into a story which contains none, or if not self-indulgence it is some kind of sop to contemporary audiences. Another objection is that while Johanna feels guilty about her love, we as the audience cannot blame her for it and so cannot properly sympathize with that sense of guilt.[14] There is a great dramatic advantage to Schiller's invention, however, which perhaps il-luminates his reasons for it, and that is that the experience of love, or at least sexual attraction, can be instantaneous, producing a sudden and complete change of outlook, because it affects the individual on an instinctual rather than an intellectual level. It is not only instantaneous, it is also involuntary and as such cannot be guarded against.

It is, of course, only after her encounter with Lionel that Johanna realizes what she has been doing. She is no longer blindly dedicated to a cause but rather has to look at her actions and herself in a new light, with her eyes open to the extraordinary position in which she finds herself, capable of longing to be back with her family. She experiences her calling for the first time as a burden; whereas in the past she and her mission were inseparable, now she feels herself to be facing excessive demands, as her monologue shows:

> Deine Geister sende aus,
> Die Unsterblichen, die Reinen,

> Die nicht fühlen, die nicht weinen!
> Nicht die zarte Jungfrau wähle,
> Nicht der Hirtin weiche Seele!
>
> (2601-5)

She can no longer be 'ein blindes Werkzeug' and cannot kill while looking her victim in the eye. She also has a new sense of the oddness of her own position. She can now actually look at herself and see what a strange phenomenon she is, when previously she had no sense of her own strangeness:

> Kümmert *mich* das Los der Schlachten,
> Mich der Zwist der Könige?
>
> (2606-7)

Johanna does not denounce her previous actions as wrong, in fact she longs for the old ability to act blindly. But a new spirit is in her now. She is humane in a way that she never was before. She is capable of common human feeling. As she shows Sorel before the coronation (IV, 2) she knows how Sorel must feel in seeing Karl crowned:

> Du liebst das Allerfreuende, die Sonne,
> Und was du siehst, ist deiner Liebe Glanz!
>
> (2696-7)

Similarly, in encounter with her sisters she has discovered a new gentleness, and a new need for human society. Margot says with surprise:

> Die Schwester ist nicht stolz, sie ist so sanft
> Und spricht so freundlich, als sie nie getan,
> Da sie noch in dem Dorf mit uns gelebt.
>
> (2902-4)

Her conversation with Raimond after her banishment bears witness not only to her acceptance of misfortune but also to the new ability to enter into genuine dialogue with another person. Now she can converse without simply pronouncing. When captured by the English she is able to resist any temptation to follow Lionel and desert her country's cause (even though her country has temporarily deserted her) but she does so as though the people she is addressing are real people, not simply an audience for her prophecies. She has not lost her sense of authority but she can appeal to Lionel on the grounds of reason and humanity:

Nicht lieben kann ich dich, doch wenn dein Herz
Sich zu mir neigt, so laß es Segen bringen
Für unsre Völker

Frankreich wird nimmer Englands Fesseln tragen.
Nie, nie wird das geschehen! Eher wird es
Ein weites Grab für eure Heere sein.
(3351-3, 3362-4)

She is also willing to let her people fight on their own and to rely
on their own courage and faith in their good cause. She recognizes
also that the English must fight. Each side is committed to its
separate cause. So when Lionel tries to persuade her again to desert
the French and follow him she says:

Spare deine Worte!
Die Franken rücken an, verteidge dich!
(3399-400)

These are no longer the words of a fanatic but of someone who is
committed to her country's good in spite of its failure to acknowledge her service to it. There is therefore a progression in the
play from one mode of action to another. Johanna dies in the end
because she is no longer invulnerable, but at the same time she has
learnt to see herself and to recognize the true nature of commitment.
There are therefore two Johannas in the play, but a weakness of the
structure of the play in contrasting the two Johannas must be that
the first Johanna is remote and rather implausible as a creation by
comparison with the second, who, though still stylized as a character, shows much greater contact with the world of normal human
feeling.

In spite of the dramatist's lack of concern for historical authenticity and his introduction of elements such as the 'schwarzer Ritter',
the play nevertheless suggests a number of perspectives on broad
historical issues raised by the subject matter, namely the nature of
commitment and the phenomenon of sainthood and national
feeling. The widespread critical recognition of the unacceptable
aspects of Johanna's mission (i.e. her implacability in battle and
suppression of mercy) leads to the need to re-examine the beginning
of the play in order to discover what the nature of commitment is.
One could almost regard the Montgomery incident as a critique of
mindless commitment. Certainly it brings to light the moral
ambiguity of that commitment. The helpless Montgomery pleads

for his life but Johanna is implacable, maintaining that Montgomery has been given into her power and she *must* kill him. For this scene Schiller has adopted Greek iambic trimeter. Schiller may have employed this metre for the monumentalizing effect it has, so stressing the way that Johanna is entirely at the mercy of the force which compels her to fight. Both she and Montgomery are in a helpless position:

> weggerissen von der heimatlichen Flur,
> Vom Vaters Busen, von der Schwestern lieber Brust
> Muß ich *hier*, ich *muß*—mich treibt die Götterstimme, nicht
> Eignes Gelüsten,—*euch* zu bitterm Harm, *mir* nicht
> Zur Freude, ein Gespenst des Schreckens würgend gehn,
> Den Tod verbreiten und sein Opfer sein zuletzt!
> (1658-63)

Perhaps she is to be pitied, as one in the grip of forces greater than herself, but there is also a sinister element. After stirring Montgomery from hopeless pleading to a vain attempt to defend himself, Johanna easily overcomes and kills him. She then offers a prayer of praise to the Virgin, surely one of the most morally disturbing speeches in the play:

> Erhabne Jungfrau, du wirkst Mächtiges in mir!
> Du rüstest den unkreigerischen Arm mit Kraft,
> Dies Herz mit Unerbittlichkeit bewaffnest du.
> (1677-9)

This speech points clearly to the de-Christianizing of the Christian context of the play.[15] The play has a superficial layer of Christian language and trappings, but side by side with them are pagan symbols and allusions to classical mythology, so that there is no sense in which Schiller is giving us here a picture of medieval piety. The Virgin becomes representative of some cruel female goddess, a sort of Amazonian Queen, who demands absolute obedience to an inhuman pattern of behaviour. The Montgomery scene cannot fail to raise questions about Johanna's conception of service. As such it recalls some of the more sinister remarks of Thibaut in the 'Prolog' about Johanna's unnatural rejection of human attachments and forms a counterbalance to the idealizing portrait of Johanna which we are given in the first act at court.

A further and more complex perspective on Johanna is provided by the scenes in the English camp. While Johanna is revered in the

French camp with almost the same awe as the Virgin herself, she is greeted with the opposite reaction among the ordinary English soldiers, who believe she is a witch. So they flee, fearing she is in league with the devil. Schiller rejects popular superstition as well as popular piety. Where he goes beyond these is in his reflection of rational reaction amongst the English commanders to what seems to them virtually an inadmissible way of conducting an honorable war. After their first defeat Talbot, enraged and frustrated, accuses Burgund's troops of responsibility for the rout, and is even more enraged when Burgund throws responsibility on to the devil.

BURGUND   Wir sind nicht von Menschen
                    Besiegt, wir sind vom Teufel überwunden.

TALBOT   Vom Teufel unsrer Narrheit

                                                    (1245-7)

Talbot is enraged by superstition but also powerless in the face of it as he sees his men flee in their next encounter with the French:

> Bin ich der einzig Nüchterne und alles
> Muß um mich her in Fiebers Hitze rasen?
>
>   (1538-9)

To Talbot Johanna is neither devilish nor divine; she embodies and unleashes the forces of unreason, against which his military skill is powerless.

This new perspective on the action—the element of objection to defeat not by arms but by superstition and unreason—is created not simply for a moment in passing but in some detail, in the figure of Talbot, who has been identified (e.g. by Garland and Sternberger[16]) as Johanna's true opponent. Talbot dies giving voice to some of the most persuasive and dramatically effective speeches of the play, speeches in which his sense of purposelessness and disillusionment is complete. His most plaintive exclamation is one which sums up his sense not only of disgust but of deep disappointment at the end:

> War unser ernstes arbeitvolles Leben
> Keines ernsthaftern Ausgangs wert?
>
>   (2337-8)

Much speculation has surrounded Talbot's final speeches. They are powerful dramatic utterances and demand to be taken seriously.

They can be dismissed as an example of Schiller's self-indulgence but this rests on the presupposition that Schiller wishes to give a wholly positive portrait of his heroine. In *Wallenstein* and *Maria Stuart* we have seen already, in the figures of Wallenstein and Elisabeth, Schiller's ability to portray characters who are, to some extent, realists in a way which shows the validity as well as the weakness of their approach to life. Max is portrayed sympathetically but not to the extent that Wallenstein loses in stature. Similarly, in *Maria Stuart*, we are invited to take Elisabeth, and her acute and immediate problems of government, just as seriously as we take Maria.

In *Die Jungfrau von Orleans* Talbot's view of the action has as much validity as Johanna's and he makes clear to us the ambiguity of dedication, the shadow side of a figure who claims to be divinely inspired, and who, intentionally or not, takes advantage of religious fervour and also superstition. H. B. Garland notes how Talbot represents Schiller's attempt to balance opposing factors in his portrayal of Johanna's world: 'though the victory is Johanna's, Talbot is not discredited'.[17] Professor Garland suggests also the parallel between *Die Jungfrau von Orleans* and *Wallenstein*, in which Schiller had also balanced opposing factors in his world of the Thirty Years War. In *Die Jungfrau von Orleans* there is not equal emphasis but there is equal integrity on each side. Taking up a similar theme, Dolf Sternberger claims that while Talbot is defeated in battle he is not defeated in the dialectic of the drama, and that Talbot is a necessary 'Kontrastfigur' to Johanna, that he modifies and conditions our view of the heroine: 'Keine Voltairesche Säure, kein umgedrehtes Fernglas ironischer Vermenschlichung (wie es nachmals von Bernard Shaw gehandelt wurde) vermochte das "edle Bild der Menschheit" so kräftig zu entzaubern, wie Schillers eigne Kontrastfigur einzugrenzen vermocht hat'.[18] Sternberger thus suggests that Schiller did not wish to bring a counterweight to bear on the heroic and inspired portrayal of Johanna by rationalizing and reducing her own mystic quality. He achieves the same effect by placing alongside her a figure whose integrity, matching her own, will provide this counterweight. This is a valuable insight into Schiller's mode of drama, and not only in *Die Jungfrau von Orleans*, because in other dramas (e.g. *Maria Stuart*, *Wilhelm Tell*) the central character can only be seen in true perspective when another is placed alongside him. Sternberger maintains that

Talbot's grand eloquence endures to the end of the play because it embodies the mystery of the play—whether such a phenomenon as Johanna comes from God or from unreason. One might paraphrase that by saying it is the mystery of whether one like Johanna can possibly be an exalted being, whether God ever actually intervenes in any sense in the world, or whether such a phenomenon, intentionally or not, is merely a means of harnessing to a particular cause those irrational elements in men which are susceptible to its power. Sternberger claims that Talbot's outcry and what it stands for is not defeated by the ending of the play but rather is still heard in the background and modifies our view of the heroine even to the end:

Das dunkle Rätsel, das in der Figur des ehedem unbezwinglichen Talbot beschlossen liegt, ... dieses Rätsel überdauert seinen Tod nicht nur, es bildet, unaufgelöst, noch den Schatten neben dem Glorienschein der verklärt entschwebenden Jungfrau, und es bleibt, unaufgelöst noch immer zurück, wenn dieser Glorienschein schon verdämmert ist.[19]

This is to extend the influence of Talbot perhaps too far. Even so, Sternberger identifies the change which Talbot's eloquence makes in our view of Johanna. She may view the world *sub specie aeternitatis* but it is not how the world views her, for her view of herself and her mission is only one view among several, Talbot's being the most dramatically impressive.

In *Wallenstein* and *Maria Stuart* both Wallenstein and Elisabeth consciously wear masks to disguise their true motives. Johanna wears no mask but this does not save her from being a highly ambiguous figure. Wallenstein and Elisabeth are entangled in their own web of conflicting appearances. Johanna appears to be nothing other than what she is, but what she is is something mysterious and inaccessible to those whom she encounters. She must, therefore, give rise to conflicting opinions which question the validity of that dedication which she displays. In *Maria Stuart* Schiller juxtaposes the two queens. While we see the problems and conflicts of the one, the other is still present in our minds, ensuring that sympathy for, and involvement with, Maria does not eliminate a sympathetic understanding of Elisabeth's problems. In *Die Jungfrau von Orleans* the idealized picture of Johanna is balanced by episodes such as that with Montgomery and by the Talbot scenes. This is irony in that the audience finds itself able to look at Johanna from a slightly more distanced viewpoint. Other perceptions of her are shown to be valid and yet the conflicting approaches to life, represented particularly by Johanna and Talbot, cannot be harmonized. They remain conflicting, and instead of trying to represent a solution which cannot exist, Schiller so juxtaposes these characters and scenes that the problem is presented but the dramatist can stand back from it.

CHAPTER 6

WILHELM TELL

Wilhelm Tell is perhaps of all Schiller's dramas the one which provokes the most widely divergent critical comment. In that respect it is similar to *Don Carlos*, about which opinions also differ fundamentally. Both plays superficially invite an idealistic interpretation, for in both Schiller seems at first sight to be championing unequivocally the cause of political liberty. On the other hand, both present obstacles to such an interpretation by the ambiguity of some of the key events (in *Wilhelm Tell* the 'Apfelschuß' and the assassination of Geßler, in *Don Carlos* the deception of Philipp by Posa). This ambiguity leads us to question the superficial interpretation and seems to cast doubt on the reliability of what is said by some of the central characters themselves. The structure of *Wilhelm Tell* adds to this difficulty because the Rütli action, led by Stauffacher and Walter Fürst, is not directly linked with the Tell action. Tell's insistence that he is acting as a private individual in killing Geßler, even though political motives are imputed to him at the end of the play, must be taken into consideration if justice is to be done to the text as it stands. How to unify these elements in the play into a coherent interpretation and at the same time to reconcile it with what Schiller himself seems to imply about his intentions as a dramatist is the central critical problem.

Wilhelm Tell and *Don Carlos* have come to us today overlaid with idealism, to some extent the legacy of the nineteenth-century elevation of Schiller. Schiller was undeniably in one sense an educator and his later plays, while obviously tailored to the practical requirements of the theatre, were not solely intended as entertainment for the contemporary theatre-going public but also to serve as models of German neo-classical drama. As a play such as *Wilhelm Tell*, the most instantly popular of Schiller's plays, became a standard school textbook in the nineteenth century, the tendency became increasingly marked to see the heroes of Schiller's plays as direct mouthpieces for Schiller's own views, and *Wilhelm Tell* is particularly susceptible to distortion of this kind. Political and social developments also conspired to distort the image of Schiller, as Muschg has observed: 'Schiller war der Abgott des um seine nationale Einigung kämpfenden Bürgertums, zuerst der vormärzlichen Liberalen, nach 1848 der siegreichen Bourgeoisie, die einen rauschenden Kult mit ihm trieb.'[1] Muschg and many others took the opportunity in 1959 to correct some of these distortions, which are clearly seen in 'Festreden' of 1859, speeches with such titles as 'Schiller als Volksdichter im edelsten Sinn'[2] and 'Wodurch ist Schiller der Lieblingsdichter der deutschen Nation geworden?'.[3] *Wilhelm Tell* naturally provided a ready supply of political slogans on the subject of national unity.

In time a reaction to this followed, either a complete dismissal of the play as out of touch with a non-idealistic age, or an attempt to look afresh at its import and to judge it by aesthetic criteria. Two main strands of critical thought are discernible, the one stressing the link between the play and Schiller's philosophical and aesthetic writings on nature, harmony and ideal societies, the other looking at the play principally as a historical drama which examines seriously the nature of political involvement. This second avenue of criticism was first explored by W. G. Moore in his article 'A New Reading of Wilhelm Tell'.[4] This article is particularly interesting because it appeared at a time when Schiller was already going out of fashion and came from a critic who, since his main interest was not German studies, was able to approach the work with fewer presuppositions. The result was an article which revealed new possibilities of interpretation. Moore recognizes that the problem of violence and rebellion finds no simple solution in *Wilhelm Tell*. Of Stauffacher's words

> Wenn der Gedrückte nirgends Recht kann finden,
> Wenn unerträglich wird die Last—greift er
> Hinauf getrosten Mutes in den Himmel
> Und holt herunter seine ewgen Rechte.
>
> (1276-9)

Moore says: 'This speech has been taken as the motto of the play but it reads more effectively as one position of its dialectic.'[5] The recognition that the participants in the action may not, after all, be stating Schiller's view, that indeed the issue is more complex than a superficial reading indicates, is an important insight of modern Schiller criticism and applies to his dramas generally. This line of interpretation does not find general acceptance, however, and in recent years there have been a number of attempts to look at the play in the light of Schiller's *Ästhetische Briefe* (cf. Martini, '*Wilhelm Tell*, der ästhetische Staat und der ästhetische Mensch'[6]) or more generally in terms of Schiller's theory of the idyll. Sautermeister,[7] Kaiser,[8] and Ueding[9] have very recently stressed the importance of Schiller's concept of the idyll in his dramatic development. For Kaiser *Wilhelm Tell* represents a progression from the arcadian in the direction of the elysian idyll:

Im dramatischen Märchen 'Wilhelm Tell' (1804) findet die Wiederherstellung der Idylle durch ein ganzes Volk für ein ganzes Volk statt, die in der Verwandlung der patriarchalischen Ordnung Attinghausens in die Brüderordnung des Rütlibundes präformativ auf die elysische Idylle hinweist.[10]

Moore's approach, however, has encouraged the more recent attempts by W. F. Mainland[11] and G. W. McKay[12] to tackle the ambiguities of the play and the problem of its structure without presupposing any links between it and Schiller's idealist philosophy or aesthetic theories. This involves an assessment of the unheroic side of Tell and a willingness to see the Parricida incident not as a miscalculation on Schiller's part but as an integral part of the drama. Mainland admits that his mode of interpretation is controversial but stresses that conventional approaches read the words but ignore the drama as an artistic whole: 'My criticism of much that I have read about *Wilhelm Tell* is that it disregards an important principle of Schiller himself, by paying too much attention to substance and too little to form.'[13] Some of Schiller's comments to Iffland[14] in defence of the Parricida scene may appear difficult to assimilate into Mainland's line of argument. However, those interpretations which rely heavily on the *Ästhetische Briefe* and the theory of the idyll (mainly discussed in *Über naive und sentimentalische Dichtung*) are assuming direct links between *Wilhelm Tell* and works written some ten years earlier. This approach tends also to raise the question why Schiller should choose a historical (rather than mythological or imaginary) setting to illustrate a state (the arcadian/elysian idyll or the aesthetic state) which has, by definition, never existed in history. In order to accept that approach it is necessary to turn decisively away from the historical aspects of the play.

Critics such as Mainland and McKay have stressed rather than avoided the historical aspects of the drama and have shown how Schiller can be seen as presenting the process of history becoming legend. The Wilhelm Tell material is historical in a different sense from all the other historical dramas which Schiller wrote. Whereas the historical dramas from *Fiesco* to *Die Jungfrau von Orleans* had incorporated a high proportion of *bona fide* historical figures, the Tell material was largely preserved in popular legend. Any attempt to get back to the original events was therefore impossible. So in this play Schiller incorporates the actions traditionally imputed to Tell i.e. the 'Apfelschuß' and the slaying of Geßler, and gives us a picture of history as it might have been. In other words the historicity of the events is unverifiable but the dramatist produces a picture of how they might possibly have been connected, not in order to set up a serious hypothesis as to the particular events, but in order to show how historical processes in general might work.[15] In the plays from *Wallenstein* onwards Schiller investigates the career of some extraordinary person and asks why that person should be considered great or memorable. While some people are mentioned only cursorily in history books, others have a more remarkable career which sets them apart. In the case of Tell, however, some 140 years elapsed between the supposed events and the first written record. Perhaps then in the case of Tell we should look for an answer to the question, 'Why is he remembered at all?'

Much criticism of the drama has suggested that Schiller's answer is that Tell is a great revolutionary hero, a man who exemplifies all that is most laudable in the Swiss: 'Einzig um die Lauterkeit und Makellosigkeit dieses Befreiungskampfes, seinen Einklang mit den ewigen naturgegebenen Gesetzen ist es ihm [Schiller] zu tun.'[16] Tell represents 'freies Bürgertum' or, in non-political terms, ideal humanity in an idealised and harmonious community. J. G. Robertson, reacting against this approach long before it went out of fashion, says:

Tell's self-satisfied sententiousness creates a prejudice against him from the start; and his creator is so insistent on his hero being regarded as an immaculate type that he neglects such opportunities as the unheroic murder of Geßler, or Tell's inhuman repudiation of the Parricida, to develop sides of Tell's personality which might have won our interest for him as a man.[17]

Although Robertson starts with a presupposition about Schiller's artistic intentions he puts his finger on the problems that an idealizing interpretation involves.

If we look back to Schiller's correspondence we may derive a clearer picture of Schiller's approach and attitude to the Tell material. In his choice of the Tell legend Schiller was obviously in step with current taste. The 'Volksstück' and the 'Familiendrama' were very popular at the time and were written by such playwrights as Kotzebue and Iffland himself. Schiller seems confident that the play will be successful if only on these grounds:

Die Actien stehen also nicht schlecht, auch bin ich leidlich fleißig und arbeite an dem Wilhelm Tell, womit ich den Leuten den Kopf wieder warm zu machen denke. Sie sind auf solche Volksgegenstände ganz verteufelt erpicht, und jetzt besonders ist von der schweizerischen Freiheit desto mehr die Rede, weil sie aus der Welt verschwunden ist.

(J7, 1913)

The picture that emerges of Schiller from his letters is a useful corrective to the image of the high-minded idealist projected by many works of criticism. This letter is revealing from a number of points of view. It shows a certain scepticism about the tastes of the theatre-going public and the knowledge that he is to some extent pandering to them. His comment about the disappearance of Swiss freedom is highly significant. It not only shows Schiller's awareness of the topicality of his subject matter in an era which was seeing another nation subjugating those around, it also cannot be free from a slight cast of irony. The much-lauded Swiss freedom is now a past reality. However hard fought the struggle, that freedom has now been abolished. One might easily argue here that if Schiller's intention was to praise unequivocally a nation's fight for freedom he would have done better to choose a nation whose freedom still existed. Indeed a certain sense of unease, almost displeasure, emerges some eighteen months later in a letter to Wilhelm von Humboldt:

Noch hoffe ich in meinem poetischen Streben keinen Rückschritt gethan zu haben, einen Seitenschritt vielleicht, indem es mir begegnet seyn kann, den materiellen Foderungen der Welt und der Zeit etwas eingeräumt zu haben. Die Werke des dramatischen Dichters werden schneller als alle andre von dem Zeitstrom ergriffen, er kommt selbst wider Willen mit der großen Masse in eine vielseitige Berührung, bei der man nicht immer rein bleibt.

(J7, 2042)

It is almost as if Schiller were saying that the poet who chooses such a potentially popular theme is asking to be misinterpreted, that one cannot choose such a theme and hope that the nuances of one's work will be noticed. Certainly the play's instant popularity made it a difficult work for Schiller to integrate into his own *œuvre*.

Schiller's death soon after the first performance of *Wilhelm Tell* meant that its fortunes were out of his hands once and for all. While it was establishing itself as Schiller's most popular work Ludwig Börne anticipated by nearly eighty years the objections made by Robertson, though Börne, while condescending to Schiller, is not hostile like Robertson to his work as a whole. In his short but trenchant essay, *Über den Charakter des Wilhelm Tell in Schillers Drama*, Börne shows how Tell is by no means a conventional heroic figure, still less an ideal type. 'Tells Charakter ist die Untertänigkeit', he says. To Börne Tell is less the simple peasant than the 'Kleinbürger'. He grovels to authority in the shape of Geßler, shoots the apple off his son's head against all impulses of morality, then shoots Geßler, not on the spot, not even in open confrontation, but from the security of an ambush, having abandoned, in true opportunist fashion, the ship entrusted to him in the storm. He inhumanly rebukes Parricida but himself has no cause to see himself as innocent of revenge, having planned and carried out the murder of Geßler after the events which originally provoked him. Börne attributes these faults to Schiller's wish to create a drama which necessarily involved such morally ambiguous and repugnant episodes as the 'Apfelschuß' and the killing of Geßler. To Börne's mind Schiller was cramped by the data of history:

Sollte ich jetzt aber auf die Frage Antwort geben, wie es denn Schiller anders und besser hätte machen können—wäre ich in großer Verlegenheit. Der dramatische Dichter, der einen geschichtlichen Stoff behandelt, kann eine wahre Geschichte nach seinem Gebrauch ummodeln ... Eine geistige Überlieferung aber darf er niemals ändern. Diese besteht nur durch den Glauben und wird zerstört, wenn der Glaube umgeworfen oder anders gerichtet wird. Eine solche Überlieferung ist das Ereignis mit Tell. Aus diesem Zwange aber entsprangen Verhältnisse, mit welchen die Kunst nicht fertig werden konnte ... Den Mann mit breiten Schultern füllt nicht ganz seine Seele aus. Warum ihn aber Schiller so behandelt, ist schwer zu erklären. Er hätte ihn können alles tun, alles ertragen lassen, was er getan und ertragen, und ihn dabei trotziger, hochsinniger, gebietender machen können.[19]

Börne makes the important point that we are dealing here not with history but with national legend, part of the spiritual heritage of a country. While history can be changed by the dramatist—'sie bleibt doch geschehen, wie sie geschah'[20]—subject matter like the

Tell legends cannot be changed because Tell does not exist apart from the legends attached to him. If these legends are omitted the play cannot legitimately be called *Wilhelm Tell*. Schiller was, in Börne's view, therefore obliged to include these morally questionable incidents, but why, he asks, did Schiller not try to alleviate the problem by making Tell into a more commanding and dignified hero?

Far from being what one critic calls 'ein charakteristisches Mißverständnis',[21] Börne's essay pinpoints the crucial problem of how we are to understand Tell's actions and Tell's character. Börne could not solve the riddle of why Tell was not more heroic because he presupposed that Schiller's idealism would inevitably lead him to create a conventional hero. From Schiller's correspondence, however, we have seen that he approached and assessed his *Wilhelm Tell* with considerable sobriety and so there is little justification for assuming that the Tell he created was not the Tell he intended to create.

Despite Schiller's scepticism about the public's taste in drama there is little doubt that he intended to give sympathetic portrayal to Tell. Describing the role to the actor Karl Schwarz Schiller says: 'Die Rolle erklärt sich selbst: eine edle Simplicität, eine ruhige gehaltene Kraft ist der Charakter ... durchaus eine edle schlichte Manneswürde' (J7, 1962). Schiller's Tell is not, however, the Tell of the *Urner Spiel*, who is a hero after Börne's conception, a leader of men as well as a man of action. The reason for this lies in the fact that Schiller has not created a pageant, but a drama.[22] Börne was right to point out the problem which arises from the dramatization of legend. The drama and the legend spring from two very different modes of presentation and it is in the task of reconciling the demands of one with the demands of the other that Börne might have found the answer to his question why Tell is as he is. The differences between drama and legend are clarified in Goethe's and Schiller's own essay, *Über epische und dramatische Dichtung*. Legends are in epic form, enshrined in narrative, often unwritten. Of the distinction between the two forms Goethe and Schiller say: 'daß der Epiker die Begebenheit als *vollkommen vergangen* vorträgt, und der Dramatiker sie als *vollkommen gegenwärtig* darstellt' (NA 21, 57). The narrator of a legend relates the events as though fully in the past whereas the dramatist recreates them before our eyes. The dramatist who wants to dramatize a legend faces parti-

cular problems because legends by their nature are enshrined un-
critically in the minds of those who share the tradition, but the
dramatist who aims to produce a drama rather than a pageant must
aim also at psychological realism and so cannot avoid the implications of the action for the human beings involved. So whereas the
narrator of a legend can relate his story without comment or censure,
the dramatist cannot avoid analysis of the action. This principle
may be the key to the heroic/unheroic Tell and to Schiller's separation of the Tell action from the Rütli-action. Schiller combines a
portrayal of the legend with a portrayal of the human crises in
which Tell is involved.

Schiller's separation of Tell from the confederates' uprising is
frequently noted as a significant departure from his sources. This
gives Schiller the opportunity to look at Tell's actions as moral as
well as political ones. The pre-eminence of the Tell action was
stressed in a letter to Iffland: 'Wenn Tell und seine Familie nicht
der interessanteste Gegenstand im Stücke sind und bleiben, wenn
man auf etwas anderes begieriger seyn könnte, als auf ihn, so wäre
die Absicht des Werks sehr verfehlt worden.'[23] Schiller also insisted
during composition on following through the separate strands of
action rather than giving Iffland the play act by act:

Gern wollte ich Ihnen das Stück Aktenweise zuschicken, aber es entsteht
nicht Aktenweise, sondern die Sache erfordert, daß ich gewisse Handlungen, die zusammen gehören, durch alle fünf Akte durchführe, und dann
erst zu andern übergehe. So z.B. steht der Tell selbst ziemlich für sich in
dem Stück, seine Sache ist eine Privatsache, und bleibt es, bis sie am Schluß
mit der öffentlichen Sache zusammengreift.

(J7, 1921)

Schiller implies that the Rütli action should not overshadow the
personal drama of Tell and his family and that care should be taken
not to blur the distinctions between one strand of action and another.

The possible significance of Schiller's separation of Tell from the
confederates is one of the frequent themes of more recent criticism
of the drama. Werner Kohlschmidt[24] indicates how Schiller's
decision to follow Tschudi in putting the murder of Geßler after
the Rütli rather than before it further emphasises how Tell is not
to be seen as a self-appointed leader of men or political activist.
Rather we are encouraged to interpret his motives and actions from
the point of view of his role as husband and father and as a morally
upright human being. Family relationships play a central part in all

of Schiller's dramas. Frequently one generation is set against another, as in the case of Max and Octavio, Don Carlos and Philipp, Ferdinand and the Präsident. This emerges in *Wilhelm Tell* not in Tell's own family but in the relationship between Attinghausen and Rudenz, but even in Tell's harmonious family there are moments when private actions assume a political dimension.

Tell's character is by no means as transparent as we are at first sight tempted to believe. He is not simply the 'model of propriety' or the 'self-sufficient psychic organism' that E. L. Stahl[25] and Ilse Graham[26] take him to be. He has in fact a very ambivalent attitude to other human beings. On the one hand he does not hesitate to do what he feels he must to save a fellow human being. He does not consider the danger when it is a case of rescuing Baumgarten nor does he stop to consider if the man is worthy of the risk he is taking on his behalf. In this he towers above the men standing helplessly on the shore as Baumgarten pleads for a rescuer. On the other hand Tell is very distrustful of human society in general, though not of its individual members. One of his remarks in the Baumgarten incident illustrates this mistrust—

> Besser ists, Ihr fallt in Gottes Hand,
> Als in der Menschen.
>
> (157-8)

Tell does indeed have the Landvogt's men in mind but his words are characteristic. Men are full of guile whereas nature, though wild, can be tackled with skill and strength.

This same attitude is evident in Tell's first conversation with Stauffacher (cf. Act I Sc. 3 1.414-45). The gulf between the two men is evident. Stauffacher believes Tell to be a necessary participant in the confederacy if it is to have any chance of success. Tell will not be drawn in, however, and firmly resists the pressure from Stauffacher to consider what to do about the Austrians. He will act if a specific task comes his way but will not be involved in discussion:

> Doch *was* ihr tut, laßt mich aus eurem *Rat*,
> Ich kann nicht lange prüfen oder wählen,
> Bedürft ihr meiner zu bestimmter *Tat*,
> Dann ruft den Tell, es soll an mir nicht fehlen.
>
> (442-5)

Tell pursues no unified line of thought; he simply rejects the idea of lending his strength to a communal effort which might restrict his freedom. He is unwilling to take any comprehensive view of events and is mistrustful of those who wish to bind him to them:

Er hat ein ganz pragmatisches, fast phantasieloses Verhältnis zum Leben und den Aufgaben, die sich ihm stellen ... Dennoch kennt er die Grenzen seiner Möglichkeiten sehr genau, und so bemüht er sich auch immer wieder, nicht in Verhältnisse zu geraten, über die er als einzelner keine Macht hat.[27]

Tell has been called by critics an aesthetic personality,[28] or a harmonious personality,[29] neither realist nor idealist, in order to establish links between him and Schiller's theoretical works. Tell is held to be a man who instinctively knows and chooses the right. Yet Tell's conversation with Stauffacher tends not to support this notion. Tell does indeed act more on instinct than on considered judgement. As a morally upright person he obeys implicitly the call of duty but is unable to analyse the ground of his sense of duty. Yet in another sense Tell is a man who wants to be relieved of moral choice. Tell is a doer rather than a talker and this is because he is unable to take a wider view of events—even to the limited extent to which that is possible. His stature is limited by the limitations of his insight into men and affairs. Tell is not a perceptive man, in fact he has, for all his distrust of human society, a great *naïveté*.

Tell's mistrust of human organizations is best illustrated in his conversations with his wife and children. In the first scene of Act III Tell reaffirms his confidence in his own ability to cope with all situations and dangers:

> Wer frisch umherspäht mit gesunden Sinnen,
> Auf Gott vertraut und die gelenke Kraft,
> Der ringt sich leicht aus jeder Fahr und Not.
>
> (1508-10)

Tell's reliance on his own power is simple and intuitive, and in accordance with this he speaks in proverbs and maxims, e.g.

> Die Axt im Haus erspart den Zimmermann. (1513)

> Früh übt sich, was ein Meister werden will. (1480)

This reliance on maxims is evident again when Tell is questioned by his son Walter on their way to Altdorf. Tell describes the land of Austria beyond the mountains but stresses how people live in fear of each other and need a ruler to protect them. The dangers of

living in the Swiss mountains are not so fearful as living at enmity
with those around:

> Ja, wohl ists besser, Kind, die Gletscherberge
> Im Rücken haben als die bösen Menschen.
>
> (1812-13)

Tell's mistrust of men is accompanied by an extreme vulnerability.
Being as a huntsman so far removed from a social existence Tell is
also guileless. He cannot understand malice or how people can be
vindictive to one another. His wife, Hedwig, is much more perceptive
than he about human reactions. She knows immediately that Tell's
encounter with Geßler on the mountain pass will make the latter
determined to humiliate Tell, just as Geßler himself was humiliated.
She also knows that his countrymen lean very heavily on Tell and
that when the time comes for confrontation he will be put in the
most dangerous position:

> Sie werden dich hinstellen, wo Gefahr ist,
> Das Schwerste wird dein Anteil sein, wie immer.
>
> (1521-2)

Hedwig's fears for Tell betray not only anxiety on his behalf but
also her recognition of the public role which her husband has
acquired. Tell himself is incapable of thinking politically—though
his actions, of course, have political implications—but he is of such
standing in his community that he has been singled out by his
fellows as their natural leader.[30] He has become in part a public
figure even before the apple-shooting incident. From the first scene
of the play we are aware of the admiration which Tell inspires.
Ruodi says:

> Es gibt nicht zwei, wie der ist, im Gebirge.
>
> (164)

Stauffacher perceives this also and so is anxious to win Tell's
support for the confederacy. Stauffacher is obviously dismayed by
the lack of response in their conversation (I, 3) and after the
'Apfelschuß' when Tell is to be taken away as a prisoner he says:

> O nun ist alles, alles hin! Mit Euch
> Sind wir gefesselt alle und gebunden!
>
> (2090-1)

Another, perhaps the key person, who sees Tell's importance to the Swiss people is Geßler. Geßler is already known for persecuting those families who seem to be in a position to rally support. Certainly Geßler's attack on Tell in the 'Apfelschußszene' is not the first instance of his victimization of the family, as we know from Hedwig, who warns Tell:

> Gemahn ihn nicht an dich, du weißt, er grollt uns.
>
> (1542)

and by implication from Walter Fürst's words after Geßler has ordered Tell's arrest:

> Es ist vorbei, er hats beschlossen, mich
> Mit meinem ganzen Hause zu verderben.
>
> (2086-7)

Some criticism[31] has drawn attention to the possibilities of personal rivalry between Geßler and Tell but Geßler is not purely concerned with personal rivalry, important though the encounter on the mountainside may have been, but also with destroying the image of Tell as leader and hero in the eyes of the people, as well as with breaking Tell's own spirit. Geßler's assault on Tell in the 'Apfel-schuß' is therefore calculated to achieve this purpose. He wants no satisfaction for the fact that Tell did not acknowledge the hat. He does not want Tell's life as a forfeit. As he says himself to Tell:

> Ich will dein Leben nicht, ich will den Schuß.
>
> (1985)

He wants Tell to shoot, kill his own son and so discredit himself. He knows that it is inhuman to make such a demand and that if Tell fails, then the moral condemnation and Tell's own remorse will break him. Alternatively, Tell can refuse, as Geßler expects, and seem powerless in front of his compatriots. Because Tell does manage to shoot what even Geßler calls the 'Meisterschuß' Geßler has to resort to out-and-out trickery and violence to take Tell captive. Though he has not managed to discredit Tell he still knows what a blow his captivity will be to the Swiss and in this he proves to be right. In the first scene of Act IV Kunz von Gersau tells a fisherman of what has happened at Altdorf. The fisherman says:

> Der Tell gefangen abgeführt nach Küßnacht,
> Der beste Mann im Land, der bravste Arm,
> Wenns einmal gelten sollte für die Freiheit.
>
> (2100-2)

So Tell is firmly rooted in the minds of the people as a man in-
dispensable to the movement for freedom even though he himself
has never counselled rebellion nor declared himself in favour of
revolt.

The 'Apfelschuß' incident is a scene which required very careful
motivation if Tell was not to seem an unnatural father. Schiller
created a situation in which Tell is forced to shoot the apple, for
if he refuses both he and his son will forfeit their lives. Geßler will
accept no other action, and intervention by Stauffacher, Rössel-
mann, then Berta and Rudenz serves only to harden his attitude. A
double perspective emerges from the 'Apfelschuß' incident which is
characteristic of the play from this point onwards. In this scene we
see Tell as a vulnerable human being struggling with the test given
to him by Geßler and the violation of his feelings and instincts as a
father. There is another aspect to the action, in which the 'Apfelschuß' features as a legendary incident, which, though horrific for
Tell as a father, is at the same time a triumph and a spectacle.
Ueding[32] stresses the classical influence in this. Tell is fulfilling the
role of the mythical hero, who is called on to perform seemingly
impossible tasks. Schiller was prevented for obvious practical
reasons from staging the 'Apfelschuß' as a straight spectacle and
having first stressed Tell's suffering he distracts the audience's
attention by the ineffective protests of other characters, particularly
Rudenz. The actual shot comes as a sudden surprise and evokes at
first disbelief and then admiration, even from Geßler himself:

> Bei Gott, der Apfel mitten durchgeschossen!
> Es war ein Meisterschuß, ich muß ihn loben.
>   (2041-2)

It is in this scene that Tell's two roles, the public/legendary and
the private are first brought together and are most clearly visible
to the audience. In completing his 'Meisterschuß' Tell is fulfilling the promise he holds for his countrymen and standing as
their representative figure. Yet we see clearly that the 'Apfelschuß'
is for him very much a 'Privatsache' in which he is in no way concerned with his public standing or representative role but solely
with his emotions as a father. Thus Tell lets his emotions speak
when Geßler questions him about the second arrow. He first
attempts to evade the question but when Geßler guarantees his life
he admits that the second arrow was for Geßler if Tell had shot his

son. So prudence and a sense of what is good for the majority in no way informs that admission. It is the admission of someone who must let his feelings speak. Before Tell is led away Stauffacher, always keenly conscious of Tell's public role, rebukes him for having made the admission to Geßler:

> O warum mußtet Ihr den Wütrich reizen! (2088)

Tell's reply shows up the inappropriateness of Stauffacher's rebuke, especially since Stauffacher himself has so far been a talker but not a doer:

> Bezwinge sich, wer meinen Schmerz gefühlt!
> (2090)

Stauffacher is dismayed because he sees his rebellion disintegrating with Tell's captivity. One can say therefore that the 'Apfelschuß' first brings together the two roles of Tell. The drama requires that the 'Apfelschuß' should not be just a spectacle but an incident with repercussions for Tell as a personality, as a moral being. Tell is also fulfilling his representative role by being the doer while others stand by helplessly, as in the Baumgarten incident.

Tell's monologue before the assassination of Geßler indicates how far this moral aspect of action, its private as opposed to its public dimension has made itself felt in Tell, a man little used to thinking outside the realm of proverb, cliché, and axiom. His thinking in the monologue is far from clear. He dwells on the way in which he feels himself to have been inwardly violated by Geßler. His thoughts were once pure and harmless but now they are thoughts of murder:

> in gärend Drachengift hast du
> Die Milch der frommen Denkart mir verwandelt.
> (2572-3)

He also feels himself bound to protect the innocent, the lives of families from such further assaults by Geßler. His vow to shoot next only Geßler is by a strange turn of logic transformed into a holy vow, which he feels bound to fulfil. He feels himself to be an instrument of God, who will no longer stand by and see Geßler violate humanity in this way:

> Es lebt ein Gott, zu strafen und zu rächen.
> (2595)

Yet Tell is aware that his job is murder and that he is in possession of a weapon which was previously used to support himself and his family in peaceful existence. His mood is grim and serious and yet there is an anticipation of achievement. Though he may be about to assassinate someone in cold blood he still feels the perfectionist's pride in anticipation of the use of his skill:

> Aber heute will ich
> Den *Meisterschuß* tun und das Beste mir
> Im ganzen Umkreis des Gebirgs gewinnen.
>
> (2648-50)

Perhaps the use of the word 'Meisterschuß' springs from Tell's own memory of Geßler's words after the 'Apfelschuß'—

> Es war ein Meisterschuß, ich muß ihn loben.
>
> (2042)

Perhaps it is rather a verbal echo which makes the audience aware of the dramatic connection between the two incidents.

Tell's thoughts then are confused and even conflicting from the point of view of strict logic but quite understandable in the character with whom Schiller has acquainted us in the play. Moral objections have frequently been raised to the assassination of Geßler[33] and it is not difficult to see why. How, we wonder, can Tell and Schiller countenance this action, where Tell waits in ambush and then shoots the defenceless Geßler in cold blood? Again the difference between legend and drama comes to light. The legendary murderer of Geßler does not stand in a morally dubious light. He is a hero, Geßler gets his just deserts, and the hearer is satisfied with this parable of justice. Not so the witness to the act in a drama who inevitably questions what he is seeing on stage and who feels himself called upon to exercise some judgement. If we look back to the 'Apfelschuß' we find an answer to the question of how Tell can countenance the action, not only because that scene provides the motivation for the assassination but also because in the assassination there is the repetition and, in one sense, completion of the former incident. In the 'Apfelschuß' Tell struggles with what seems impossible for him as a father to do. Having made the decision that it must be done, however, he goes ahead to do it with complete thoroughness. The assassination seems to be the same. Tell feels impelled to kill Geßler. He cannot fully find words for that feeling and he finds a number of justifications in his monologue which express more of an intuition than a coherent argument. Having decided to do it he does not indulge in heroics such as challenging Geßler. He would not understand such ostentation. Geßler has to be removed and is removed with the same ruthless efficiency. Werner Kohlschmidt[34] sees the assassination as being in obedience to the Kantian categorical imperative. This argument seems to impute to Tell a greater capacity for moral discernment than we have seen in him and perhaps too great an emotional detachment. Rather it is the reaction of a man of simple intuition who is himself incapable of malice. Hence what he does proceeds from a kind of innocence, the same innocence which gives him the courage to rescue Baumgarten in spite of the storm.

Schiller orchestrates the scene of the killing in such a way that Armgard and her starving children distract attention from Tell and cast an unsympathetic light on Geßler. Tell's shot is thus seen to some extent as a judgement from heaven; it is certainly taken as such by those standing by who refuse to help, saying:

> Wir ihn berühren, welchen Gott geschlagen! (2816)

Again there is the appearance of the representative Tell who, after the shooting, addresses the almost lifeless Geßler:

> Du kennst den Schützen, suche keinen andern!
> Frei sind die Hütten, sicher ist die Unschuld
> Vor dir...
>
> (2792-4)

The appearance of Tell on a high ridge above Geßler and the on-lookers gives weight to the suggestion that he has performed some act of divine retribution, certainly in the minds of the Swiss. From this moment onwards it is the public Tell who fixes himself in the minds of the people as deliverer from oppression. His very position on the high ridge suggests the kind of statue that he is to become in the popular mind. It is this process which W. F. Mainland has in mind when he says of Tell's story that it is 'a Wallenstein in re-verse'.[35] By this he perhaps means that whereas the reputation of Wallenstein after his death was in the hands of his enemies, who had in fact brought about his downfall, Tell's reputation, by contrast, is determined by the approval of those surrounding him and those who come after him, the people who created his legend and ensure that posterity will also regard him as a hero. From the beginning of the play we have seen Tell chosen as hero; the killing of Geßler and the subsequent insurrection seal his position as ideal leader in the eyes of the people. This is, of course, particularly promoted by Stauffacher, who after the capture of Zwing Uri says to the jubilant people—

> Wo ist der Tell? Soll *er* allein uns fehlen,
> Der unsrer Freiheit Stifter ist?
>
> (3082-3)

The very next scene (V, 2) opens with Hedwig and the children, who await Tell's return. This is the place where Tell the human being re-emerges, where our interest in Tell should be most fully engaged, as Schiller claimed he intended. Tell is joyful to see his wife and children again and seems to have put behind him the various tribulations of the play. Hedwig, however, who is always more alive than Tell to the problems in any situation, reminds him that he is not the same Tell who left her:

> Wie—*wie* kommst du mir wieder?—Diese Hand
> —Darf ich sie fassen?—Diese Hand—O Gott!
>
> (3141-2)

Tell is unperturbed by this and reassures Hedwig of his moral blamelessness:

> Hat euch verteidigt und das Land gerettet,
> Ich darf sie frei hinauf zum Himmel heben.
>
> (3143-4)

The encounter with Parricida follows, however, and Tell is not allowed to escape consideration of the fact that he has committed a murder.

Much controversy surrounds the Parricida incident. Interesting and formally satisfying interpretations of the scene are given by W. F. Mainland and G. W. McKay, in which they stress how the Parricida incident, far from exculpating Tell, actually brings the moral problem of his murder into sharp focus. Such interpretation is rejected by those who, like Vander Meulen,[36] appeal to Schiller's correspondence with Iffland[37] and his comments there about the Parricida scene, which seem to point to the purpose of the scene as a justification of Tell's action. Let us look at the actual words of Schiller: 'Parricidas Erscheinung ist der Schlußstein des Ganzen.

Tells Mordthat wird durch ihn allein moralisch und poetisch aufgelößt.'[38] Schiller's first sentence in no way refutes, in fact it promotes, the idea that the arrival of Parricida gives a more complete perspective in the final act. The second sentence emphasizes the first and stresses that Tell's assassination of Geßler cannot be seen in true moral, poetic, or historical perspective until the scene with Parricida. This is not to say that we necessarily have to see the scene in terms of black and white, the wholly bad and the wholly good, but merely that the juxtaposition of the two characters with their differing motives and yet similar deeds gives a broader perspective on the Tell action. If this is indeed the case then it is not surprising that Schiller should so persistently have stressed its importance and insisted on its inclusion in the first production. The next sentence is, however, more difficult to deal with:

Neben dem ruchlosen Mord aus Impietaet und Ehrsucht steht nunmehr Tells nothgedrungne That, sie erscheint schuldlos in der Zusammenstellung mit einem ihr so ganz unähnlichen Gegenstück und die Hauptidee des ganzen Stückes wird eben dadurch ausgesprochen, nämlich; Das Nothwendige und Rechtliche der Selbsthilfe in einem streng bestimmten Fall.[39]

Schiller certainly seems to be saying that the Parricida incident is designed to show up the blamelessness of Tell's action. The problem with the argument itself is, of course, that it makes the scene superfluous. Tell is justified already in the play. We have already been encouraged to see him as a good man doing what he feels he must. Schiller has so designed the 'Apfelschuß' and the assassination incident with its preceding monologue that 'das Nothwendige und Rechtliche' are sufficiently apparent. Given this argument, the Parricida incident is indeed misconceived because it inevitably raises questions which would otherwise have lain dormant. For this reason it is frequently omitted from productions to this day, especially in Switzerland, where the play is treated usually as a pageant.

Perhaps, however, we can give Schiller's words a less superficial interpretation without distorting their sense. Certainly there is a difference between the two murderers. As they confront each other as people the moral differences between them are certainly of vital importance to Tell who cannot bear to think of himself as being in the same category as Parricida. It seems that Schiller realized that his play could become just a pageant, just another *Urner Spiel*, a glorification of a legend, which, once put on stage, could be seen as a hopelessly superficial treatment of the subject of political assassination. It is as though with the Parricida incident Schiller recognized the need to save the play from superficiality and to give some kind of moral perspective on Tell's action. He perhaps recognized also that the play could be taken all too easily as a justification of assassination and hence he puts in the proviso of 'in einem streng bestimmten Fall'. We could say from Schiller's words that his intention was to show how in one particular instance a man was led to consider murder necessary and justified. However, Schiller gives no easy answers to moral dilemmas in any of his later dramas; all characters share a certain ambiguity and Tell is no exception. Although Schiller talks of 'das Nothwendige und Rechtliche der Selbsthilfe in einem streng bestimmten Fall' as being the 'Hauptidee' of the play, the pattern of the later plays suggests that central ideas are usually put up for discussion and surveyed from a number of points of view.

Throughout discussion of the play so far there has been mention of its epic and dramatic aspects and the two roles of Tell which correspond to these. Tell's appearance in the final act with his wife and children reintroduces the private dimension of Tell's life. Although Tell puts aside Hedwig's dismay at his changed state Parricida reminds him of it yet again and so in the Parricida incident we are reminded that Tell must bear responsibility as an individual human being for the murder of another human being. Up to the encounter with Parricida it looked as though Tell was going to avoid looking at the morality of his present position.

Parricida tends immediately to engage the audience's sympathy by his wretched state and we half expect to see Tell show compassion towards him. This certainly is what Parricida expects but he misjudges his man in Tell by trying to make Tell see a similarity between the two murders:

> Bei Euch hofft ich Barmherzigkeit zu finden,
> Auch Ihr nahmt Rach an Eurem Feind.
>
> (3173-4)

Tell, as we have seen, is not a man to waver from any standpoint which he has taken up. Tell believes in his moral purity and we as the audience believe in it too, inasmuch as we know Tell to be a man without malice, who was drawn into the sphere of public action much against his will, who was motivated not by a desire for revenge but from a sense of outraged humanity.

Yet Parricida has obviously touched a sensitive spot. Tell's vehement reply to Parricida,

> Unglücklicher!
> Darfst du der Ehrsucht blutge Schuld vermengen
> Mit der gerechten Notwehr eines Vaters?
>
> (3174-6)

shows his urgent need to preserve his sense of moral purity. However, we as the audience see only too clearly that the very resolve and determination with which Tell hunted down Geßler, not immediately after the 'Apfelschuß' but later by deliberate ambush, suggest revenge and cannot be called 'Notwehr'. Börne says of Tell's self-justification:

Doch Tell irrt. Aus Ehrsucht hat er freilich den Landvogt nicht getötet, doch mit Notwehr ... kann er sich nicht entschuldigen. Damals wenn er, um den Schuß von seinem Kinde abzuwenden, den Bogen nach Geßlers Brust gerichtet hätte, wäre es Notwehr gewesen, später war es nur Rache ...[40]

We sympathize to some extent with Tell's need to maintain some distance from Parricida and he is right in sensing that Parricida's argument is only superficial and takes no account of their individual situations. Yet Parricida can be excused for making the comparison in absence of any knowledge of Tell, for appearances suggest a strong similarity between the two deeds and Tell could easily be a ruthless assassin from any account of the events themselves.

Yet in repudiating Parricida's argument Tell is also rejecting the now wretched man himself. He senses this, and just as Parricida gives up hope of finding mercy Tell says:

> Und doch erbarmt mich deiner...   (3190)

Whatever he meant by 'das Nothwendige und Rechtliche der Selbsthilfe' Schiller shows in the Parricida incident that 'Selbsthilfe', however morally justified and necessary it may appear, must involve even the most upright and unassuming of men in a kind of ambiguity. Parricida can be seen as a sort of accuser, the voice that suggests to Tell he is a common murderer. Tell may be convinced of his own innocence but the audience is made aware of his ambiguity.

The Parricida incident therefore places Tell's assassination in a broader moral and historical context. The fact that it is Parricida himself, not merely some stranger, who confronts Tell emphasizes the historical context of the events. Parricida reminds us that there is a world beyond the bounds of Switzerland, a world which none the less impinges on Tell's world. The fact that this broader historical perspective is needed was confirmed in 1966 by Friedrich Dürrenmatt who, commenting on a Zürich production which omitted the Parricida scene, said:

Parricida brauchte nicht aufzutreten, Tell war von vornherein vom Zuschauer, vom Patrioten gerechtfertigt. Die Szene, die das Stück erst in die Geschichte Europas einordnet, dieser große Einfall der Begegnung zweier Mörder, der ihm seine wahre Dimension gibt, fiel dahin.[41]

The encounter of the two men then raises the question of innocence and guilt, self-defence and murder against this historical background.

Tell's innocence springs from a very simple outlook on moral matters, an intuitive rather than a logical approach to them. Tell shows the moral outlook of his community whereas Parricida comes from outside the community and does not necessarily share its moral outlook. He offers the view that Tell and he have something in common. Not only have they both killed their enemy, but they have both liberated others from him. Parricida says to Tell:

> Auch ich
> Hab einen Feind erschlagen, der mir Recht
> Versagte—Er war Euer Feind wie meiner—
> Ich hab das Land von ihm befreit.
>
> (3152-5)

Parricida is clutching at straws here for he knows that he did not murder his uncle in order to free Switzerland but to gain his inheritance. Yet in another sense he is making a very important observation on events. Both he and Tell have indirectly brought about the liberation of Switzerland. Parricida in fact speaks truer than he realizes for, as we shall see, the Emperor posed the real threat to Swiss freedom and so Parricida has freed Switzerland more effectively than Tell in shooting Geßler. While Parricida is consciously usurping the role of liberator, in the sense that Swiss freedom was far from his thoughts in murdering the Emperor, Tell has unconsciously usurped it, in that his act of assassination may have given the confederates impetus to begin their insurrection but he did not intend it as such, nor has it brought about liberation, for Geßler, evil though he was, was by his own admission only a servant of the Emperor:

Sagt, was Ihr wollt, ich bin des Kaisers Diener
Und muß drauf denken, wie ich ihm gefalle.
(2709-10)

Thus the historical perspective in the Parricida incident is extremely important because it raises the question of how far justice has been done in the movement of history, a question asked in *Wallenstein* and in all the later dramas. Superficially we could say that Tell's story is an instance of a man who acts morally on the impulse of his conscience and that while the deed itself is usually regarded as a crime there are occasions when it has to be done; Tell is vindicated in the end through the acclamations of his countrymen and in his legend. Future generations have seen the good man that he is and honoured him. He also makes a good hero because of his famous circus trick, the 'Apfelschuß'. Parricida, on the other hand, has murdered from revenge and resentment. So he reaps his just rewards—to be banished from human society and to take the lonely path of the penitent. Thus Fritz Martini says:

Der fürstliche Neffe und Mörder seines Kaisers, jetzt zur Maske des ärmsten Büßers verdammt, macht dramatisch sinnfällig, was ein Mord aus menschlicher Schuld, der ein nur egoistisch ungeduldiger Rechtsanspruch, nur eine Gewalttat gegen die Pflichten der Natur, nur eine unbesonnene, wilde Wahnsinnstat war und nichts als seinen engsten selbstischen und entfesselten Zweck kannte, bewirkt. Er verjagt den Täter aus jeder Harmonie der Gemeinschaft mit dem Menschen, mit der Natur, mit den sittlichen und göttlichen Ordnungen.[42]

This is, however, rather a superficial judgement and one which would be surprisingly superficial in one so aware as Schiller of the complexity of historical judgements and the folly of trying to claim that people receive their just deserts. The case of *Wallenstein* illustrates this insight perfectly and it was precisely the lack of justice and vindication in Schiller's view of history in the play which so appalled Hegel.[43]

If we are to accept the superficial judgement on Tell and the vindication of history we are in fact accepting the view put forward by the confederates, who have limited insight into what is happening. We as the audience are obliged to hold together the strands of action and to take a more complex view. Tell does not suffer the fate of the lonely outcast, Parricida, because he already enjoys the approbation of his community, and the assassination seems to him and to them morally justified. Conscience can be at peace. However, Tell cannot rightfully be called the saviour of his people in strictly logical terms. It is an illusion, a popular one, that Tell has freed the country, but not one which can be justified on historical grounds. Parricida's removal of the Emperor has been far more effective in securing Swiss freedom. What is more, the confederates actually admit this, when the news of the Emperor's death arrives (V, 1) just after the capture of Zwing Uri, but scarcely realize what they are saying. On hearing of the fate of Duke Johann, Walter Fürst says:

> So trägt die Untat ihnen keine Frucht!
> Rache trägt keine Frucht!
>
> (3011-12)

Stauffacher does not simply moralize, however; he seems to grasp what the news of Albrecht's death means to them:

> Den Mördern bringt die Untat nicht Gewinn,
> *Wir* aber brechen mit der reinen Hand
> Des blutgen Frevels segenvolle Frucht.
> Denn einer großen Furcht sind wir entledigt;
> Gefallen ist der Freiheit größter Feind.
>
> (3015-19)

The moral opportunism of his speech is quite breathtaking.[44] Stauffacher admits that they will take advantage of the deed which brought no happiness to those responsible for it. Stauffacher admits himself here that the Emperor was freedom's greatest enemy and yet cheerfully goes on, seconds later, to rally the Swiss to go to acclaim Tell as 'unsrer Freiheit Stifter' (3083). Stauffacher is aware of the larger forces at work on the Swiss. His moralizing and that of the confederates is the more incongruous, however, as we look back in the play to the Rütli, where again we catch a glimpse of the world outside Switzerland. It is in the Rütli scene that we first hear of Parricida and his accomplices in the later murder. The behaviour of the Emperor towards Parricida is taken as evidence of the Emperor's lack of justice as Konrad Huhn reports on his recent attempt to petition against the Landvögte:

> Die edeln Herrn von Wart und Tegerfeld
> Die riefen mir und sagten: Helft euch selbst,
> Gerechtigkeit erwartet nicht vom König,

Beraubt er nicht des eignen Bruders Kind,
Und hinterhält ihm sein gerechtes Erbe?
(1338-42)

These words are taken up by the confederates as confirmation of
the need to act, even though they reject extreme measures. It is
ironical in retrospect that they are encouraged by the very people
whose behaviour they later condemn.

What sort of justice is then operating in the play? It is too simple
to say that Tell and Parricida get their just deserts. After all, Tell
has committed a murder which goes entirely unpunished, in fact
unreproached. More than that, he is elevated to a position in the
community which it is doubtful he deserves. Parricida, on the other
hand, has a valid claim to have liberated the Swiss, whether he
appreciates its extent or not, and yet finds himself entirely wretched
and outcast. The reason for this discrepancy would seem to be the
very particular place which Tell occupies among his people and the
particular moment in history when Tell found himself forced to
act. It is the conjunction of these forces which gives Tell his special
place in the scheme of history. Alongside this however must go an
admission that no principle of justice is operating, but rather that
by its movement history forces some people to the fore. They themselves and, in this case, others too have a sense that they have
made history, but in fact history has made them. Tell is the perfect
example of how a man can perform deeds of extremely limited
effectiveness in strict causal terms and yet find himself hailed as
one who has given national history a new direction. Parricida, by
contrast, finds himself unable in any way to capitalize on his
murder of the Emperor. No one seems prepared to condone it. This
may be because, unlike Tell, no one has any vested interest in
Parricida beyond the lords who persuaded him to join them. Schiller
seems to indicate that such twists of history, whereby people can
literally get away with murder, are unpredictable. One cannot in
the process of acting impose the interpretation one chooses on a set
of events. The operation of complex circumstances goes beyond the
control of any one person.

In accepting Tell's murder without any sign of moral disapproval
while wholeheartedly condemning Parricida, the confederates
might be charged with inconsistency, even hypocrisy. The reason
for the discrepancy is not in any conscious discrimination but in
Tell's position in the community and in the partiality of judgement

to which the confederates, being themselves bound up in the circumstances of action, are inevitably subject.

On the Rütli the confederates meet to discuss how to free the
land from tyranny and restore the old order. They exhibit quite
soon a certain moral squeamishness in the face of possible action.
They first have to convince themselves that no other course is open
to them than to expel the Austrians. Walter Fürst draws a distinction
between changing the old order for a new one and simply safe-
guarding the old order; the latter is the confederates' intention.

> Die alten Rechte, wie wir sie ererbt
> Von unsern Vätern, wollen wir bewahren,
> Nicht ungezügelt nach dem Neuen greifen.
>
> (1353-5)

The deep-rooted conservatism of the confederates emerges here;
they certainly do not wish to consider themselves revolutionaries.
Yet an uprising is an uprising, whatever the reasons behind it, and
it is this fact which the confederates try to avoid considering. In
addition, the uprising is to be bloodless as far as possible. Fürst
says:

> Die Vögte wollen wir mit ihren Knechten
> Verjagen und die festen Schlösser brechen,
> Doch, wenn es sein mag, ohne Blut.
>
> (1366-8)

The Emperor is to be shown that the Swiss have considered open
rebellion only as a last resort:

> Es sehe
> Der Kaiser, daß wir notgedrungen nur
> Der Ehrfurcht fromme Pflichten abgeworfen.
>
> (1368-70)

This is hard to accept as a realistic appraisal of the Emperor's
reaction. It must be wishful thinking on Fürst's part to suppose
that an Emperor who has already denied the country its ancient
charter and has sent governors like Geßler would bother to scrutinise
the moral attitudes of the confederates. Fürst may be putting the
case in these terms in order to persuade his countrymen of the
moral justification for the uprising, perhaps also to persuade
himself. Certainly the leaders are unwilling to admit that it is
very difficult to separate personal from altruistic motives in such

a case. This is clearly illustrated in the case of Melchtal whose father has suffered brutal treatment from the Landvogt's men on his account. On the Rütli he says to Stauffacher:

> O Herr Stauffacher! Ich hab ihn
> Gesehn, der *mich* nicht wiedersehen konnte!
> Die Hand hab ich gelegt auf seine Augen,
> Und glühend Rachgefühl hab ich gesogen
> Aus der erloschnen Sonne seines Blicks
>
> (986-90)

Stauffacher obviously finds this a disturbing idea and reproves Melchtal:

> Sprecht nicht von Rache. Nicht Geschehnes rächen,
> Gedrohtem Übel wollen wir begegnen.
>
> (991-2)

Again a sense of anxiety about the nature of involvement in action emerges. Stauffacher perhaps would like to believe that altruism can be the only pure motivating force in the uprising. However, the very presence of Baumgarten, let alone Melchtal, should indicate to him that motivation is bound to have its personal aspect which cannot be separated from feelings of duty or patriotism. Certainly Stauffacher feels the danger of things getting out of hand and he hopes that a conservative policy will prevent gratuitous acts of violence. Fürst later commends Melchtal after the capture of Zwing Uri because Melchtal has resisted the temptation to retaliate:

> Wohl Euch, daß Ihr den reinen Sieg
> Mit Blute nicht geschändet!
>
> (2912-13)

Fürst is clearly pleased to think that he and the other confederates can sleep easily in their beds without bloodshed on their consciences. Yet Fürst here has only very limited vision. The audience recognizes that the uprising has not been 'ohne Blut', for Tell has committed a murder in what was essentially 'eine Privatsache'.

If the confederates, so anxious about the moral effects of involvement in political action, wish to feel sure of their moral purity, why then are they so ready to accept Tell as saviour of the country, in spite of what he has done? The answer must lie in part in the fact that no one will believe any ill of Tell, the focus of all their hopes and their ideal figure-head. Even deeper than this, however, may be some unconscious gratitude for what Tell has done in taking on himself the morally questionable action. By doing so he has saved them from having to bear that guilt themselves. This must be what underlies Stauffacher's words after the capture of Zwing Uri:

> Wo ist der Tell? Soll er allein uns fehlen,
> Der unsrer Freiheit Stifter ist? Das Größte
> Hat *er* getan, das Härteste erduldet.
>
> (3082-4)

It is not that the confederates condone murder, therefore, but that in condemning Parricida they are able to stand back from the murder of the Emperor. The murder of Geßler is too close to them to be viewed critically or objectively and in condemning Tell their own ease of conscience would be put at risk.

In Schiller's later dramas it is a virtual rule of life that any political action involves moral compromise. Men's actions are by very definition not true expressions of their personalities but are made necessary by the force of circumstances. No one who is thus forced to act can maintain his moral purity. Such is the painful discovery of Max Piccolomini and Johanna. In the dramas from *Wallenstein* onwards this problem of the entanglements of the political world and the discrepancy between personality and action is worked out with tragic consequences, until *Wilhelm Tell*. By contrast with Wallenstein, Maria, Elisabeth, and Johanna, Tell at first sight seems to escape the consequences of his actions and tragedy is avoided. Schiller has chosen not to break with the legend, which has no tragic implications. The avoidance of tragedy is not problematic to critics who see Schiller's dramas as progressing towards the idyll. Those who, like Reinhold Schneider, see in Schiller a particular attachment to tragedy, and the struggle for freedom as usually giving rise to that tragedy, find Schiller's apparently happy ending more surprising: 'es ist schwer zu begreifen, daß in diesem einen und einzigen Falle die Realisierung der Freiheit in der Geschichte ohne Tragik abgehen soll.'[45] Tragedy is avoided in *Wilhelm Tell* through the precise constellation of circumstances surrounding Tell's murder of Geßler and also through the presentation of Tell's personality. Tell's limited intellect would not allow him to perceive the anomalous position in which he finds himself at the close of the play. It encourages him to accept his own self-justifications about Geßler's murder. However, the Parricida scene reflects, through the wretched Parricida, the tragic guilt which *can* be felt by a man who has become a murderer and which Tell, being a man in other circumstances has, by the decree of history, been able to avoid.

This does not mean, however, that Tell escapes all consequences of his actions. W. F. Mainland indicates the significance of Tell's cross-bow,[46] which is finally taken from him to become a museum-piece. This shows how the community forms a sense of its own history through the preservation of objects such as the cross-bow and Geßler's hat, but it also shows how Tell himself has become something of a museum-piece. The cross-bow can be said to represent the 'normal' life of Tell the hunter. It is this very normal existence which now no longer seems possible. The cross-bow is a loss to Tell, who says to his wife in Act III:

> Mir fehlt der Arm, wenn mir die Waffe fehlt.
>
> (1536)

Now his cross-bow is gone permanently. Tell seems to have lost the ability to carry on with his former life. Mainland, therefore, interprets the final scene of the play, where Tell stands silently among his jubilant countrymen, as an ending which leaves open the verdict on Tell and hints at the possible distress behind the façade. McKay sees the final silence as being a picture of Tell in his legendary setting, receiving the acclaim which his compatriots believe to be his due.[47] Certainly the last scene shows popular history's verdict on Tell. It shows how the legend expunges the private dimension to Tell's life. It is a timeless scene in that sense, because Tell stands in that scene as he will always be, though not, notably, until we have seen him with Parricida.

What can we then infer from *Wilhelm Tell* about the nature of political involvement? Tell's story demonstrates how a man is drawn into the sphere of public action despite all his attempts to keep himself outside it and despite his own lack of concern for politics. It is therefore ironical that the very man who wanted to keep aloof is forced into the limelight, not because he is finally persuaded to take up the political cause but because his private moral judgement leads him to act in a way which happily suits the purposes of the political group. Schiller presents the Swiss cause as unequivocally good but also brings to light the way in which a man can unintentionally bring about good, even through actions which seem neither strictly connected with that good, nor to be morally good in themselves.

  Private motivation as a spur to political action has been touched on in connection with the confederates' anxiety about moral purity. In fact Tell is only one of a group of characters who commit themselves to involvement in public action for personal motives. We have noted Stauffacher's reproach to Melchtal for speaking of revenge:

> Sprecht nicht von Rache. Nicht Geschehnes rächen,
> Gedrohtem Übel wollen wir begegnen.
>
> (991-2)

Stauffacher fears that God will not be on their side if their motives are not pure but if he were merely to look around him on the Rütli he might ask himself how many of those men were there for purely altruistic reasons. Baumgarten is present, for example, and it would be most dangerous to claim that personal experience of oppression played no part in his decision to join the confederates. It is interesting that Melchtal is one of the most active and enterprising of the confederates, who with Rudenz is the prime force in executing the plans for the uprising. Equally significant is the part which Rudenz himself plays. He had been seduced on to the Austrian side through his pursuit of Berta. When she makes it clear that she sympathizes with the Swiss and wishes Rudenz would rather fight for his country's tradition and independence Rudenz engages himself energetically on the side of the confederates. He reproves them after Attinghausen's death for delaying and himself leads the men who captured one of the castles. Together with Melchtal he rescues Berta from the burning Zwing Uri. It seems from the play, therefore, that those who are willing to commit themselves most wholeheartedly to a cause are not moved by abstract and altruistic reasons but by personal involvement.[48] The fact that people who enter into dangerous political activity do so not for abstract ideas of justice or the good of the country but for personal reasons was recognized by Schiller long before *Wilhelm Tell*, indeed as far back as *Fiesco*. At the beginning of the book version of the play the characters are listed along with a detailed description of their salient traits. As the play progresses these characteristics emerge and become linked with various personal reasons for their involvement in Fiesco's conspiracy. Significantly, the only character who seems to be acting from purely altruistic motives is Verrina and he is perhaps the least convincing of all the characters.

It has become evident in discussion of *Wilhelm Tell* how the pronouncements of the participants in the action of the play cannot be taken to express any absolute or objective truth about the nature of the events. We are familiar with this principle in Schiller's drama, for it is quite evident from *Wallenstein* onwards that the participants in any complex situation cannot see in full what is happening around them, nor escape their own presuppositions in interpreting it. W. F. Mainland has pointed out how the loose, episodic structure of *Wilhelm Tell* has in the past been frequently criticized.[49] Mainland's contention is that the episodic structure is a deliberate choice on Schiller's part to show how the various strands of action eventually meet and how on a set of unconnected events a retrospective interpretation can be imposed which brings those unconnected events together into a pattern. Of the later plays Mainland says: 'His [Schiller's] later plays, and especially *Wilhelm Tell*, would probably be of greater interest to the twentieth century if there were more frank admission of the irony in Schiller's own disposition.'[50] It is certainly true to say that Schiller's reputation has suffered at the hands of critics who have taken at face value all idealistic or patriotic statements made by characters in the play. The possible irony in the later drama may spring from Schiller's disposition; certainly it is a principle on which the later drama is built. It was noted that in the *Wallenstein* trilogy the dramatist creates his own 'little world'. The way in which he makes his characters behave conforms to his conception of how life and history are governed. The dramatist, however, stands aloof from his world. No single character can therefore be said to have a God's-eye view of events. This is reserved for the dramatist, the creator of that world and, by extension, for the spectator.

In *Wilhelm Tell*, perhaps more than in any other of Schiller's dramas, we as the audience share the dramatist's panoramic view of events. Because the strands in the drama are separate and over-lap only occasionally, we as the audience see what the characters cannot, and can see how false interpretations are being put on the events. This relationship between the audience and the play implies a certain ironic distance. By ironic distance we do not imply that the audience fails to take the characters in the play seriously; the implication is that the audience recognizes that true insight into how history is made and legend is formed comes only from watching events as from above and seeing the variety of viewpoints, all partial and limited, held by the participants. We have already noted the fact that the Tell theme is not given tragic treatment; Schiller called the play a 'Schauspiel'. One of his reasons for avoiding a tragic treatment may have been that a figure such as Tell is so inextricably bound to his legend. He does not exist apart from it. The legend has it that Tell is a hero. What Schiller can be said to have done is to show what sort of reality might lie behind the legend.

Because we stand back with Schiller from the drama we have to piece together the various strands of action and see how the juxtaposition of these lines of action modifies our view of events. One interpretation is placed alongside another so that no single statement can be said to contain the whole truth of the matter. The truth seems in fact to lie beyond what any individual can perceive. The juxtaposition of the Tell and Rütli action produces just such an ironical effect. It is only through realizing that Tell is involved in a 'Privatsache' that we can see the process of distortion of Tell's motives by the confederates. It is only through looking at the Tell action that we see the inadequacy of the Rütli confederates' attitude to political action. Tell counsels passive acceptance of oppression but acts when the time is right; the confederates counsel controlled action but are too circumspect and miss the proper moment. The confederates condemn bloodshed and in particular the murder of the Emperor but accept Tell, in spite of what he has done. It is by maintaining this panoramic view of the action that we as the audience can piece together the true causal relationships between events but also see simultaneously how these relationships are being misapprehended by characters in the play. This is what can be seen as the fundamentally ironic standpoint of the dramatist (and audience) to the world of his play. Within that are specific instances of different types of irony, particularly, in the case of the confederates, the irony of self-betrayal where characters unwittingly expose their real attitudes. The prime example of this is Fürst's remark to Melchtal after the fall of Zwing Uri:

> Wohl Euch, daß Ihr den reinen Sieg
> Mit Blute nicht geschändet.
>
> (2912-13)

Fürst gives away his own failure to grasp what has happened to Tell in the process of the uprising and his own fear of moral guilt.

In 'On the Irony of Sophocles' Thirlwall indicates how a sense of irony arises when two parties contend an issue, both convinced of the justice of their cause:

> Here the irony lies not in the demeanour of the judge but is deeply seated in the case itself ... the liveliest interest arises when by inevitable circumstances characters, motives, and principles are brought into hostile collision, in which good and evil are so inextricably blended on each side, that we are compelled to give an equal share of our sympathy to each, while we perceive that no earthly power can reconcile them.[51]

This description corresponds well to the situation of Tell and Parricida. It is a different kind of irony from that distance maintained by the dramatist from the action, though the dramatist's aloofness brings it fully to light. It is rather the irony of two opposing and limited views of the same issue which are opposing not merely because each contender cannot see the whole story but because the issue is itself so complex that it seems to go beyond the powers of human judgement. Such is the issue of the comparative guilt and innocence of Tell and Parricida. There can be no simple question of right or wrong in this scene, which makes clear the ambiguity of human action. In the Parricida scene we see Schiller the historian surveying the forces that have put these two men in their present position and the moral aspects of each man's actions. History seems to have vindicated one rather than the other but the historian, who is not satisfied merely with legend, has to leave the issue finally undecided.

In spite of this cast of irony, in fact to some extent as a result of it, the dramatist is not unsympathetic to his characters. He portrays the confederates and Tell as trying to act morally and responsibly in spite of their limitations. His own uncritical outlook, but more particularly his particular position among his countrymen has saved Tell from becoming a tragic figure but Demetrius may be seen to act as a counterpart to him, so indicating the re-emergence of Schiller's tragic vision of the individual's involvement in the movement of history.

CHAPTER 7

DEMETRIUS

It has become usual to begin any piece of work on *Demetrius* with
the observation that this fragment has produced a great confusion
of interpretations and to quote Emil Staiger, who said, 'Die
Verwirrung [der Schiller-Forschung] erreicht ihren Gipfel in den
Interpretationen des *Demetrius*.'[1] The fact that attempts at interpretation often begin in this way points to the fact that *Demetrius*
remains a work fraught with obvious critical problems, most of
them insoluble. *Demetrius* is a fragment, and in spite of the large
quantity of documents relating to it which Schiller left, there is very
little which can safely be said about the work as a whole. Interpretations tend rather, as Fritz Martini suggests, to spring more
from the critics' pre-established view of Schiller than from the
limited amount of text and the varying indications of the sketches
and notes: '[Die Schwierigkeiten] haben sich in der Geschichte der
kontroversen Demetrius-Deutungen niedergeschlagen, die wie ein
Konzentrat der Geschichte des Schiller-Verständnisses und der
Geschichte der literaturwissenschaftlichen Methoden erscheinen.'[2]
This is also true, of course, of attempts at interpretation of any of
Schiller's dramas and virtually unavoidable when one is dealing
with a fragment.

Debate centres on a particular issue—whether *Demetrius* marks a
new departure in Schiller's tragic drama, whether its tragic vision is
the same as that of the other dramas, or whether we cannot possibly
tell from the material available.[3] The idealistic interpretation,
represented by Cysarz,[4] lays stress on Demetrius as a typical
Schillerian hero, typical in that he is pure and noble but becomes
fatally involved in the world of politics. The realist approach
stresses the apparent new departure by Schiller in *Demetrius*, in
his presentation of a hero whose idealism is defeated and whose
heart, far from being an authentic guide, misleads him. Fricke[5]
puts forward this argument and points to the Kleistian features of
the play, with its exploitation of misleading appearances. Kurt

May[6] surveys both of these points of view and comes to the conclusion that neither can be maintained with any certainty or even reasonable confidence, a view supported later by Fowler.[7] The same is true of the view of history conveyed by the play. The idealist approach is to suggest that in the *schöne Seele* Romanow there is a ray of hope at the end. The realist approach is to stress Schiller's introduction in his *Szenar* of another potential usurper in the final scene, who 'kann die Tragödie schließen, indem er in eine neue Reihe von Stürmen hinein blicken läßt' (NA 11, 226), so that history repeats itself.[8] Such problems are clearly insoluble and to take up a definite standpoint requires a selective reading of Schiller's notes, which inevitably ignores contrary indications. The purpose, therefore, of this short chapter on *Demetrius* is not to offer any new contributions to these particular controversies, but rather to look primarily at the scenes which stand virtually completed and to see how far they reflect the preoccupations and method which have emerged in the course of the previous chapters.

Schiller's choice of and approach to the Demetrius material is illuminated to some extent if we look at his interest in, and final rejection of, the Warbeck plan. Schiller first came upon the Warbeck material while at work on *Maria Stuart*. He notes to Goethe how he thinks the material could be used:

Nun ist zwar von der Geschichte selbst so gut als gar nichts zu brauchen, aber die Situation im Ganzen ist sehr fruchtbar, und die beiden Figuren des Betrügers und der Herzogin von York können zur Grundlage einer tragischen Handlung dienen, welche mit völliger Freiheit erfunden werden müßte.

(J6, 1491)

He does not pursue the plan immediately, however, and though some scenes were written and considerable plans made, Warbeck was finally superseded by *Demetrius*. Schiller might, of course, have returned to it, if he had lived, but it seems more likely that he found the material unsatisfactory, and though simpler than *Demetrius*, it did not have the same scope or topical interest.[9] In the *Szenar* to *Demetrius*, which he composed between November 1804 and March 1805, there is a comparison of the two dramatic plans. Schiller lists the advantages and drawbacks in each case. Against *Warbeck* are the following:

1. Betrug als Basis repugniert.
2. Margaretha hat keine Gunst und bedeutet doch viel.

3. Stoff hat Unwahrscheinliches und schwer zu motivierendes.
4. Lücken im Plan.
5. Kein rechter Schluß.
6. Keine rechte Handlung.   (NA 11, 179)

Schiller seems, therefore, to have had very fundamental difficulties with the Warbeck material, especially in view of points 1, 5, and 6.

The problems he sees in the Demetrius material are largely of a different order:

1. Daß es eine Staatsaction ist[.]
2. Daß es abentheuerlich und unglaublich ist.
3. Daß es fremd und ausländisch ist.
4. Die Menge u. Zerstreuung der Personen schadet dem Intereße.
5. Die Größe und der Umfang, daß es kaum zu übersehen.
6. Die Schwierigkeiten es zu executieren auf den Theatern.
7. Die Unregelmäßigkeit in Absicht auf Zeit und Ort[.]
8. Die Größe der Arbeit.

                                                    (NA 11, 179)

These problems, concerned with the scope of the work and its political nature, are very similar to those which Schiller had when planning his *Wallenstein*: 'Es ist im Grund eine Staatsaction und hat, in Rücksicht auf den poetischen Gebrauch, alle Unarten an sich, die eine politische Handlung nur haben kann, ein unsichtbares abstractes Objekt, *kleine* und *viele* Mittel, zerstreute Handlungen, einen furchtsamen Schritt ...' (J5, 1134). Schiller obviously was in the process of attempting a different solution to some of these problems in *Demetrius* from his solution in *Wallenstein*. *Demetrius*, for example, has more of an epic quality, with movement from place to place and an extended time-scale. However, the problems he faced with *Demetrius* were essentially problems he had faced and solved before. We shall, of course, never know whether *Demetrius* would, like *Wallenstein*, eventually have burst the confines of a five-act drama.

The advantages which Schiller sees in the material are the following:

1. Die Größe des Vorwurfs und des Ziels.
2. Das Interesse der Hauptperson[.]
3. Viele glänzende dramatische Situationen.
4. Beziehung auf Rußland.
5. Der neue Boden auf dem es spielt.
6. Daß das meiste daran schon erfunden ist.

7. Daß es ganz Handlung ist[.]
8. Daß es Viel für die Augen hat.

(NA 11, 179)

Point 7, 'Daß es ganz Handlung ist', stands in implied contrast to what Schiller then puts as a disadvantage of the Warbeck plan, where there was 'keine rechte Handlung'. Schiller suggests that of the two plans *Demetrius* has been developed into a full dramatic plot, where there is a 'Kette von Begebenheiten', to use the term of the *Rheinische Thalia* preface to *Don Carlos* (NA 4, 217). The theatrical considerations in all of these lists are evident, but are especially clear above. *Demetrius* is to be a visually exciting play (8) with gripping encounters (3) played out in a setting which is new to the audience (4/5). (Point 5 would seem to be in contradiction to one of the disadvantages of the material, number 3 'Daß es fremd und ausländisch ist'. Schiller's audience was already used to a variety of foreign settings—Spain, France, England—and it is hard to see how the setting of *Demetrius* would seem more foreign than others.)

Like so many of the documents which complement the limited text of *Demetrius*, these remarks can carry only limited weight. What they do indicate is why the Demetrius plan appealed more at that moment to Schiller than the Warbeck plan and possibly which compositional difficulties he felt he could overcome and which he felt he could not.

If we turn to the place of the *Demetrius* fragment in Schiller's dramatic work it is clear that Schiller still maintained his interest in the role of the individual in the movement of history. There are recent critics who stress Schiller's move after *Wallenstein* away from history towards the idyll, a development culminating in *Wilhelm Tell*. A certain corrective to this view must result from a consideration of *Demetrius*, in which Schiller presents the phenomenon of a man whose finest qualities are exploited for political ends by those who want to profit from the changing times. One of the reasons why some critics have seen a realistic turn in *Demetrius* is that in this play the hero himself cannot trust his own heart.[10] He may be upright but his perception of himself is still false. In these circumstances there can, it is claimed, be no scope for sublime choice. Again, this is a matter for speculation but the fact that this view finds support suggests strongly how far Schiller was concerned with the way in which the individual can be trapped and manipulated

in the world of politics. Indeed Schiller's first drafts of the play
were the Sambor scenes, where Demetrius (Grischka) is 'discovered'.
Despite their dramatic effectiveness as an opening, Schiller rejected
them in favour of the Reichstag opening, where Demetrius appears
immediately as a political figure.

Thematically, *Demetrius* indicates the enduring fascination for
Schiller of the usurper in history and his interest in the question
of legitimacy of government. Comparisons with *Wallenstein* spring
immediately to mind. *Demetrius* is a play where role-playing by the
characters is an important element, as it was in *Wallenstein* also.
This aspect of *Demetrius* has been explored by Kommerell. In his
essay 'Schiller als Psychologe'[11] he notes how in *Demetrius* the role
and the one who plays it are one. Demetrius believes himself to be
the Czarovich and behaves with the dignity and nobility which he
feels befit that calling. In *Wallenstein*, by contrast, the hero tries
out various roles, but in the end only one, that of the traitor, is
forced on him. In the case of Demetrius, his role is given him by
the combination of historical forces which bring him to prominence,
and while he still believes in its authenticity, there is no discrepancy
between his role and himself. He becomes it completely. In this is
illustrated again that view of personality and action which also
emerges from *Wallenstein*, namely that what a man seems to be
affects what he is, so that one cannot speak of people having surface
roles and true selves. They and their roles become indistinguishable.
Just as we cannot talk about the real Wallenstein, we cannot talk
about the real Demetrius. His role is laid on him by historical
forces beyond his control and he becomes it.

While, however, Demetrius guilelessly plays the role into which
he has been manipulated, he is watched by others who are conscious of their own public role and that of Demetrius. While he acts
out his role, Marina, and perhaps Odowalsky, observe him. When
we see Demetrius at the Reichstag we are aware of no conscious
dissembling on his part. When Marina and Odowalsky confer
together, however, we experience a change of perspective. We as
the audience are drawn into Marina's observation of Demetrius as
one playing a part. This is a technique which alerts us as the audience
to the fact that Demetrius is an unintentional usurper. We see his
public performance and then look at it through the eyes of those
whose advantage Demetrius is unconsciously promoting. Marina
regards him as with superior insight when she says:

Mag er
Der Götterstimme folgen, die ihn treibt,
Er glaub an sich, so glaubt ihm auch die Welt ...
(639-41)

Demetrius inevitably, in spite of his nobility, takes on the appearance of a pawn in the political game. So, if *Wallenstein* showed
how a man discovers himself at the mercy of the ambiguous appearances he has given, as a result of his attempt to maintain his
freedom, *Demetrius* shows how a man can be manipulated into a
role without being aware of it: 'Es ist wohl der einzige Fall, daß
Schiller diesen unheimlichen Vorgang, der dem Wunsch des
Menschen, sich als seine eigene Bedingung zu verstehen, so un-
bequem ist—den Vorgang, wie *man gemacht wird*, von Augenblick
zu Augenblick zerlegt und abgeschildert hat.'[12]

Demetrius plays his role in the first act and is watched by Marina
as from a superior standpoint. As we look at him through her eyes,
we as the audience experience a certain sense of distance as we
perceive the possibility of his being manipulated. This effect is a
form of dramatic irony, though less explicit than what is usually
understood by the term. We experience through the sharing of
Marina's standpoint with regard to Demetrius that same sense of
greater insight and panoramic vision which is one of the characteristics of the operation of irony in drama. This is not to say that
Demetrius is no more than a pawn. In the first act Schiller invests
him with dignity, which gives him an appearance of freedom and a
certain strength. He is not, however, any more than Wallenstein,
'der Täter seiner Taten'.

Comparisons with *Wallenstein* are instructive for another reason.
Just as it is impossible, almost irrelevant, to decide whether Wallenstein is guilty or not, so it is with Demetrius. Considerable critical
attention has been devoted to Demetrius himself as a character and
critics have attempted to decide whether Demetrius is a self-
deceiver[13] and therefore in some sense to blame for his delusion.
This is another unanswerable question, and Fritz Martini[14] has
recently pointed away from concern with Demetrius as a 'character'
to his position in the movement of events.

An explicit statement linking *Demetrius* in some sense with *Die
Jungfrau von Orleans* is made in Schiller's letter to Körner of 25
April 1805, some two weeks before his death: 'Der Stoff ist historisch
und so wie ich ihn nehme, hat er volle tragische Größe und könnte

in gewissem Sinne das Gegenstück zu der Jungfrau v. Orleans heißen, ob er gleich in allen Theilen davon verschieden ist' (J7, 2052). The connection with *Die Jungfrau von Orleans* occurred to Schiller at at least one other point during composition, where in the 'Szenar' he likens Boris's despair at Demetrius' uprising to that of Talbot. With reference to the letter to Körner (above), May says that Schiller's words are so qualified and conditional as to efface the comparison as soon as it is made.[15] While it is unwise to develop full interpretations on this basis, it is nevertheless evident that there are points of contact between these two dramas. Interestingly, these points of contact spring from the nature of the two plays as historical drama, an aspect of *Die Jungfrau von Orleans* which has been somewhat neglected, and yet one which, to judge by these comments by Schiller on the two plays, the dramatist himself fully recognized and acknowledged. Both plays deal with a hitherto unknown person who at a specific historical moment is called upon to play a public role, fired by a sense of his/her absolute right to play that role. The use of the word 'Götterstimme', in connection with the driving force in either person's life, provides an immediate link, though the word is employed with different connotations in either case. Johanna says to Montgomery, 'mich treibt die Götterstimme, nicht/Eignes Gelüsten' (1660-1); Marina says of Demetrius, 'Mag er/Der Götterstimme folgen, die ihn treibt' (639-40). Of the sense in which one play is 'ein Gegenstück' to the other, Szondi says it is 'weil die Götterstimme, die in beiden Werken einen Menschen aus der Unschuld der Natur in die Wirren der Geschichte und in den Untergang stößt, Jeanne d'Arc zur Märtyrerin macht, Demetrius aber zum Betrüger und Despoten.'[16] This is not entirely correct, however. Johanna leaves her country idyll to take up arms. Demetrius, however, is not called out of an idyllic setting. He is about to be executed, albeit perhaps unjustly, and Szondi himself in the same essay points out the irony that Demetrius' rescue from execution is in fact the first step towards his eventual destruction— 'Rettung und Vernichtung (sind) tragisch verbunden'.[17] Whereas Johanna's 'Götterstimme', or at least her belief in it and dedication to it, is finally vindicated, Demetrius' is found to be false, and instead of leading his country to victory, he has plunged it into renewed chaos. (Both Demetrius and Johanna share a certain political *naïveté*.)

The other reference to *Die Jungfrau von Orleans* in connection with *Demetrius* is the comparison in the 'Szenar' of Boris's position with that of Talbot. Here we can form only very limited conclusions, since there is no actual text for these scenes. Boris is described as a man who can be implacable towards those whom he perceives as enemies to himself, but essentially he is an able and just ruler, 'ein schätzbarer Fürst und ein wahrer Vater des Volks' (NA 11, 211). He has come to power through a crime but has distinguished himself as a ruler. He is enraged to think that a usurper, whom he himself has brought to life by disposing of the real Dmitri, is going to bring to nothing his efforts as a ruler. To the Patriarch he says, 'Muß ich durch dieses Gaukelspiel untergehen, muß ich wirklich?' (NA 11, 210). In this sense he is close to Talbot: 'Es ist etwas incalculables, göttliches, woran sein Muth und seine Klugheitsmittel erliegen. (Talbots Situation in der Johanna).' Both Boris and Talbot have to suffer the destruction of what they consider to be their life's work by the intervention of an extraordinary force, the legitimacy of which they deny. As dramatic characters they have it in common that they are antagonists who preserve their nobility. Though both defeated they maintain their integrity. In the case of *Die Jungfrau von Orleans* we have seen how Talbot's vision of life and his reaction to Johanna modify our view of her. Perhaps Schiller had something comparable in mind in his conception of Boris's role, but this again is a matter for speculation.

Although one ends tragically and the other happily, there are salient parallels to be drawn between *Demetrius* and *Wilhelm Tell*. Indeed, in the final analysis, these parallels are perhaps more telling than the more obvious ones with *Wallenstein* or *Die Jungfrau von Orleans*. The three plays *Die Jungfrau von Orleans*, *Wilhelm Tell*, and *Demetrius* have it in common that they all portray the arrival on the historical scene of a previously unknown person. In the case of Johanna, her insight into her calling, its origin and its historical roots are not examined. She remains an extraordinary phenomenon. This is not so with Demetrius and Tell. They are swept to prominence by historical forces which are beyond their control, as part of a process which becomes apparent to the audience, though not to the participants in the action. Both plays deal with the way in which a man is forced into a role which has been designed for him. In *Wilhelm Tell* Schiller shows how a number of factors join together at a particular moment to force a man into the role of liberator of his country. The coincidence of these factors is largely fortuitous. Stauffacher, the popular historian, steers the Swiss people into a

particular interpretation of events, but they have already unconsciously chosen Tell to be their hero. The murder of the Emperor,
the event which actually secures Swiss freedom, coincides by pure
chance with Tell's murder of Geßler, but is quickly assimilated into
the popular interpretation of events. Tell himself is not alive to the
fact that he is being wrongly elevated to the role of national hero.
The final tableau suggests that he accepts it as his natural position,
and the role in which his compatriots wish to see him. What was in
Wilhelm Tell a series of happy coincidences, interpreted in a spirit
of unconscious opportunism, becomes in *Demetrius* conscious
manipulation and exploitation, both of the hero himself, and of the
historical moment. This is evident in the first act of the play, in
which we discover the various vested interests behind Demetrius'
rise. Marina is concerned for her own advancement and Odowalsky
supports her for purely private reasons, rather than from conviction
about the pretender's claim. Others join the cause because they
seek booty from Russia. The King, Sigismund, claims to be moved
by Demetrius' story (483-7) but according to Marina (664-76) he
hopes only to gain more control over the nobility by encouraging
Marina's powerful father to waste his strength in Russia. The
various reasons for the support given to Demetrius in Act I are
joined in Act II by Marfa's desire for revenge and her willingness
to foster belief in the pretender as a way of crushing Boris:

> wär er auch nicht meines Herzens Sohn,
> Er soll der Sohn doch meiner Rache seyn:
>
> (1162-3)

By a reverse process, Demetrius' loss of confidence when the
deception is revealed to him accounts only in part for his later
downfall. Rather he is disabused at the very moment when those
forces which brought him to prominence are ready again to break
up. He depends on Polish support, which alienates the Russians.
Odowalsky, in protection of Marina's interests, encourages his
unpopularity with the Russians, while Marfa has had her revenge
and no longer needs Demetrius. So the process of disillusionment
and deterioration into a despot is matched by the dissolution of the
forces which brought Demetrius to power: 'im Geschick der
Herrscher Demetrius und Boris zeichnet sich die Situation der Zeit
ab, sie erhält aus ihnen ihre Kennzeichen. Das Geschick dieser
Usurpatoren konnte sich nur in dieser Zeit vollziehen und nur sie
konnte beide hervorbringen.'[18]

CONCLUSION

Schiller's change to historical drama with *Don Carlos* marks the beginning of a vital transition in his method of presenting character and action. His earlier method of character portrayal was an exploration of the contradictions within certain types of personality. Such a personality is Fiesco. That play cannot, however, properly speaking be considered a historical drama because it does not correspond to an authentic political world. The main character is able to manipulate others round him because there is essentially very little interaction between them. In *Don Carlos* Schiller was concerned in the later stages of his conception of the play to present the clash of ideologies at a crucial moment in history, as well as to present the relationships within a ruling family. In the course of composition, more by intuition than by conscious design, Schiller moves towards a portrayal of the interaction of character and event. The political world in *Don Carlos* becomes a world where characters act less from pre-established personality and more as a response to the pressures of the situation. So the ambiguity which was previously inherent in the idealist personality becomes the ambiguity of the world of action itself.

Don Carlos showed to Schiller his need to come to terms both with the nature of history and with the nature of the drama if he was going to execute a play according to his conception of it. Up to *Don Carlos* Schiller had been able to create dramas in a spontaneous way. However, he found with *Don Carlos* that the dramatic form he had chosen for it—the static tableau form—could not satisfactorily be adapted to his new conception of the subject matter. The main period of historical writing, from 1787 to 1792, gave Schiller scope for experimenting with the portrayal of historical figures and for discovering how history and historical drama are related to each other. In the *Abfall der Niederlande*, as in *Don Carlos*, Schiller discovered that historical movement cannot adequately be described in terms of actions proceeding from fixed personalities. Rather he found that he had to abandon that approach and admit to a far greater complexity in the material than he had at first acknowledged. The study of history made Schiller aware of the extreme dependence of historical figures on circumstances beyond their control and on the movement of events which pushes them to prominence and then brings about their downfall. The discipline of historical writing, as well as supplementing what he felt to be his incomplete general education, fostered Schiller's growth towards greater objectivity of judgement and more particularly of presentation. This quest for greater objectivity manifests itself also in the theoretical writings and in the later dramas. Although the *Geschichte des Dreißigjährigen Kriegs* still has a Protestant bias, and while Schiller idealizes Gustavus Adolphus while exaggerating the villainy of Tilly, Schiller no longer finds in history a confirmation of his preconceptions and he is open to reversing his judgements by the end of the work. It was in developing his ability to treat material in a more distanced way that Schiller could develop his accompanying perception of the ambiguity of history and politics and express this later in the drama.

By sharpening his perception of the dependence of historical characters on their circumstances, the study of history made Schiller move in *Wallenstein* even more decisively away from his early drama in his presentation of character. In *Wallenstein* Schiller shows that he has turned away from the idea that certain personalities are inherently tragic. Indeed, Schiller seems to approach the play without any image of Wallenstein as a character in mind. What the central figure intrinsically is, is irretrievably obscured by the masks which he adopts and by what later, through the pressure of circumstances, he is forced to do and to say. Actions, therefore, can no longer be taken to proceed from a certain personality. This is characteristic of Schiller's conception of the political world, which is most fully articulated in *Wallenstein* and *Maria Stuart*. This representation of how personality and action are related is the product also of Schiller's emphasis on tragic situation, as opposed to tragic character. It is in the historical circumstances themselves that the characters find themselves trapped, rather than in the implications of their own personalities as realized in action. This is not to say that they are victims, for they find decision and assertion of the will thrust upon them, and it is in the decisions and in the way that they bear the consequences of those decisions that they appear tragic. This is true of Maria and Wallenstein and, in part, of Elisabeth.

In spite of the fact that Schiller sees into the extreme dependence of historical figures on their circumstances, he is nevertheless able to present in the drama the phenomenon of greatness. It is not historical greatness, however, but human greatness, which occupies him in *Wallenstein* and *Maria Stuart*. The reverse is the case in *Die Jungfrau von Orleans* and *Wilhelm Tell*. After *Maria Stuart* Schiller turns to the phenomenon of folk or popular heroes, before returning to the political world of *Demetrius*. He shows in Johanna and Tell how certain people are brought to prominence by the circumstances of the time from the previous obscurity of their lives. This is particularly true of Tell, who never wished to be anything other than a private individual; but by a historical accident he becomes a folk hero, in spite of the limited insight he has into the circumstances which have brought this about.

Wallenstein and *Maria Stuart* present the dilemmas of characters who are more than conscious of the problems of political action and involvement. In *Die Jungfrau von Orleans* and *Wilhelm Tell* Schiller examines the phenomenon of characters who fulfil a public role on the stage of history but are not very self-aware. While, as we noted, Schiller avoids the political world to a great extent in *Die Jungfrau von Orleans*, he nevertheless presents the problems surrounding commitment to a political cause. In Johanna, the dawn of self-awareness makes her conscious of that problematic side to commitment and to the extraordinary nature of her own position. In *Wilhelm Tell* the lack of self-awareness of the hero prevents him from having any potentially tragic or destructive insight into his guilt as a murderer and into the ambiguity of his position as supposed national liberator. *Demetrius*, though largely a matter for speculation, may be seen as a counterpart to *Wilhelm Tell*, in so far as the theme of self-awareness and disillusionment is worked out in the realm of power politics, this time with a tragic outcome.

A corollary to Schiller's interest in presenting characters within the political and historical world is his concentration on role. One could almost say that Schiller is more interested in role than in personality, personality being elusive and emerging, as in the case of Maria Stuart, only when the character is stepping outside history, or, in the case of Tell, where a character remains himself oblivious to the public sphere of action and behaves always essentially as a private individual. The matter of role is closely linked to the matter of self-awareness. All characters who are active on the stage of history and politics have public roles. They have certain functions to fulfil as monarchs or generals. Such roles are forced upon them in some instances, and characters such as Elisabeth are conscious of the public nature of such roles and the limitations of unequivocal appearances.

Yet within these public roles is another sort of role-playing, which is the manipulation of role by the person himself or by others. This is the adoption of roles as masks to suit the purposes of the person concerned. Wallenstein and Elisabeth fear to be seen as what they are because they know that they lose their freedom of action by doing so. This consciousness of role is not felt by Johanna before her crisis or by Tell. They both feel themselves committed to certain types of action, but they do not experience a sense of themselves as public figures whose private desires are opposed to the public function they fulfil. They are as they seem. Yet Johanna does have a political role, and she is manipulated by others, though she tries to resist this. She rejects the attempts of the court to fit her into what they regard as a more normal existence, being conscious only of her private sense of mission. Her self-doubt and guilt coincide with apparent fulfilment of her mission and with her consequent political expendability and so she can be banished. Her sense of personal renewal coincides with her renewed political usefulness as a leader in the new national crisis, but she never fully grasps this sequence of events. Tell himself is also unaware of having a public role, but the different strands of action of the play show how in spite of himself circumstances conspire to force him to prominence, how he is unconsciously manipulated by his community into the role which it has chosen for him.

All of Schiller's later historical dramas are historical in different ways. The sense of objective distance between himself and the material—a quality lacking in the early drama and in part provided by the study of history—is, however, significantly present in all of the later historical plays. It is, in fact, through this ability to hold himself aloof from the play that Schiller exhibits his skill as a historical dramatist—his technique of juxtaposing differing views of the action, letting the characters speak for themselves and not for him and allowing the audience to enjoy a superior standpoint and to judge the action as from above. Differing moral approaches (Max's and Octavio's, Burleigh's and Shrewsbury's, Maria's and

Elisabeth's, Posa's and Philipp's, even Talbot's and Johanna's) emerge from the plays and each is allowed its own validity. In this way Schiller is able to take the historical and political world and make it transparent through art. Schiller exploits the theatrical experience of the play which the audience enjoys. He portrays a world of human involvements through a stylized and compressed form of drama. While the vividness with which these human involvements are enacted draws the audience sympathetically into the play, the stylizing techniques act as a counterbalance to this, reminding the audience of the nature of the play as an artefact. The technique of juxtaposition increases the audience's sense of standing outside and above the action, viewing it as a whole. Through this interplay of involvement and detachment Schiller brings to light the complexity of the historical world.

NOTES

LIST OF ABBREVIATIONS

DU   *Der Deutschunterricht*
DVjs   *Deutsche Vierteljahrsschrift für Literaturwissenschaft und Geistesgeschichte*
EG   *Etudes Germaniques*
GLL   *German Life and Letters*
GQ   *German Quarterly*
GR   *Germanic Review*
GRM   *Germanisch-Romanische Monatsschrift*
Jahrbuch   *Jahrbuch der Deutschen Schillergesellschaft*
JEGP   *Journal of English and Germanic Philology*
MLQ   *Modern Language Quarterly*
MLR   *Modern Language Review*
PEGS   *Publications of the English Goethe Society*
Reden 1955 *Schiller. Reden im Gedenkjahr 1955*, ed. B. Zeller (Deutsche Schillergesellschaft), Stuttgart, 1955
Reden 1959 *Schiller. Reden im Gedenkjahr 1959*, ed. B. Zeller, Stuttgart, 1961

INTRODUCTION

1. K. Berger, *Schiller: Sein Leben und seine Werke*, 2 vols., Berlin, 1890; L. Bellermann, *Schillers Dramen. Beiträge zu ihrem Verständnis*, 3 vols., Berlin, 1908; J. Minor, *Schiller. Sein Leben und seine Werke*, 2 vols., Berlin, 1890.
2. In *DU* 12 (1960), 91-118.
3. Ibid. 91.
4. G. Sautermeister, *'Maria Stuart'*, in *Schillers Dramen. Neue Interpretationen*, ed. W. Hinderer, Stuttgart, 1979, p. 195.
5. G. Storz, *Der Dichter Friedrich Schiller*, Stuttgart, 1959, p. 14.
6. K. May, *Friedrich Schiller: Idee und Wirklichkeit im Drama*, Göttingen, 1946.
7. See p. 44.
8. In *Jahrbuch* 3 (1959), 34-70.
9. Ibid. 45.
10. Frankfurt a.M., 1934.
11. In *Geist und Buchstabe der Dichtung*, Frankfurt a.M., 1942, pp. 132-99.
12. Ibid., p. 142.
13. Oxford, 1954.
14. In *Jahrbuch* 4 (1960), 2-41.
15. In *Reden 1955*, pp. 192-213.

16. See p. 16, and Chapter 1, n. 7.
17. *Friedrich Schiller. Medicine, Psychology and Literature*, Oxford, 1978, especially pp. 314-38.
18. See Chapter 2, pp. 42-4, 59 and notes 2, 6, 12, 15, 16.
19. For such views, see Chapter 2, pp. 36 f.; also Chapter 4, p. 106 and n. 7; W. Witte, introduction to *Maria Stuart*, London, 1965, p. xxxi.
20. U. Wertheim, *Schillers 'Fiesko' und 'Don Karlos'. Zu Problemen des historischen Stoffes*, Weimar, 1958, pp. 10 f.
21. Ibid., pp. 106 f.
22. *Historical Drama. The Relation of Literature and Reality*, Chicago and London, 1975.
23. Ibid., p. 133.
24. Ibid., p. 37.
25. Ibid., p. 5.

CHAPTER 1

1. F. M. Fowler, 'Schiller's *Fiesco* Re-Examined', *PEGS* 40 (1970), 1-29.
2. K. May, *Friedrich Schiller: Idee und Wirklichkeit*, pp. 33 f.
3. I. A. Graham, *Schiller's Drama: Talent and Integrity*, London, 1974, pp. 9 f.
4. G. Storz, *Das Drama Friedrich Schillers*, Frankfurt a.M., 1938, p. 87.
5. U. Wertheim, *Schillers 'Fiesko' und 'Don Karlos'*, p. 107.
6. P. Böckmann, 'Politik und Dichtung', pp. 201 f.
7. The *Thalia* version and the 1787 version are in NA 6; the Hamburger and Rigaer Bühnenfassungen and the final approved version of 1805 are in NA 7(1). The *Thalia* scenes are also printed in *Schillers Don Karlos. Edition der ursprünglichen Fassung und entstehungs-geschichtlicher Kommentar von Paul Böckmann* (Stuttgart, 1974). Böckmann gives the continuation of the play from Act III, 7 in the 1787 'Buchfassung', along with Act I of the 1787 version, with notes on variations between it and the *Rheinische Thalia* version. Line references in this chapter correspond to the final approved version of 1805.
8. For changes between the 1787 and 1805 versions see the discussion of Philipp's role on pp. 26 f.
9. *Historical Drama*, p. 124.
10. *Don Carlos*, ed. H. B. Garland, London (Harrap), 1949, p. xxi. Garland sees in this 'proof of the dualism which is the play's chief defect'.
11. *Schillers Don Karlos*, p. 438. Gerhard Storz in his essay, 'Der Bauer-bacher Plan zum *Don Carlos*', *Jahrbuch* 8 (1964), 112-29, also states that Schiller was aware of the political dimension of the action at this stage but was not anxious to develop it (pp. 117 f).
12. *Schillers Don Karlos*, p. 577.

13. Posa's rise to prominence may be the result of Schiller's increased awareness of Philipp's historical role and tragic potential. For this, see U. Wertheim, pp. 169 f., and G. Orton, *Schiller: Don Carlos, Studies in German Literature 8*, London, 1967, pp. 8 f.

14. *GR* 26 (1951), 196-214.

15. *Schillers Leben und Werke*, Berlin, 1865, p. 68.

16. *Schiller und seine Zeitgenossen*, Leipzig, 1859, p. 103.

17. R. Gottschall, 'Schillers Ideale, die Ideale des deutschen Volks', in *Schiller-Reden, nebst Goethes Epilog*, Ulm 1905, pp. 114-19 (p. 119).

18. Berger (see Introduction, n. 1), p. 519; Bellermann suggests that the play can be appreciated only by those who accept the idealism of Posa and Carlos (II, 256).

19. G. Steiner, *The Death of Tragedy*, London, 1961, pp. 176, 179 f.

20. O. Seidlin, 'Schiller, Poet of Politics', in *A Schiller Symposium*, ed. L. Willson, Austin, 1960, pp. 29-48 (p. 34).

21. M. Kommerell, *Der Dichter als Führer in der deutschen Klassik*, Berlin, 1928, p. 210.

22. 'Friedrich Schiller's Marquis Posa' (n. 14).

23. *Schiller: Don Carlos* (n. 13).

24. 'In Defense of Marquis Posa', *GR* 36 (1961), 205-20.

25. Wertheim, pp. 182 f.

26. Orton, p. 20.

27. *Schillers Don Karlos*, pp. 481 f.

28. Ebstein, p. 215.

29. *Schillers Don Karlos*, pp. 379 f.

30. Ibid., pp. 385 f.

31. *Das Theater des Herrn Diderot*, transl. G. E. Lessing, in *Werke* (Hempelsche Ausgabe), Elfter Teil, p. 280.

32. Garland, *Don Carlos*, p. xxi.

33. P. Szondi, '*Tableau* und *coup de théâtre*' in *Lektüren und Lektionen*, Frankfurt a.M., 1973, pp. 13-36 (pp. 21 f).

34. Ibid., p. 23.

35. *Wallensteins Tod*, line 161.

36. In *Schiller*, from *Selected Essays*, ed. M. Gilbert, Oxford, 1955, p. 23 (my italics).

37. Philipp is made to know it too. Schiller brings the defeat of the Armada forward in time by some twenty years, so that it coincides with the action of the play. So Philipp is aware of his declining power when he says, 'Die Welt/Ist noch auf einen Abend mein' (5082-3).

38. Although Schiller quotes these lines as though they were one speech, they are in fact drawn from various speeches made by Carlos in the final scene, lines 5310-13, 5320-1, 5313-17, 5294-8.

39. B. von Wiese, *Schiller*, Stuttgart, 1959, p. 273.

40. In 'The Dramatic Image', in *Tradition and Creation. Essays in honour of E. M. Wilkinson*, Leeds, 1978, pp. 63-76 (p. 71).

41. My italics.

CHAPTER 2

1. G. G. Gervinus, *Geschichte der deutschen Dichtung*, 5 vols., völlig umgearbeitete Auflage, Leipzig, 1871-4, vol. 5, p. 411.
2. J. Janssen, *Schiller als Historiker*, Freiburg, 1863.
3. K. Hoffmeister, *Schillers Leben, Geistesentwicklung und Werke im Zusammenhang*, 5 vols., Stuttgart, 1838-42, vol. 2, p. 200.
4. D. Regin, *Freedom and Dignity*, The Hague, 1965, p. 48.
5. See R. Fester, SA 13, p. XII.
6. K. Tomaschek, *Schiller in seinem Verhältnisse zur Wissenschaft*, Vienna, 1862, p. 4; Dewhurst and Reeves, pp. 37f.
7. A. Ward, *Book Production, Fiction and the German Reading Public 1740-1800*, Oxford, 1974, pp. 29-58.
8. *Schiller-Kommentar*, 2 vols., Munich, 1969, vol. 2, p. 39.
9. L. S. Mercier, *Portrait de Philippe II, Roi d'Espagne*, Amsterdam, 1785, pp. v f.
10. *Der Dichter Friedrich Schiller*, p. 156.
11. See Regin, pp. 49 f.
12. *Friedrich Schiller (1759-1805)* : *The Poet as Historian*, Keele, 1966, pp. 5 f.
13. For surveys of historiography in the eighteenth century, see E. Fueter, *Geschichte der neueren Historiographie*, Munich, 1936, pp. 334-414; also J. W. Thompson and B. J. Holm, *A History of Historical Writing*, 2 vols., New York, 1942, vol. 2, pp. 3-131.
14. R. Buchwald, *Schiller*, 2 vols., Neue Ausgabe, Wiesbaden, 1954, vol. II, pp. 123 f; Regin, p. 65.
15. F. Überweg, *Schiller als Historiker und Philosoph*, ed. M. Brasch, Leipzig, 1884, p. 105.
16. Simon, p. 15.
17. e.g. Janssen, pp. 24 f., and Tomaschek, p. 76.
18. Überweg, p. 113.
19. Janssen, p. 63.
20. *Idee und Wirklichkeit im Drama*, p. 63.
21. 'Der amerikanische Unabhängigkeitskampf im Spiegel der zeitgenössischen deutschen Literatur', in U. Wertheim and E. Braemer, *Studien zur deutschen Klassik*, Berlin, 1960, pp. 71-114 (p. 113).
22. Janssen, p. 59.
23. Letter to Schiller, 2 Nov. 1788, in *Briefwechsel zwischen Schiller und Körner* (Von 1784 bis zum Tode Schillers), 4 vols., Stuttgart/Berlin, 1892, vol. 1, p. 276.
24. Janssen, p. 51.
25. See H. A. Walter, 'Die Stellungnahme Schillers zu Goethes *Egmont*'', in *GQ* 32 (1959), 330-40 (pp. 332, 334).
26. J. M. Ellis, 'The Vexed Question of Egmont's Political Judgement', in *Tradition and Creation* (see above, Chapter 1, n. 40), pp. 116-30 (p. 116).
27. In *Sturm und Drang: Kritische Schriften*, ed. E. Loewenthal, Heidelberg, 1949, p. 743.

28. Walter, p. 334.
29. Ellis, p. 116.
30. This point is discussed fully at the opening to Chapter 3, in connection with Schiller's stage version of *Egmont*.
31. Koopmann, *Schiller - Kommentar*, vol. 2, p. 20.
32. R. J. Collingwood, *The Idea of History*, London, 1946, pp. 104 f.
33. Regin, p. 59.
34. Ibid., pp. 63-7; K. H. Hahn, however, decisively rejects the idea that Herder's influence can be traced in this, or any of Schiller's lectures ('Schiller und die Geschichte', *Weimarer Beiträge* 16 (1970), 39-69).
35. Buchwald, vol. 2, p. 127.
36. The 1802 ed. is in SA 15, where there are full notes on Schiller's cuts.
37. See J3, 528.
38. Tomaschek, pp. 105-8.
39. Überweg, pp. 139 f.
40. Janssen, p. 117.
41. Überweg, p. 139.
42. May, p. 73.
43. In *Jahrbuch* 4 (1960), 98-109 (p. 104).

CHAPTER 3

1. In *Remains, Literary and Theological*, 3 vols., ed. J. S. Perowne, London, 1878, vol. 3, p. 9.
2. See D. C. Muecke, *Irony*, in *The Critical Idiom* 13, general editor J. D. Jump, London, 1970, pp. 21 f.
3. For concise treatments of this subject see G. P. Gooch, *Germany and the French Revolution*, London, 1920, pp. 208-29; J. Droz, *L'Allemagne et la Révolution Française*, Paris, 1949, pp. 172-81; M. Boucher, *La Révolution de 1789 vue par les écrivains allemands ses contemporains,* Paris, 1954, pp. 95-113.
4. Boucher, p. 104.
5. E. Genast, *Aus dem Tagebuch eines alten Schauspielers*, 2 vols., 2nd ed., Leipzig, 1862, vol. 1, pp. 112 f.
6. To Eckermann, 18 Jan. 1825, in J. P. Eckermann, *Gespräche mit Goethe in den letzten Jahren seines Lebens*, new ed., edited by F. Bergemann, Wiesbaden, 1955, p. 133.
7. A. Glück, *Schillers Wallenstein*, Munich, 1976, p. 145.
8. *Schiller*, Zürich, 1967, p. 39.
9. C. Heselhaus, 'Wallensteinisches Welttheater', *DU* 12/2 (1960), 42-71 (p. 43).
10. Ibid., p. 45.
11. Thirlwall, p. 9.
12. W. Witte, *Schiller*, Oxford, 1949, p. 148.
13. R. Marleyn, '*Wallenstein* and the structure of Schiller's tragedies', *GR* 32 (1957), 186-99 (p. 198).
14. e.g. E. L. Stahl, pp. 88 f.; May, pp. 99 f.
15. F. Strich, 'Schiller und Thomas Mann', *Neue Rundschau* 68 (1957), 63 f.

16. See Muecke, pp. 19 f. By mentioning the Schlegels I am not suggesting that Schiller's aloofness as a dramatist is to be considered a form of 'romantische Ironie'.
17. Thirlwall, p. 8.
18. Ibid., p. 9.
19. See G. G. Sedgewick, *Of Irony, Especially in Drama*, University of Toronto Studies: Philology and Literature Series 10, Toronto, 1935 (especially pp. 28-30).
20. *The Dry Mock*, Berkeley, 1948, p. 47.
21. D. Worcester, *The Art of Satire*, Cambridge, Mass., 1940, p. 141.
22. See E. Frenzel, *Stoffe der Weltliteratur*, Stuttgart, 1962, p. 657.
23. 'Schiller als Psychologe', p. 141.
24. Ibid., p. 142.
25. Letter to Schiller, 8 Dec. 1798, in *Der Briefwechsel zwischen Schiller und Goethe*, ed. E. Staiger, 2 vols., Frankfurt a.M., 1966, vol. 2, pp. 711 f.
26. Witte, p. 160.
27. G. A. Wells, 'Astrology in Schiller's *Wallenstein*', *JEGP* 68 (1969), 100-15.
28. 'Wallenstein: Sein und Zeit', in *Von Goethe zu Thomas Mann. Zwölf Versuche*, Göttingen, 1963, pp. 120-35 (p. 123).
29. In 'Politik und Dichtung'. Böckmann, like Seidlin, stresses Wallenstein's desire for control over events (pp. 211-13). His use of the words 'geschichtliche Konstellation' implies the link with astrology, though he does not make it explicit.
30. Glück, pp. 43 f.
31. W. Hinderer, '*Wallenstein*' in *Schillers Dramen. Neue Interpretationen*, pp. 142 f.
32. *Schiller als Gestalter des handelnden Menschen*, p. 18.
33. Glück, p. 45.
34. I. A. Graham, *Talent and Integrity*, pp. 125 f.
35. 'Politik und Dichtung', p. 211.
36. O. Ludwig, *Dramatische Studien*, selected by R. Petsch, Dresden, 1923, p. 177. Ludwig sees this and other appeals to 'Notwendigkeit' as Schiller's sop to a sentimental age and audience.
37. H. B. Garland, in *Schiller the Dramatic Writer*, Oxford, 1969, notes the use of stichomythia and tirade throughout this Act, which, he suggests, emphasize Buttler's choral function in it (pp. 172-6).
38. W. Silz, 'Chorus and Choral Function in Schiller', in *Schiller 1759/ 1959. Commemorative American Studies*, Urbana, 1959, pp. 147-70 (p. 164); also W. Silz, 'The Character and Function of Buttler in Schiller's *Wallenstein*', in *Studies in Germanic Languages and Literatures, in memory of F. O. Nolte*, ed. E. Hofacker and L. Dieckmann, Washington, 1963, pp. 77-91 (p. 83).
39. *Schiller als Gestalter des handelnden Menschen*, p. 15.
40. For a discussion of Schiller and the Baroque, see W. Rehm, 'Schiller und das Barockdrama', *Deutsche Vierteljahrsschrift* 19 (1941), 311-353.

41. See Garland, *Schiller the Dramatic Writer*, pp. 153-6.
42. Ibid., pp. 172 f.
43. 'Chorus and Choral Function', pp. 162 f.
44. R. D. Miller, *The Drama of Schiller*, Harrogate, 1966, p. 98.
45. C. Heselhaus, 'Die Nemesis-Tragödie: *Fiesco—Wallenstein—Demetrius*', *DU* 5 (1952), 40-59 (p. 52).
46. Ibid.
47. May, p. 164.
48. B. von Wiese, p. 677.
49. G. W. F. Hegel, 'Über Wallenstein', in *Sämtliche Werke* (Jubiläumsausgabe), ed. H. Glockner, Stuttgart, 1927-30, vol. 20, pp. 456-8.
50. Ibid., p. 456.
51. Ibid.

CHAPTER 4

1.   *The Death of Tragedy*, p. 181.
2.   *Schiller*, Bern, 1950, p. 363.
3.   *Das historische Drama in Deutschland*, Stuttgart, 1969, pp. 59 f.
4.   *Der Dichter Friedrich Schiller*, pp. 330-3. Storz, however, sees disadvantages in the form Schiller has chosen, especially in the character of Mortimer, whom he considers poorly integrated into the action.
5.   A. Beck, '*Maria Stuart*', in *Das deutsche Drama vom Barock bis zur Gegenwart. Interpretationen*, 2 vols., ed. B. von Wiese, vol. 1, pp. 305-21.
6.   Storz, pp. 331 f.; G. Sautermeister, '*Maria Stuart*', in *Schillers Dramen. Neue Interpretationen*, pp. 174-216 (p. 180 f.).
7.   H. Koopmann, *Friedrich Schiller*, Sammlung Metzler 51, vol. 2 (1794-1805), p. 47.
8.   See Storz, pp. 335 f.
9.   Sengle, pp. 59 f.
10. For a discussion of Schiller's presentation of rulership, see Stephen Spender, 'Schiller, Shakespeare and the Theme of Power', in *A Schiller Symposium*, pp. 51-61.
11. R. D. Miller, *The Drama of Schiller*, p. 102.
12. W. Witte, *Schiller*, pp. 165-72.
13. O. Ludwig, *Dramatische Studien*, p. 180.
14. Ibid.
15. Gerhard, p. 363.
16. Steiner, p. 182.
17. I. A. Graham, 'The Structure of the Personality in Schiller's Tragic Poetry', in *Bicentenary Lectures*, ed. F. Norman, London, 1960, pp. 104-44.
18. W. F. Mainland, *Schiller and the Changing Past*, London, 1957, pp. 57-86; see also Spender for a discussion of experimental government.

19. Sautermeister, pp. 176 f.
20. Ibid., p. 201.
21. See C. David, 'Le personnage de la reine Elisabeth dans la *Maria Stuart* de Schiller', in *Deutsche Beiträge zur geistigen Überlieferung* 4 (1961), 9-22 (esp. 11 f).
22. William Robertson, *History of Scotland during the Reigns of Queen Mary and James VI until his Accession to the Crown of England*, 2 vols., 6th ed., London, 1771, vol. 2, pp. 132-6.
23. e.g. G. A. Wells, 'Villainy and Guilt in Schiller's *Wallenstein* and *Maria Stuart*', in *Deutung und Bedeutung—Studies in German and Comparative Literature Presented to K. W. Maurer*, ed. B. Schludermann, The Hague, 1973, pp. 100-17; also J. L. Sammons, 'Mortimer's Conversion and Schiller's Allegiances', *JEGP* 72 (1973), 155-66, esp. p. 163.
24. *Schiller and the Changing Past*, p. 81.
25. e.g. Stahl, p. 109; Sammons, pp. 163 f.
26. For a discussion of the quarrel and the gradual dropping of formality, see W. Ross, 'Der Streit der Königinnen', *Wirkendes Wort* 5 (1954-5), 356-62.
27. Sammons, p. 163.
28. 'Schiller als Psychologe', *Geist und Buchstabe der Dichtung*, p. 177.
29. See J. B. Black, *The Reign of Elizabeth 1558-1603*, The Oxford History of England, 8, 2nd ed., Oxford, 1959, pp. 385 f.
30. Sammons, p. 166.
31. Sautermeister, p. 203.
32. 'Schiller: Poet of Politics', in *A Schiller Symposium*, p. 47.

CHAPTER 5

1. G. B. Shaw, *Saint Joan. A Chronicle Play in Six Scenes and an Epilogue*, London, 1924, p. xxviii.
2. Ibid.
3. W. C. Sellar and R. J. Yeatman, *1066 And All That*, London, 1930, pp. 46 f.
4. L. Bellermann, *Schiller*, Leipzig, Berlin, Vienna, 1901, pp. 217 f.
5. *The Drama of Schiller*, p. 118.
6. G. Storz, 'Die Jungfrau von Orleans' in *Das deutsche Drama I*, pp. 322-38.
7. E. J. Engel and W. F. Mainland, introduction to *Die Jungfrau von Orleans*, London/Edinburgh, 1963, p. xv.
8. T. Sellner, 'The Lionel Scene in Schiller's *Jungfrau von Orleans*', *GQ* 50 (1977), 264-82.
9. I. A. Graham, 'Friedrich von Schiller: A Portrait of Maturity', *GLL* New Series, 14 (1960-1), 151-9, also *Schiller's Drama: Talent and Integrity*, pp. 171-91.
10. Stahl, p. 117.
11. *Talent and Integrity*, p. 176.
12. Ibid., pp. 181 f.

13. F. M. Fowler, 'Sight and Insight in Schiller's *Die Jungfrau von Orleans*', *MLR* 68/2 (1973), 367-79.
14. e.g. Witte, 'Joan's own attitude towards her lapse and its consequences is ... made perfectly clear; but can we share it?' (p. 178).
15. See D. E. Allison, 'The Spiritual Element in Schiller's *Jungfrau* and Goethe's *Iphigenie*', *GQ* 32 (1959), 316-29; P. Grappin, 'La *Jeanne d'Arc* de Schiller', *EG* 10 (1955), 119-27.
16. H. B. Garland, *Schiller Revisited*, London, 1959; D. Sternberger, 'Talbot, der einzig Nüchterne', in D. S., *Figuren der Fabel. Essays*, Berlin, 1950, pp. 129-40.
17. Garland, pp. 14 f.
18. Sternberger, p. 138.
19. Ibid., p. 129.

CHAPTER 6

1. W. Muschg, 'Schiller: Die Tragödie der Freiheit', in *Reden 1959*, p. 218.
2. F. J. Egenter, Stuttgart, 1959.
3. *Festrede, gehalten am 10. November 1859 von W. Wiedasch*, Hanover, 1859.
4. In *German Studies Presented to H. G. Fiedler*, Oxford, 1938, pp. 278-92.
5. Ibid., p. 289.
6. See above, Introduction, n. 2.
7. G. Sautermeister, *Idyllik und Dramatik im Werk Friedrich Schillers*, Stuttgart (Bern, Cologne, Mainz), 1971.
8. G. Kaiser, *Wandrer und Idylle—Goethe und die Phänomenologie der Natur in der deutschen Dichtung von Geßner bis Gottfried Keller*, Göttingen, 1977, especially pp. 82-106.
9. G. Ueding, '*Wilhelm Tell*' in *Schillers Dramen. Neue Interpretationen*, pp. 271-93.
10. Kaiser, p. 93.
11. *Wilhelm Tell*, ed. W. F. Mainland, London, 1968.
12. G. W. McKay, 'Three Scenes from *Wilhelm Tell*', in *The Discontinuous Tradition. Studies in Honour of E. L. Stahl*, ed. P. F. Ganz, Oxford, 1974, pp. 99-112.
13. Mainland, pp. xii f.
14. See F. Schnapp, 'Schiller über seinen *Wilhelm Tell*, mit unbekannten Dokumenten', *Deutsche Rundschau* 206 (1926), 101-11.
15. Cf. Ueding, p. 274, for whom the play presents the goal rather than the processes of history.
16. Gerhard, p. 402.
17. *Schiller after a Century*, Edinburgh and London, 1905, pp. 119 f.
18. L. Börne, *Gesammelte Schriften*, 12 vols., Hamburg/Frankfurt, 1862, vol. 4, pp. 315-25.
19. Ibid., pp. 323-5.
20. Ibid., p. 324.

21. H. Koopmann, *Schiller II*, p. 78.
22. The play is, of course, frequently staged as a pageant, particularly in Switzerland. See n. 41.
23. Schnapp, p. 108.
24. W. Kohlschmidt, 'Tells Entscheidung', in *Reden 1959*, pp. 87-101.
25. Stahl, p. 146.
26. 'The Structure of the Personality in Schiller's Tragic Poetry', p. 130.
27. Ueding, p. 278.
28. e.g. Graham, 'The Structure of the Personality'; Martini, 'Der ästhetische Staat und der ästhetische Mensch'.
29. Garland, *Schiller Revisited*, p. 15.
30. See McKay, pp. 105 f.
31. See R. Plant, 'Geßler and Tell: Psychological Patterns in Schiller's *Wilhelm Tell*', *MLQ* 19 (1958), 60-70.
32. Ueding, p. 281.
33. See Robertson (n. 17), and more recently F. G. Ryder, 'Schiller's Tell and the Cause of Freedom', *GQ* 48 (1975), 407-54.
34. 'Tells Entscheidung', pp. 95 f.
35. Mainland, p. xii.
36. In 'The Theological Texture of Schiller's *Wilhelm Tell*', in *GR* 53 (1978), 56-62; also Koopmann, *Schiller II*, p. 79.
37. See above, n. 14.
38. Ibid., p. 108.
39. Ibid.
40. Börne, p. 323.
41. 'Schillers *Wilhelm Tell*', in *Theaterschriften und Reden*, Zürich, 1966, p. 324.
42. Martini, p. 117.
43. See Chapter 3, pp. 104 f., for a discussion of Hegel's 'Über Wallenstein'.
44. See Mainland, p. 162.
45. R. Schneider, 'Tragik und Erlösung im Weltbild Schillers', in *Reden 1955*, p. 297.
46. Mainland, p. lxvii.
47. McKay, p. 112.
48. See M. Ives, 'In Tyrannos! Rebellion and Regicide in Schiller's *Wilhelm Tell* and Joszef Katona's *Bánk Bán*', *GLL* New Series 30 (1976-77) 269-82.
49. Mainland, pp. x f.
50. Ibid., p. xxvi.
51. See Chapter 3, n. 17.

CHAPTER 7

1. E. Staiger, *Die Kunst der Interpretation*, Zürich, 1955, p. 136.
2. F. Martini, '*Demetrius*', in *Schillers Dramen. Neue Interpretationen*, pp. 316-47 (pp. 316 f.).
3. For a survey of the critical debate, see F. M. Fowler, 'The Riddle of Schiller's *Demetrius*', in *MLR* 61 (1966), 446-54.

4.   H. Cysarz, *Schiller*, Halle, 1934, pp. 389-401.
5.   G. Fricke, 'Die Problematik des Tragischen im Drama Schillers', *Jahrbuch des Freien Deutschen Hochstifts* (1930), pp. 3-69.
6.   K. May, 'Die "realistische Wendung" und "neue Tragik" in Schillers *Demetrius*' in *GRM* Neue Folge 1 (1950-1), 258-75.
7.   See n. 3.
8.   Benno von Wiese (*Schiller*) sees Romanow as giving hope for the return of legitimate government. He reconciles this with the arrival of a new potential usurper by suggesting that legitimate government is constantly threatened (p. 808).
9.   See W. Witte, '*Warbeck* and *Demetrius*'. *GLL* New Series 8 (1955), 296-303; also in W. Witte, *Schiller and Burns and Other Essays*, London, 1959, pp. 48-56.
10. P. Szondi, 'Demetrius', in *Versuch über das Tragische*, Frankfurt a.M., 1961, p. 91.
11. *Geist und Buchstabe der Dichtung*, pp. 183-8.
12. Ibid., p. 185.
13. e.g. Szondi, 'So ist Demetrius von Anfang an das Opfer nicht bloß der Umstände, sondern auch seiner selbst' (p. 90).
14. Martini, p. 319.
15. May, p. 273.
16. Szondi, p. 91.
17. Ibid., p. 90.
18. Martini, p. 319.

BIBLIOGRAPHY

I. SCHILLER'S WORKS

i. *Collected Works*

Schillers Werke (Nationalausgabe), ed. J. Petersen, G. Fricke, H. Schneider, L. Blumenthal, and B. von Wiese, Weimar, 1943-, 1 ff.

Schillers Sämtliche Werke (Säkular-Ausgabe), ed. E. von der Hellen, 16 vols., Stuttgart, 1904-5.

ii. *Individual Works* (in alphabetical order of editor)

BÖCKMANN, P., *Schillers Don Karlos. Edition der ursprünglichen Fassung und entstehungsgeschichtlicher Kommentar von Paul Böckmann*, Stuttgart, 1974.

ENGEL, F. J., and W. F. MAINLAND, edd., *Die Jungfrau von Orleans*, London and Edinburgh, 1963.

GARLAND, H. B., ed., *Don Carlos*, London, 1949.

MAINLAND, W. F., ed., *Wilhelm Tell*, London, 1968.

WITTE, W., ed., *Maria Stuart*, London, 1965.

iii. *Correspondence*

Schillers Briefe, ed. F. Jonas, Kritische Gesamtausgabe, 7 vols., Stuttgart, 1892-6.

Der Briefwechsel zwischen Schiller und Goethe, ed. E. Staiger, 2 vols., Frankfurt a.M., 1966.

Der Briefwechsel zwischen Schiller und Körner (Von 1784 bis zum Tode Schillers), introduced by L. Geiger, 4 vols., *c.* 1892.

II. OTHER CONTEMPORARY SOURCES

ECKERMANN, J. P., *Gespräche mit Goethe in den letzten Jahren seines Lebens*, new ed. ed. F. Bergemann, Wiesbaden, 1955.

GENAST, E., *Aus dem Tagebuch eines alten Schauspielers*, 2 vols., 2nd ed., Leipzig, 1862.

LENZ, J. M. R., *Anmerkungen übers Theater*, in *Sturm und Drang. Kritische Schriften*, ed. E. Loewenthal, Heidelberg, 1949, pp. 715-45.

LESSING, G. E., *Das Theater des Herrn Diderot*, in *Werke* (Hempelsche Ausgabe), 23 vols., Berlin, 1868-79, Elfter Teil.

MERCIER, L. S., *Portrait de Philippe II, Roi d'Espagne*, Amsterdam, 1785.

III. SECONDARY LITERATURE

(This section contains all the works referred to in the text, supplemented by a small number of others which have been found helpful.)

ALLISON, D. E., 'The Spiritual Element in Schiller's *Jungfrau* and Goethe's *Iphigenie*', *GQ* 32 (1959), 316-29.

AYRAULT, R., 'La figure de Mortimer dans *Maria Stuart* et la conception du drame historique chez Schiller', *EG* 13/14 (1958-9), 313-24.

BECK, A., *'Maria Stuart'*, in *Das deutsche Drama vom Barock bis zur Gegenwart. Interpretationen*, ed. Benno von Wiese, 2 vols., Düsseldorf, 1958, vol. 1, pp. 305-21.

BELLERMANN, L., *Schiller*, Leipzig, Berlin, Vienna, 1901.

—— *Schillers Dramen: Beiträge zu ihrem Verständnis*, 3 vols., Berlin, 1908.

BERMAN, J., 'Schiller's Mortimer and the Gods of Italy', in *Oxford German Studies* 8 (1973/4), 47-59.

BERGER, K., *Schiller: Sein Leben und seine Werke*, Berlin, 1890.

BÖCKMANN, P., *Schillers Geisteshaltung als Bedingung seines dramatischen Schaffens*, Neue Ausgabe, Darmstadt, 1965.

—— 'Politik und Dichtung im Werk Friedrich Schillers', in *Reden 1955*, pp. 192-213.

—— 'Gedanke, Wort und Tat in Schillers Dramen', *Jahrbuch* 4 (1960), 2-41.

—— 'Untersuchungen zur Entstehungsgeschichte des *Don Karlos*', in *Schillers Don Karlos. Edition der ursprünglichen Fassung und entstehungsgeschichtlicher Kommentar*, Stuttgart, 1974, pp. 379-623.

BÖRNE, L., 'Über den Charakter des Wilhelm Tell in Schillers Drama', in *Gesammelte Schriften*, 12 vols., Hamburg/Frankfurt, 1862, vol. 4, pp. 315-25.

BOUCHER, M., *La Révolution de 1789 vue par les écrivains allemands ses contemporains*, Paris, 1954, pp. 95-113.

BRUMFITT, J., *The French Enlightenment*, London, 1972.

BUCHWALD, R., *Schiller. Leben and Werk,* 2 vols., Neue Ausgabe, Wiesbaden, 1954.

CASSIRER, E., *Die Philosophie der Aufklärung*, Tübingen, 1932.

COLLINGWOOD, R. J., *The Idea of History*, London, 1946.

CYSARZ, H., *Schiller,* Halle, 1934.

DAVID, C., 'Le personnage de la reine Elisabeth dans la *Maria Stuart* de Schiller', in *Deutsche Beiträge zu geistigen Überlieferung* 4 (1961), 9-22.

DEWHURST, K., and N. REEVES, *Friedrich Schiller. Medicine, Psychology and Literature*, Oxford, 1978.

DROZ, J., *L'Allemagne et la Révolution Française*, Paris, 1949, pp. 172-81.

DÜRRENMATT, F., 'Schillers *Wilhelm Tell*', in *Theaterschriften und Reden*, Zürich, 1966, pp. 324-6.

EBSTEIN, F., 'In Defense of Marquis Posa', *GR* 36 (1961), 205-20.

EGENTER, F. J., *Schiller als Volksdichter im edelsten Sinn. Ein Denkzeichen für seine Verehrer*, Stuttgart, 1859.

ELLIS, J. M., 'The Vexed Question of Egmont's Political Judgment', in *Tradition and Creation. Essays in Honour of E. M. Wilkinson*, ed. C. P. Magill, B. A. Rowley, C. J. Smith, Leeds, 1978, pp. 116-30.

FOWLER, F. M., 'The Riddle of Schiller's *Demetrius*', *MLR* 61 (1966), 446-54.

—— 'Schiller's *Fiesco* Re-Examined', *PEGS* 40 (1970), 1-29.

—— 'Storm and Thunder in Gluck's and Goethe's *Iphigenie auf Tauris* and in Schiller's *Die Jungfrau von Orleans*', *PEGS* 43 (1972), 28-56.

—— 'Sight and Insight in Schiller's *Die Jungfrau von Orleans*', *MLR* 68/2 (1973), 367-79.

—— 'The Dramatic Image' in *Tradition and Creation. Essays in honour of E. M. Wilkinson* (see above, Ellis), pp. 63-76.

FREY, J. R., 'Schillers Schwarzer Ritter', *GQ* 32 (1959), 302-15.

FRICKE, G., 'Die Problematik des Tragischen im Drama Schillers', *Jahrbuch des Freien Deutschen Hochstifts*, 1930, pp. 3-69.

FUETER, E., *Geschichte der neueren Historiographie*, Munich, 1936.

GARLAND, H. B., *Schiller Revisited*, London, 1959.

—— *Schiller the Dramatic Writer*, Oxford 1969.

GERHARD, M., *Schiller*, Berne, 1950.

GILLE, K. F., 'Das astrologische Motiv in Schillers *Wallenstein*', *Amsterdamer Beiträge zur neueren Germanistik*, 1 (1972), 103-18.

GLÜCK, A., *Schiller's 'Wallenstein'*, Munich, 1976.

GOOCH, G. P., *Germany and the French Revolution*, London, 1920, pp. 208-29.

GOTTSCHALL, R., 'Schillers Ideale, die Ideale des deutschen Volks', in *Schiller-Reden nebst Goethes Epilog*, Ulm, 1905, pp. 114-19.

GRAHAM, I. A., 'The Structure of the Personality in Schiller's Tragic Poetry', in *Bicentenary Lectures*, ed. F. Norman, London, 1960, pp. 104-44.

—— 'Friedrich von Schiller: A Portrait of Maturity', *GLL* 14 (1960-61), 151-9.

—— *Friedrich Schiller's Drama: Talent and Integrity*, London, 1974.

GRAPPIN, P., 'La *Jeanne d'Arc* de Schiller', *EG* 10 (1955), 119-27.

GRONICKA, A. von, 'Friedrich Schiller's Marquis Posa', *GR* 26 (1951), 196-214.

GUTMANN, A., 'Schillers *Jungfrau von Orleans*: Das Wunderbare und die Schuldfrage', *Zeitschrift für deutsche Philologie,* 88 (1969), 560-83.

HAHN, K. H., 'Schiller und die Geschichte', *Weimarer Beiträge*, 16 (1970), 39-69.

HAMBURGER, K., 'Schiller und Sartre. Ein Versuch zum Idealismus-Problem Schillers', *Jahrbuch* 3 (1959), 34-70.

HEGEL, G. W. F. 'Über Wallenstein', *Sämtliche Werke* (Jubiläumsausgabe), ed. H. Glockner, Stuttgart, 1927-30, vol. XX, pp. 456-8.

HESELHAUS, C., 'Die Nemesis-Tragödie: *Fiesco—Wallenstein—Demetrius*', *DU* 4 (1952), 40-59.

—— 'Wallensteinisches Welttheater', *DU* 12 (1960), 42-71.

HEYN, G., *Der junge Schiller als Psychologe*, Zürich, 1966.

HINDERER, W., '*Wallenstein*', in *Schillers Dramen. Neue Interpretationen*, ed. W. Hinderer, Stuttgart, 1979, pp. 126-73.

HOFFMEISTER, K., *Schillers Leben, Geistesentwicklung und Werke im Zusammenhang*, 5 vols., Stuttgart, 1838-42.

HOFMANNSTHAL, H. VON, 'Schiller', in *Selected Essays*, ed. M. Gilbert, Oxford, pp. 20-5.

IVES, M. C., 'In Tyrannos! Rebellion and Regicide in Schiller's *Wilhelm Tell* and Joszef Katona's *Bánk Bán*', *GLL* New Series, 30 (1976-77), 269-82.

JANSSEN, J., *Schiller als Historiker*, Freiburg, 1863.

KAHN, L. W., 'Freedom: an Existentialist and an Idealist View (Sartre's *Les Mouches* and Schiller's *Wilhelm Tell*)', *PMLA* 64 (1949), 5-14.

KAISER, G., *Wandrer und Idylle. Goethe und die Phänomenologie der Natur in der deutschen Dichtung von Geßner bis Gottfried Keller*, Göttingen, 1977, pp. 82-106.

KOHLSCHMIDT; W., 'Tells Entscheidung', in *Reden 1959*, pp. 87-101.

KOMMERELL, M., *Der Dichter als Führer in der deutschen Klassik*, Berlin, 1928.

—— *Schiller als Gestalter des handelnden Menschen*, Frankfurt a.M., 1934.

—— 'Schiller als Psychologe', in *Geist und Buchstabe der Dichtung*, Frankfurt a.M., 1942, pp. 132-99.

KOOPMAN, H., *Friedrich Schiller*, 2 vols., Sammlung Metzler 50/51, Stuttgart, 1966.

—— *Schiller-Kommentar*, 2 vols., Munich, 1969.

LINDENBERGER, H., *Historical Drama. The Relation of Literature and Reality*, Chicago and London, 1975.

LINN, R. F., 'Wallensteins Innocence', *GR* 34 (1959), 200-8.

LUDWIG, O., *Dramatische Studien*, ausgewählt von R. Petsch, Dresden, 1923.

MAINLAND, W. F., *Schiller and the Changing Past*, London, 1957.

MANN, G., 'Schiller als Historiker' in *Jahrbuch* 4 (1960), 98-109.

MARLEYN, R., '*Wallenstein* and the structure of Schiller's tragedies', *GR* 32 (1957), 186-99.

MARTINI, F., '*Wilhelm Tell*: der ästhetische Staat und der ästhetische Mensch', *DU* 12 (1960), 91-118.

—— '*Demetrius*', in *Schillers Dramen. Neue Interpretationen*, ed. W. Hinderer, Stuttgart, 1979, pp. 316-47.

MAY, K., *Friedrich Schiller: Idee und Wirklichkeit im Drama*, Göttingen, 1948.

—— 'Die "realistische Wendung" und "neue Tragik" in Schillers *Demetrius*', *GRM* Neue Folge, 1 (1950/1), 258-75.

McKAY, G. W., 'Three Scenes from *Wilhelm Tell*' in *The Discontinuous Tradition. Studies in Honour of E.L. Stahl*, ed. P. F. Ganz, Oxford, 1974, pp. 99-112.

MILLER, R. D., *The Drama of Schiller*, Harrogate, 1966.

MINOR, J., *Schiller. Sein Leben und seine Werke*, 2 vols., Berlin, 1890.

MOORE, W. G., 'A New Reading of *Wilhelm Tell*', in *German Studies Presented to H. G. Fiedler*, Oxford, 1938, pp. 278-92.

MUECKE, D. C., *Irony*, in *The Critical Idiom*, 13, general editor J. D. Jump, London, 1970.

MUSCHG, W., 'Schiller—Die Tragödie der Freiheit', Berne, Munich, 1959, also in *Reden 1959*, pp. 218-39.

NEUBAUER, J., 'The Idea of History in Schiller's *Wallenstein*', *Neuphilogus* 56 (1972), 451-63.

ORTON, G., *Schiller: Don Carlos*, Studies in German Literature, 8, London, 1967.

PALLESKE, E., *Schillers Leben und Werke*, Berlin, 1865.

PLANT, R., 'Geßler and Tell: Psychological Patterns in Schiller's *Wilhelm Tell*', *MLQ* 19 (1958), 60-70.

REGIN, D., *Freedom and Dignity. The Historical and Philosophical Thought of Schiller*, The Hague, 1965.

REHM, W., 'Schiller und das Barockdrama', *DVjs* 19 (1941), 311-53.

ROBERTSON, J. G., *Schiller after a Century*, London, 1905.

ROSS, W., 'Der Streit der Königinnen', *Wirkendes Wort* 5 (1954/5), 356-62.

RYDER, F., 'Schiller's *Tell* and the Cause of Freedom', *GQ* 48 (1975), 407-54.

SAMMONS, J. L., 'Mortimer's Conversion and Schiller's Allegiances', *JEGP* 72 (1973), 155-66.

SAUTERMEISTER, G., *Idyllik und Dramatik im Werk Friedrich Schillers. Zum geschichtlichen Ort seiner klassischen Dramen*, Stuttgart, 1971.

—— *'Maria Stuart'* in *Schillers Dramen. Neue Interpretationen*, ed. W. Hinderer, Stuttgart, 1979, pp. 174-216.

SCHMIDT, J., *Schiller und seine Zeitgenossen*, Leipzig, 1859.

SCHNAPP, F., 'Schiller über seinen *Wilhelm Tell*. Mit unbekannten Dokumenten', *Deutsche Rundschau* 52 (1926), 101-11.

SCHNEIDER, R., 'Tragik und Erlösung im Weltbild Schillers', in *Reden 1955*, pp. 276-302.

SEDGEWICK, G. G., *Of Irony, Especially in Drama*, University of Toronto Studies—Philology and Literature Series, 10, Toronto, 1935.

SEIDLIN, O., 'Schiller: Poet of Politics', in *A Schiller Symposium*, ed. L. Willson, Austin, 1960, pp. 29-48.

—— *'Wallenstein*: Sein und Zeit', in *Von Goethe zu Thomas Mann. Zwölf Versuche*, Göttingen, 1963, pp. 120-35.

SELLAR, W. C., and R. J. YEATMAN, *1066 and All That*, London, 1930.

SELLNER, T. F., 'The Lionel Scene in Schiller's *Jungfrau von Orleans*: a psychological interpretation', *GR* 50 (1977), 264-82.

SENGLE, F., *Das historische Drama in Deutschland. Geschichte eines literarischen Mythos*, new ed., Stuttgart, 1969.

SHAW, G. B., Preface to *Saint Joan: A Chronicle Play in Six Scenes and an Epilogue*, London, 1924.

SILZ, W., 'Chorus and Choral Function in Schiller', in *Schiller 1759/1959. Commemorative American Studies*, Urbana, 1959, pp. 147-70.

—— 'The Character and Function of Buttler in Schiller's *Wallenstein*', in *Studies in Germanic Languages and Literatures in memory of F. O. Nolte*, ed. E. Hofacker and L. Dieckmann, Washington, 1963, pp. 77-91.

SIMON, W. M., *Friedrich Schiller (1759-1805): The Poet as Historian*, Keele, 1966.

SINGER, H., '"Dem Fürsten Piccolomini"', *Euphorion* 53 (1959), 281-302.

SPENDER, S., 'Schiller, Shakespeare and the Theme of Power', in *A Schiller Symposium*, ed. L. Willson, Austin, 1960, pp. 51-61.

STAHL, E. L., *Friedrich Schiller's Drama: Theory and Practice*, Oxford, 1954.

STAIGER, E., *Die Kunst der Interpretation*, Zürich, 1955.

—— *Schiller*, Zürich, 1967.

STEINER, G., *The Death of Tragedy*, London, 1961.

STERNBERGER, D., 'Talbot, der einzig Nüchterne', in D.S., *Figuren der Fabel. Essays*, Berlin, 1950, pp. 129-40.

—— 'Macht und Herz oder der politische Held bei Schiller', in *Reden 1959*, pp. 310-29.

STORZ, G., *Das Drama Friedrich Schillers*, Frankfurt a.M., 1938.

—— *Jeanne d'Arc und Schiller. Eine Studie über das Verhältnis von Dichtung und Wirklichkeit*, Munich, 1946.

——*Der Dichter Friedrich Schiller*, Stuttgart, 1959.

——*'Die Jungfrau von Orleans'*, in *Das Deutsche Drama vom Barock bis zur Gegenwart* (see above, A. Beck), vol. 1, pp. 322-38.

—— 'Der Bauerbacher Plan zum *Don Carlos'*, *Jahrbuch* 8 (1964), 112-29.

STRICH, F., 'Schiller und Thomas Mann', *Neue Rundschau* 68 (1957), 60-83.

SZONDI, P., 'Schiller: Demetrius', in P.S., *Versuch über das Tragische*, Frankfurt a.M., 1961, pp. 89-97.

—— '*Tableau* und *coup de théâtre*,' in P.S., *Lektüren und Lektionen*, Frankfurt a.M., 1973, pp. 13-36.

THIRLWALL, C., 'On the Irony of Sophocles', in *Remains Literary and Theological*, ed. J. S. Perowne, 3 vols., London, 1878, vol. 3, pp. 1-57.

THOMPSON, A. R., *The Dry Mock*, Berkeley, 1948.

THOMPSON, J. W. and B. J. HOLM, *A History of Historical Writing*, 2 vols., New York, 1942, vol. 2, pp. 3-131.

TOMASCHEK, K., *Schiller in seinem Verhältnisse zur Wissenschaft*, Vienna, 1862.

ÜBERWEG, F., *Schiller als Historiker und Philosoph*, ed. M. Brasch, Leipzig, 1884.

UEDING, G., *'Wilhelm Tell'*, in *Schillers Dramen. Neue Interpretationen*, ed. W. Hinderer, Stuttgart, 1979, pp. 271-93.

VANDER MEULEN, R., 'The Theological Texture of Schiller's *Wilhelm Tell'*, *GR* 53 (1978), 56-62.

WALTER, H. A., 'Die Stellungnahme Schillers zu Goethe's *Egmont'*, *GQ* 32 (1959), 330-40.

WARD, A., *Book Production, Fiction and the German Reading Public 1740-1800*, Oxford, 1974.

WELLS, G. A., 'Astrology in Schiller's *Wallenstein'*, *JEGP* 68 (1969), 100-15.

—— 'Villainy and Guilt in Schiller's *Wallenstein* and *Maria Stuart'*, in *Deutung und Bedeutung—Studies in German and Comparative Literature Presented to K. W. Maurer*, ed. B. Schludermann, The Hague, 1973, pp. 100-17.

WERTHEIM, U., *Schillers 'Fiesko' und 'Don Karlos'. Zu Problemen des historischen Stoffes*, Weimar, 1958.

—— 'Der amerikanische Unabhängigkeitskampf im Spiegel der zeitgenössischen deutschen Literatur', in U.W. and E. Braemar, *Studien zur deutschen Klassik*, Berlin, 1960, pp. 71-114.

WIEDASCH, W., 'Wodurch ist Schiller der Lieblingsdichter der deutschen Nation geworden?', Festrede, gehalten am 10. November 1859, Hanover, 1859.

Wıᴇsᴇ, B. ᴠᴏɴ, *Schiller*, Stuttgart, 1959.

—— 'Schiller as an Historian and Philosopher of History', in *Bicentenary Lectures*, ed. F. Norman, London, 1960, pp. 83-103.

Wıʟᴋıɴsᴏɴ, E. M., *Schiller: Poet or Philosopher?*, Special Taylorian Lecture 1959, Oxford, 1961.

Wıᴛᴛᴇ, W., *Schiller*, Oxford, 1949.

—— '*Warbeck* and *Demetrius*', *GLL* New Series 8 (1955), 296-303; also in W. W., *Schiller and Burns and Other Essays*, London, 1959, pp. 48-56.

Wᴏʀᴄᴇsᴛᴇʀ, D., *The Art of Satire*, Cambridge, Mass., 1940.

INDEX

Abel, J. F., 37, 42, 84

Beck, A., 106
Bellermann, L., 1, 17, 131 f.
Berger, K., 17 f.
Beulwitz, C. v., 6, 36
Böckmann, P., 4, 11, 16, 20, 24, 88, 90
Börne, L., 147 f., 161
Böttiger, K., 102
Bougeant, G. H., 59
Buchwald, R., 57

Chemnitz, B. P. v., 59
Collingwood, R. J., 56
Condorcet, N. A. de, 54
Crusius, S. L., 35, 41, 42
Cysarz, H., 174

Dalberg, W. H. v., 3, 9, 10, 13, 16, 23, 24, 29
Dewhurst, K., and N. Reeves, 5
Diderot, D., 24, 28
Dürrenmatt, F., 162

Ebstein F., 18, 21, 22
Ellis, J. M., 51, 53
Engel, F. J., and W. F. Mainland, 132
Euripides, 106, 110

Fowler, F. M., 9, 32, 134, 175
French Revolution, 17, 72 f.
Fricke, G., 174

Garland, H. B., 16, 91, 100, 138 f.
Genast, A., 74
Gerhard, M., 106, 109, 117, 145
Gervinus, G. G., 36
Gibbon, E., 40, 42, 54
Glück, A., 76, 88
Goethe, J. W. v., 54, 72, 74 f., 88, 100, 106 f., 110, 129 f., 148, 175
  Egmont, 51-3, 74-6, 129
  Götz von Berlichingen, 7
  Über epische und dramatische Dichtung, 148
  Zum Schäkespears Tag, 52

Göschen, G. J., 58, 60, 130
  Historischer Kalender für Damen, 35, 57
Graham, I. A., 9, 90, 110, 132 f., 150
Gronicka, A. v., 17 f.

Hamburger, K., 3 f.
Hegel, G. W. F.,
  'Über Wallenstein', 104 f., 163
Herder, J. G., 15
  Auch eine Philosophie, 56 f.
Heselhaus, C., 77 f., 103
Hinderer, W., 88
Hoffmeister, K., 36
Hofmannsthal, H. v., 30
Huber, L. F., 35, 37, 39
Humboldt, W. v., 55, 146
Hume, D., 42

Iffland, A. W., 144, 146, 149, 158

Janssen, J., 36, 44, 47 f., 59

Kaiser, G., 144
Kant, I., 3, 56 f., 157
Kohlschmidt, W., 149, 157
Kommerell, M., 4, 18, 85, 121, 178 f.
Koopmann, H., 38, 92, 106, 148
Körner, C. G., 15, 35-7, 40 f., 48, 55, 57, 74 f., 179 f.
Kotzebue, A. v., 146

Lenz, J. M. R.,
  Anmerkungen übers Theater, 52
Lessing, G. E., 24
Lindenberger, H., 7, 15 f.
Ludwig, O., 91, 109

Mainland, W. F., 112, 116 f., 132, 144, 157, 169, 171
Mann, G., 68
Marleyn, R., 79
Martini, F., 1 f., 144, 163, 174, 179, 182
May, K., 3, 9, 44, 64, 104, 175, 180
McKay, G. W., 144, 158, 169
Mercier, L. S., 38 f.

Miller, R. D., 101, 107 f., 131
Montesquieu, C de S., Baron de, 42
Moore, W. G., 143
Möser, J. J., 43
Müller, J. v., 43
Muschg, W., 143

Niebuhr, C., 36

Orton, G., 18, 20 f.

Palleske, E., 17
Plutarch, 37
Pütter, J. S., 42, 54, 59

Quicherat, J., 127

Reeves, N., *see* Dewhurst
Regin, D., 36, 41, 56
Reinwald, H. F. H., 30
Robertson, J. G., 145
Robertson, W., 40, 42, 114

Sammons, J. L., 119
Sartre, J. P., 3
Sautermeister, G., 106, 113, 144
Schiller, Christophine, 55

SCHILLER, J. F. C.
　*Allgemeine Sammlung Historischer
　　Memoires*, 35, 37, 62
　Ästhetische Briefe, 1, 73, 78, 97, 105,
　　124, 144
　Belagerung von Antwerpen, Die, 70 f.
　Braut von Messina, Die, 108
　Briefe über Don Carlos, 14-17, 19,
　　21, 23-5, 27, 30 f., 33, 35, 40

　Demetrius, 127, *174-82*, 185
　*Des Grafen Lamoral von Egmont
　　Leben und Tod*, 54
　Don Carlos, 1, 3-12, *13-34*, 38-40,
　　49-51, 55, 61, 68, 79 f., 86, 92, 105,
　　119, 128, 142, 150, 177, 183, 187

　Egmont (Bühnenbearbeitung), 75
　*Etwas über die erste Menschengesell-
　　schaft*, 57

　Fiesco, Die Verschwörung des, 5 f.,
　　9-13, 22, 24, 27, 29, 39, 46, 49 f.,
　　145, 170, 183

Geisterseher, Der, 41
*Geschichte der Französischen Un-
　ruhen*, 61
*Geschichte der merkwürdigsten
　Rebellionen und Verschwörungen*,
　41
*Geschichte des Abfalls der Nieder-
　lande*, 3, 5 f., 16 f., 31, 34, *35-54*,
　56 f., 59-62, 64, 68, 70, 183
*Geschichte des Dreißigjährigen
　Kriegs*, 5 f., 35, 37, *57-70*, 74 f., 79,
　84, 87, 101, 103, 184

Horen, Die, 70

Jungfrau von Orleans, Die, 6, 29, 39,
　65, 79, 108, 114, *127-41*, 145, 168,
　179-81, 185-7

Kabale und Liebe, 12, 14, 22, 27, 45,
　77, 79, 86, 150

'Mädchen von Orleans, Das', 128
Maria Stuart, 1 f., 7, 39, 53 f., 80,
　92-4, *106-26*, 127 f., 130, 139 f.,
　168, 175, 184-7

Räuber, Die, 2, 9, 12, 22, 37, 55, 72,
　77, 79, 86
Rheinische Thalia, Die, 14, 26, 35,
　39, 177

Thalia, Die, 14, 16, 25, 35, 38 f., 50,
　57

Über Anmut und Würde, 2, 124
Über das Erhabene, 108
Über das Pathetische, 2
Über die tragische Kunst, 2
*Über Egmont, Trauerspiel von
　Goethe*, 51-4
*Über epische und dramatische Dicht-
　ung*, 148
*Über naive und sentimentalische
　Dichtung*, 3, 102, 105, 113, 144

Verbrecher aus verlorener Ehre, Der,
　84-6
Verschwörung des Fiesco, Die, see
　Fiesco

Wallenstein, 2, 5-9, 11, 29, 31, 49,

54, 68, 70, *72-105*, 106-8, 112 f.,
113, 120, 122, 126, 128, 130, 139,
145, 150, 163, 168, 176-9, 181, 184-6
Warbeck, 106, 175-7
*Was heißt und zu welchem Ende
studiert man Universalgeschichte?*,
55-7
Wilhelm Tell, 1, 46, 127, 129, 139,
142-73, 177, 181 f.

Schlegel, A. W. and F., 81
Schlözer, A., 42
Schmidt, J., 17
Schmidt, M. I., 42, 54, 59
Schneider, R., 168
Seidlin, O., 18, 88, 126
Seller W. C. and R. J. Yeatman, 129
Sellner, T., 132
Sengle, F., 106 f.
Shakespeare, W., 7, 13, 52, 100, 109
Shaw, G. B., 128, 139
Silz, W., 91, 100
Simon, W. M., 41, 43
Spittler, L. T. v., 42
Stahl, E. L., 4, 132 f., 150
Staiger, E., 77, 174
Steiner, G., 18, 106, 109 f.
Sternberger, D., 138-40

Storz, G., 2 f., 9 f., 41, 106, 131
St. Réal, C. V., Abbé de, 14, 38
Strich, F., 80
Szondi, P., 28, 180

Teutscher Merkur, 35, 44, 55
Thirlwall, C., 72, 78, 81, 173
Thompson, A. R., 83
Tomaschek, K., 59
Tschudi, A., 149

Überweg, F., 43 f., 59
Ueding, G., 144
Urner Spiel, 148, 159

Vander Meulen, R., 158
Voltaire, 37, 40, 42, 127, 139

Ward, A., 37
Watson, R., 16, 37, 39 f.
Wells, G. A., 88
Wertheim, U., 6, 10, 19, 45
Wieland, C. M., 35, 41 f.
Wiese, B. v., 32, 104
Witte, W., 79, 88, 108 f.
Worcester, D., 83

Yeatman, R. J., *see* Sellar